Mind Game

Discover Your Golf Identity

**The Insights, Secrets & Decisions
that Allow You to Become a Better Player**

By **Stu Ingraham**
and **Bob Ockenfuss**

Copyright ©

2015

Table of Contents

Appendix

Acknowledgments

As I look back upon my career as a golf professional, I feel extremely lucky to have been involved with a sport I am passionate about. As a teacher, I enjoy helping people to improve their skills. As a player myself, the competitive aspect excites me. Very importantly, not many people can truly say they love their job. I have been very fortunate to have had many people and situations influence and enhance my playing, teaching and overall career. First and most importantly, I want to thank my mother and father. No resources have proven to be more helpful than the natural ability, love and opportunity they bestowed upon me. Thank you from the bottom of my heart. I must also thank and recognize my two coaches, Fred Sherk at Cedar Crest High School and the late Hal Morrisson at East Tennessee State University. Over the years, two influential golf professionals, Mike Swisher and Ted McKenzie, gave me opportunities, support and a true understanding of the golf industry. Among other things, they helped me increase my knowledge of the game. I enjoyed my time and experience working at three different golf facilities, Lebanon Country Club, Waynesborough Country Club and Overbrook Golf Club. I am greatly indebted to Bev and Mike Owsik and family for the opportunity and support they gave me in the spring of 2008 to change my career path as a head golf professional. At that time, I became the director of instruction at the M Golf Driving Range and Learning Center, where I am today. I feel very fortunate to have had close friends, family and colleagues who have supported and stood by me both on and off the golf course. These people include John Gross, Rick Gleeson, Jim Farrelly, Russ Baribault, Rich Driscoll, Anne Deluca, Donald Kurz, Red Davidson and Byron Driscoll. Thanks to a few caddies over the years, Bob Donato, Fran McCabe, Bill Ruddy, Jim Wellman, Ann Blasko, Dan McAnally and Jeff Owsik, all of whom put up with my expression and personality. I want to give special recognition to Chuck and Nancy Wojciehowski at Capt'n Chucky's Crab Cake Company for all of their assistance. Special thanks to Paul Pizzi for his creative graphic art talents used in the terrific design of the front and back covers. To my co-author, Bob Ockenfuss, a retired public school teacher and coach, thank you for your patience, knowledge, dedication, insights and writing ability. Thanks also to his lovely wife, Judy, for her skills in editing this book. There aren't enough words to thank all of my students who, over the past thirty-two years, have trusted me with sharing my knowledge, experiences and secrets with them. You have provided me with insights that have helped me to become a better coach and instructor. Finally, as always, thanks to my three wonderful children, Adam, Ashley and Stu, for their understanding, patience, selflessness and inspiration through the challenges I have had and sacrifices I have had to make as a golf professional. Thank you for supporting me through this special journey. Love, Dad.

Golf Instructional Conversations
with Stu Ingraham

Introduction

Unique insights to better golf

This book is meant to be *unlike any other golf instruction book* out on the market today! The question and answer organizational presentation format along with the types of information covered is representative of this fact.

Most golf instruction manuals and/or books are geared and written to better understand the so-called perfect swing. After taking a journey through this book, chapter by chapter and page by page, the reader will truly come to understand why P.G.A. tour players are the best in the world. Understanding how to improve the mechanics of the swing is only a small part or percentage of how to improve a player's game.

Over all, I have been *involved in* the great game of golf for over forty years. I was introduced to the sport at age eight and was fortunate enough to play both junior and high school golf. I won the Pennsylvania Interscholastic Athletic Association high school championship, subsequently earned a scholarship to East Tennessee State University and was named to the college All-America third team during my senior year. In 1985, on my third attempt at Q-school, I finished ninth and earned my playing card on the P.G.A. Tour. I have been a golf professional for the past thirty-three years (since 1982), and have been a member of the P.G.A. since 1987.

It is my opinion that very few golf professionals in America have had the opportunity to walk my walk. Over the course of my career, I have had many experiences and been exposed to many situations. As a club professional, I have been fortunate enough to have given over nineteen thousand individual golf lessons and over five hundred clinics and camps to players of all levels. At the same time, after having played on the 1986 P.G.A. Tour, I have competed in eight major championships. My greatest single golf accomplishment was being the low club professional in the 1993 P.G.A. Championship. As of 2015, I will have played in twenty-four P.G.A. Professional National Championships, in over five hundred Philadelphia P.G.A. section tournaments and have been a member of two United States P.G.A. Cup Teams, the equivalent of the Ryder Cup for club professionals.

Some well-known teachers have taught the game of golf, but they themselves have never competed on a high level. Some players have played the tour but have never really been teachers. My advantage is that I have done *both*. To my knowledge, no one has ever written a book from this perspective.

As a golf professional, I have decided to put together this book/manual with the intention of influencing you, the reader, to cross over the bridge and become a better golfer. This is an opportunity for people who really love golf to benefit from my years of insights and experiences as both a player and teacher. I feel that now is the time for me to share the secrets and insights that I know about this wonderful game with all of you fellow golfers and enthusiasts.

There are many choices to be made with the goal of improving your golf game. Some of them are quite expensive, costing hundreds or even thousands of dollars. One could attend a golf camp or school or have a video analysis done of their swing. One might even schedule time with a professional sports psychologist, such as Bob Rotella. However, for less than the cost of a single lesson, I am going to expose you to practical information no one has ever thought to share with you before. Your life and your golf game will definitely change when you begin to digest the information expressed within these pages.

Exactly how might a reader benefit from being exposed to such information? What topics will be covered? My answer lies in creating the format of asking a sample of questions and then giving my responses to them. How do you handle nerves away from the golf course? Have you ever spent time at home or in your hotel room with a two-shot lead in either your club championship or the state amateur and wondered how to approach the situation? Is it alright to be insecure about your next round? How might you manage your game better? What foods should you eat or stay away from? What drinks can you consume? Is it your desire to be able to improve from a ten to a five handicap? Have you ever had the shanks or the yips? Is one of your goals to hit the ball a bit farther but don't know how? What thoughts do you need to have in order to hit a successful bunker shot? In terms of club fitting, do you have the correct clubs in your hands? Do they match your needs concerning factors such as age, physical condition and flexibility? What about your driver and irons? Are your irons adjusted to the correct lies and lofts? Have you been matched with the proper shafts in all of your clubs? How different are you from the best players in the world in handling matters of insecurity, trust, happiness and confidence? If you answer, "Yes!", to any one of these questions, then you owe it to yourself to see what answers I have for you in the following chapters.

As a point of clarification, instructional information presented in this manual/book is mentioned from the perspective of a right-handed golfer. This book has something for enthusiasts at all levels of the game. Some parts of chapters and certain details are geared towards the better player, so the information presented could apply to scratch golfers and even L.P.G.A. and P.G.A. Tour-level players. The somewhat simplicity of other chapters would benefit a high handicapper or a true beginner. The point is, all players can benefit from its contents. It is almost meant to be treated like a cookbook which might be opened up to various favorite recipes. When you are struggling with chipping, go to the chipping chapter. When you can not get out of the sand, go to the bunker chapter. If you are struggling with the yips, read what I have to say about solving that problem. Whatever your identity, this book has something of value for you. Use it like a manual and/or a cookbook to benefit the future of your golf game.

During my years of instruction, I feel that I have been able to learn much from my students. Most importantly, I have learned that a teacher has to consider each student as an *individual*. It all begins with and depends on the *identity* of the student. How can they be helped to *identify* who they are as a golfer? What does the player bring to the table in terms of personality, strengths and weaknesses, equipment, ball flight, beliefs and fears? Does the information presented match what the individual student needs to hear and work on to help them improve their game? What suits one will not work for all students. How can what is presented maximize their enjoyment in playing the game? This is really the unique feature of the journey that I present in this book. What is not intended is to rehash the faulty, generalized commandments that have been created by society that you have heard in the past. Instead, while utilizing an *individualistic* approach, my experience has shown me how students learn in different ways and sometimes have physical limitations. They see, feel and react to what is presented in different ways. I have seen how players have been able to progress in their level of play from one stage to the next. In order for this to happen, there must be a healthy dialogue back and forth between instructor and student so as to help them establish his/her identity. Doing so will help establish what the player is looking to accomplish. The instructor will be able to assess where each student is presently in their development in order to help them build a plan of improvement for the future. In my approach to the game, I avoid teaching in a "cookie cutter" instruction method but am still able to discuss solid fundamentals which will lead to improved play.

My hope is to present educational information that will help golfers at *all* levels maximize their opportunity to become better players. This book will neither describe perfect positions in the golf swing nor compare your swing to that of Ernie Els. However, what you will receive is a multitude of unique insights into how to play better golf. My single biggest goal is to get inside your *brain* and share with you many aspects and situations that will allow you to make correct decisions both on and off the golf course. Such knowledge will enable you to have the proper ability and *mindset* to use that famous green light approach in your next round of golf. Thinking it, positively or negatively, makes it so! If you are excited to become a better player, this book will meet your needs.

Respectfully,

Stu Ingraham
P.G.A. golf professional

Getting Started

Chapter One
How to Take a Lesson

On the simplest level, how and where might I begin to learn to play golf?

There are a variety of ways in which people can be introduced to the game of golf. A large percentage probably begin by hitting balls for the first time somewhere on a practice or driving range. As a youngster, one's family members or friends might already play the game. While in high school or college, many younger people played team sports, such as baseball, basketball, football and soccer. Now, when they are older and entering the work world, they find their businesses involve golf. Their companies have outings, and they want to learn how to play. Newly retired persons might want to develop a hobby. They discover their knees are not good enough to play tennis, so they turn to golf. An introduction to golf can come at any time during one's lifetime.

What can I learn from written and audio-visual materials?

There are many books and magazines in print. There are also "glitzy" video productions and instruction programs to watch on television. There are many game-improvement "training devices" being hawked on the market. One can also find much information on the internet. However, much of the information presented is both conflicting and confusing. In fact, there is a lot of "bad" information out there, and it is hard to sort out the truth from fiction. Many such offerings feature one-size-fits-all solutions to instruction. These types of presentations can not possibly take the place of the necessary one-on-one instruction given by a qualified and trusted instructor. They may even delay or all together halt improvement. Since each golfer is an individual, adjustments are impossible to make without a trained eye that sees the flight of the ball.

Suppose I am "bitten by the golf bug". What might be a logical next step?

If you are just starting out and are not yet ready to make a commitment, you might consider group lessons, a clinic or a golf camp. Again, the selection of a qualified instructor is a must! There are several advantages to such a group program. The cost is lower. The other participants will be golfers who more than likely have the same level of experience and proficiency as you have. There is not as much pressure to perform, and you might even develop friendships with potential playing partners. The experience is fun because the atmosphere is more relaxed. The instructor divides time among several people. He or she may cover a general topic with the entire group and then work individually with group members. While working individually with one member, other members of the group are able to practice on what is being taught. Over time, all parts of the game are covered. It is a great, nonthreatening way to get a start in the game.

What factors does a player need to weigh before considering individual lessons?

Such lessons focus on individual needs and abilities. The instructor works with you alone. With that in mind, there are several things to consider. How frequently do you play? Do you play once a year, several times a month or several days a week? How serious are you about the game? What kind of a commitment in both time and money are you willing to make? How much time are you willing to put into practicing what you have learned?

Why is it important to consider what type of student you are?

As it is with all walks of life, everyone is an individual when it comes to golf. Each of us has a different learning style. Some of us are auditory and learn through our sense of hearing. Most of us are visual and learn through sight. Still others are kinesthetic-tactual and learn by doing. Such awareness is important for both the instructor and the student. Does the student have any physical limitations? Are you realistic about your abilities?

How do I go about selecting an instructor?

You should interview him or her about their background and experience. A face-to-face meeting would be most beneficial. Think about what is important to you as a student? What is their teaching philosophy? Are they able to work around your schedule? What is the fee structure? What is the length of time for a lesson? How often should I come for lessons? Does the teacher have a systems approach to the game or will they work with the swing I have right now? What if I have to cancel a lesson? How much information will be covered at any one time?

What questions might an instructor ask a student at their first meeting?

Some instructors actually have the student complete an individual questionnaire prior to the first meeting. They will then go over it with the student to begin their first lesson. Here is a sampling of what might be asked? What is your golf history and experience? What scores do you *actually* shoot? What *realistic* expectations and goals do you have? What specifically do you want to improve? What is your level of commitment to the game? How much time do you have to practice? What are your strengths and weaknesses? What is your most frequent miss? What does the flight of the ball look like --- hook, straight or slice? The instructor might even ask you to fill out a *chart* indicating your shot patterns for a recent round. Do you have any physical limitations? What is your learning style? How far do you *honestly* hit the ball with individual clubs? Are you able to maneuver the ball right-to-left and left-to-right?

On the day of the lesson, how early should I arrive? Once at the location for the lesson, what should I do to get ready?

Make sure you allow enough time to reach the destination of your lesson. Be prompt! The instructor will probably have a full schedule to keep and you do not want to keep them waiting for you. Arrive at least twenty minutes early. First go through your stretching routine. Then hit enough warm up shots before the lesson starts so that you are loose and ready to begin. Concentrate on problem areas rather than what you already do well.

During the lesson itself, what should the student be doing?

There should be a sense of teamwork between instructor and student.

Communicate to the instructor what you have been working on during practice time.

Clearly indicate to the instructor what part of your game you want to improve and work on today.

Actively participate in the lesson! Give eye contact and be a good listener. Really listen to each instructional comment without thinking about some other topic. Do not make the lesson a one-way street. As a student, do not be afraid to ask questions yourself. There should be give and take between teacher and student within a lesson. Ask for clarification if you do not understand what the instructor is communicating to you.

The instructor might provide the student with notes summarizing key points of the lesson. The student might take notes themselves. However, a better scenario would have the student purchase a voice recorder to use during instruction. Good quality recorders are available that are able to save four hundred continuous hours or more of instruction. This would allow both instructor and student to make maximum use of their lesson time. Confusion about what was said is avoided. The student is able to play back the lesson at a later time and possibly even transcribe notes. In the process, nothing is missed or left to conjecture. The student is able to intently listen to what the instructor has to say knowing the conversation has been recorded for future referral.

Besides full-swing instruction, what other types of instruction exist?

There are many parts of the game to work on besides hitting full shots. Pick the game apart and identify those areas. Do not forget the mental side of the game. Players should work on pitching, chipping and sand shots. Putting should definitely be on the list since it often represents thirty-five to forty-five percent of the shots taken on the course during a round. Wedge play and hitting half or knockdown shots is important. How do you perform from one hundred yards and in? Do you have a second serve tee shot you can rely on when it is required? Are you able to creatively fade or draw the ball on demand? Are you able to control the trajectory of the ball when necessary? Are you willing to take a lesson when the weather is bad or the winds are up? Are on-course playing lessons available? Are my current clubs right for me? If not, can you perform a club-fitting for me?

How should I spend my time between lessons?

Work on specific areas which have been covered during lessons between you and your instructor. Put yourself in the present. Do not revert back to what your golf buddies have been telling you is important. Be sure to practice but do not neglect playing. Do not exclusively be a range rat. Golf is played one-shot-at-a-time on the golf course! Stick to the game plan!

Do you truly know how far you hit each club in your bag? This knowledge becomes important in the club selection process during a round, especially on a strange course. Hit a test sample of shots with each club and use a laser range-finding device to calculate average distances. Not many players complete this task!

Work on maneuvering the ball. If your tendency is to hit fades, work upon drawing the ball. If your tendency is to hit draws, work upon fading the ball. Work on varying the trajectory, alternating between high, medium and low.

In addition to lessons and/or competitions, what steps can I take in order to continue my advancement as a player?

Once you have played the game and have become an avid golfer, there are a number of things you can do to grow your game beyond lessons. At your own club, observe and play with better players. Ask them questions about their game and the steps they have taken to improve. The National Collegiate Athletic Association and the United States Golf Association hold regional tournaments, qualifiers and finals around the country. You can watch very good collegiate and high level amateurs at these events. Another good place to begin might simply be to watch television coverage of either an L.P.G.A. or a P.G.A. tournament on the Golf Channel or on one of the major networks. Such tournaments are aired on a weekly basis during all seasons of the year. A better choice might be to actually attend one of these events in person whenever the situation presents itself. At such a tournament, there are many opportunities to get up-front-and-personal with the pros. As a spectator, you can walk the course with the players and see how they deal with the various situations they encounter. You will see they make mistakes too and do not always hit the ball perfectly. You will witness how they manage themselves around the course, how they can work the ball to hit draws and fades, how they hit high and low shots and how they save strokes by hitting all sorts of trouble shots. Be sure to spend time at the practice range, the chipping area and the putting green. Before the round, you will see how the pros warm up. After the round is over, they will work on parts of the game that gave them difficulty. All of these places present an opportunity for any golfer to see how the best-of-the-best go about their craft.

Chapter Two
Grip, Setup and Posture

What is the single most important *fundamental* in golf?

The ***grip*** is the single most important fundamental to focus on in the development of one's game, especially for someone who wants to become a more accomplished player. Think of it this way.

The grip dictates exactly and directly the flight of the golf ball.

It is the only connection a player has with the club. The grip exerts a direct influence on the face of the club. The angle of the club face at impact controls eighty-five percent of the initial direction of the golf ball. The next most important factor on shot direction and curvature is the path of the club head.

After an introduction to the game, and as one improves as a player, one's golf swing and setup will be developed over time around ball flight. That is how the golf swing will adjust and change. Ball flight will help to dictate what the player does in order to counterbalance their fears. What actually first influences their golf swing is their grip. Their grip totally affects ball flight, the starting direction of the ball and their fears concerning the golf swing. The grip starts everyone down the road of adjustments. Everything develops around the grip and club face.

What is the *right grip*? That is impossible to say until I have seen a player's ball flight. Everyone is different because body type, strength and the insecurities a person possesses are such an individual thing. Until I see a player's ball flight, I will not change their grip. Once I see a distinctive ball flight, grip changes can be suggested. How often will this be the case? Probably 90% of the time! The grip will have to be adjusted to match the player's needs. That is the key! It is very important! The grip is the single most important part of the game, bar none. There is not even a close second.

Another important factor worth mentioning is *grip tension*. Grip pressure should be somewhat light, something like holding a tube of toothpaste or a small kitten. The lighter the pressure, the more release and power the player will have. On the other hand, the tighter and firmer the pressure, the weaker the release will be and the less power it will generate.

After that, the **setup** is the second most important part of this whole program.

Can you suggest a visual cue that will help me properly position my hands on the golf club?

Certainly! One needs simply to visualize the circular face of a clock dial and relate grip hand placement to its twelve hourly positions. For example, the twelve o'clock position would represent a neutral grip. In the information which follows, I will be describing this position from the vantage point of a right-handed golfer.

In relation to this, please describe a *strong* grip.

This does not refer to the amount of tightness, looseness, tension or pressure on the grip of the club. Instead, as mentioned above, it has to do with the position of the hands on the grip. When viewed from above, a strong grip would have the hands appear to be turned to the right. The left hand would be palm-down on top of the grip and the right hand would be under the club. Another way of saying this is that the hands would be rotated in a clockwise fashion to a one or two o'clock position on the grip and away from the target relative to a neutral position. In this way, a player would see more knuckles on their left hand. Such a grip would produce a closing effect on the club face during the swing, and would create a hooking, drawing, right-to-left ball flight.

Now, please describe a *weak* grip.

Again, the amount of tightness, looseness, tension or pressure on the grip of the club is not the issue. As is the case with the strong grip, it has everything to do with hand position on the grip. When viewed from above, a weak grip would have the hands appear to be turned to the left with the right hand more on top of the club. The hands would be rotated in a counterclockwise fashion to a ten or eleven o'clock position on the grip and toward the target relative to a neutral position. A player would see almost no knuckles on their left hand. Such a grip would produce an opening effect on the club face during the swing, and would create a slicing, fading, left-to-right ball flight.

What is the second most important *fundamental* in golf?

My answer is the ***distance*** one sets up at address from the golf ball. Why? Sometimes coming over the top of the ball is due to a weak left *(leading)* hand. Most importantly, however, ninety-eight percent of the golfers in the world do so because they stand too far away from the ball. No matter who we are, as an athlete, our number one goal is *not* to hit it as close to the hole as possible. *In simple terms, it is to make contact with that little white ball sitting there.* So, if it sits 3 1/2 inches too far away, what are we going to do to get there? Are we going to jump to hit it? Are we going to move to hit it? Or are we going to come over the top to hit it? Guess what? We are coming over the top to hit it! And we will hit it --- absolutely! As a good player, we are still going to come over the top. We are still going to make contact. But now our golf swing will change from what we were taught and what we hoped to do to make contact, because that is the ultimate goal, to hit the ball. *Our second goal is to make the swing our golf pro said we should make. And our third goal is to get the ball close to the hole.* Goal number one -- making contact --- is what no one really talks about!

Assuming we have correct-fitting clubs, the key rule of thumb, in terms of measuring distance from the ball, is to be set up approximately one fist from the butt (end) of the club to one's body in the proper posture address position. It could be a fist and 1/4 for the driver if indeed the club fits you properly in terms of length when correctly setting up to the ball. *If the length of the club is not correct, improper accommodations have to be made in both posture and setup.* If a player's club fit does meet their build, then the great rule of thumb will work. From that point forward, they will have the ability to make a proper turn, to enter the ball from the inside quadrant and make a balanced swing resulting in a good golf shot. That will happen if their equipment fits them properly and if they set up to the ball with good posture.

What determines good posture?

I want to keep this as uncomplicated and simple as possible. Positions should not be overanalyzed. Athleticism should be the focal point. Good posture starts from the bottom up. The feet should be placed approximately shoulder-width apart. There should be a very slight flex in both knees. One's bottom should be stuck out slightly causing one to bend slightly forward from the hips. This allows the arms to hang down naturally from the shoulders. As long as the factors of club length and the distance from the ball are correct, everything will fall into place.

How does ball position influence ball flight?

Ball position should be one of the major starting points for most golfers. Here are my basic rules of thumb for *most* players concerning this topic. The ball is placed off of the left heel for the driver. The ball is moved back slightly for fairway woods. Hybrids and mid-irons are left-center. High-irons and wedges are placed in the middle for full shots. In order to hit the ball higher, the ball should be moved more forward in the stance. It is just the reverse to hit lower shots, so in that case, the ball should be placed further back in the stance. Better players tend to use more lower body and weight transfer during their swings than the standard player or beginner. As a whole, beginners need to play the ball further back in their stance than the better player who tends to drive their legs and can play the ball more forward.

How important is proper aiming and alignment?

It's very important because every shot involves a target. For a normal shot, a right-handed player wants their feet, legs, hips, shoulders and eyes to be aligned parallel left of the target. This allows for a proper swing path to take place. In this situation, it is helpful to visualize a *railroad track* when accomplishing this task. The left or inside rail represents the proper placement of one's feet, legs, hips, shoulders and eyes to be parallel left in relation to the distant target. The right or outside rail represents the target line with the ball resting on this line. This basic rule is true for all golf shots from the drive to the putt. In my opinion, there are two reasons golfers struggle with aim and alignment. First, they don't understand the parallel railroad track concept, and they misalign themselves either too far right or left of the target. Second, aiming *across one's body line* instead of facing the target is sometimes quite difficult to conceptualize. Let us consider several sports situations in which the aiming process is quite different. Basketball players and bowlers aim at a target while they are facing the target. Hunters wouldn't be successful shooting a rifle at a target if their eyes were continuously parallel to the target line instead of somewhat facing the target. Golfers are different because golf is a side along game. Subsequently, golfers must aim across their body line in order to hit shots toward a target. Golfers should consider using a nearby intermediate target which is on the target line inbetween the ball and the distant target in order to correctly set up to the ball when hitting shots.

Chapter Three
Proper Club Fitting and Equipment

It seems that as each year goes by, proper fitting of golf equipment becomes more and more important. Equipment today is far superior to that which was produced fifteen to twenty years ago. As a player, if you do not use the most updated equipment and you are not fitted properly, you will never be able to maximize your ability.

I frequently hear golfers say they need to learn to swing properly and to improve their game before they buy new clubs. That is like saying I am not going to buy a new car before I can parallel park perfectly. New equipment and proper fitting are paramount to success. The higher the handicap, the more important this choice is.

Golf clubs are like tools for a carpenter, electrician, plumber or mechanic. A player must have the correct-fitting tool for the task at hand. One wrench size does not fit all bolts!

Would you rather be playing with perfectly fit, ten-year-old golf clubs or brand new clubs which are fitted improperly?

I would rather be playing with ten-year-old clubs which fit perfectly.

Considering the last fifteen players you fit for new clubs, how many needed a different fit than the one for their current set?

All fifteen! Rather than simply buying off the rack, each and every player should be individually and properly fit for their clubs. Each player should carefully go through the various steps of the fitting *process*. This is because every golfer has an individual body type with proportional differences involving the length of their trunk, legs and arms. Factors which are evaluated in the fitting process include shaft type and length, lie angle, loft angle and grip size.

Sale price, such as buying last year's $399 model for $150 at the end of the season, should not be the number one priority when considering the purchase of new clubs. This approach leaves out the important fitting factors of shaft type and flex, length, lie, loft, total weight, swing weight, type of club head and grip size. Remember, a player does not want to get rid of a new club within a year due to a careless, less than thorough purchasing approach. New clubs should last at least five to ten years. Even if the player spends a little more money and takes the time to go through the proper fitting process, it is a good thing. This is true especially if it costs the player five to ten thousand dollars per year to play a sport they truly enjoy and love.

Is the size of the grip important?

Absolutely! It is a very important club fitting variable when attempting to understand why you hit the ball left, right or straight. For discussion purposes, we will consider the right-handed golfer. Grips which are too large may inhibit wrist and hand action and cause the ball to weakly slice to the right. On the other hand, grips which are too small may induce an over-active wrist and hand action and cause the ball to go almost anywhere, but normally hooked to the left. What, then, is the proper grip size? Remember, there are both men's and women's grips. For the right-handed player, while holding one's club with the left hand in the correct hitting posture, the middle two fingers should lightly touch the palm. There should neither be a gap between the fingers and the palm nor should the fingers be digging into the palm. In a proper fitting, there should be a definite correlation or direct relationship between the correct size of a player's golf glove and the size of the grip to be installed on their clubs. The most common glove size is medium to medium large. Therefore, most players should use a standard sized grip installed with one wrap of tape. In my opinion, unless the player is faced with debilitating arthritis, I am not in favor of oversized jumbo grips. Today, the biggest fault I see is that in getting their clubs regripped, almost every golfer incorrectly has grips installed that are either mid- or jumbo-sized. The bottom line is that most people simply need standard-sized grips on their clubs.

What alterations were needed the most?

The clubs needed to be *longer* and more *upright* in lie!

Impact tape can be affixed to the *face of a club* being evaluated for the optimum fitting **length** for each individual player. A fitter might routinely begin the process with a six or seven iron because this most commonly represents the club manufacturer's demo club. As a general rule, when clubs are too long, the point of impact is too close to the heel. When clubs are too short, the point of impact is too far out on the toe. The length of the club is correct when the point of impact is in the middle of the club face or fractionally toward the toe. The better a player maintains posture throughout the swing, the easier it is to calculate optimum club length and obtain consistent ball flight. Keep in mind, when setting your iron on a firm surface at address, the toe should be slightly up in the air. This is known as a *static fit*. During the golf swing, due to centrifugal force, the shaft actually bows downward slightly (about one degree), thus flattening the lie angle. Scuff marks of properly-fitted clubs should be at the center of the sole mid-way between the heel and the toe and directly under the middle of the club face.

Besides length, what other factors should be considered in the club fitting process?

Lie, *the angle in degrees between the club shaft and ground at address*, can be checked by affixing impact tape to the *sole of the club* and hitting balls off of a lie board. This is known as the *dynamic fitting process*. Ball flight and the scuff marks on the impact tape are evaluated. Should the scuff marks be located toward the heel and ball flight is consistently to the left of the target, the existing lies are too upright and need to be flattened. Should the scuff marks be located toward the toe and ball flight is consistently to the right of the target, the existing lies are too flat and need to be made more upright.

Every single golf club has loft, from the driver on down to the putter. **Loft** is *the angle in degrees of the face of the club with respect to the shaft.* In other words, the degree of the loft angle of the club is relative to the *vertical plane* rather than the ground. A properly adjusted, finely-tuned set of irons should have a three to four degree separation in loft between clubs. This will create the proper distance gaps between adjacent clubs in the set. For example, the traditional loft for a 3 iron is 21 degrees, a six iron is 31 degrees and a pitching wedge is 47 degrees.

The lies and lofts of each iron should be checked and "fine tuned" periodically due to the constant contact with the ball and ground at impact while practicing and playing. This is especially true with malleable, forged clubs. A Mitchell machine can be used by a trained club fitter to periodically check these specifications.

How long does it take to be fit properly for clubs?

A general fit for the average recreational player might only take about ten to fifteen minutes! Because it is their livelihood, a more detailed fit, such as a touring pro desires, would consume a longer period of time. Such a fit would utilize a launch monitor to evaluate swing speed, ball speed, smash factor, launch angle, trajectory and ball flight pattern. This information would be used to select the proper combination of shaft type and flex, shaft length and club head type for a new set of clubs. Especially if the fitting is accomplished without the use of a launch monitor, tape or special decals would be placed both on the face and sole of the club in order to evaluate centeredness of impact and correctness of lie angle.

What is your simple procedure for fitting someone?

There are several steps to the process. I first talk to the student for a few minutes about the history of their game. I then examine their old equipment. I study their setup and posture. As they hit shots on the practice range, I watch their ball flight in relationship to trajectory height, distance and curvature of the ball. I measure the distance from the ground to their hands hanging at their side in relationship to mine. This will indicate the proper length of club. Remember, I play this game for a living. I sometimes have the player hit *three to five balls* off of a hitting board using a six or seven iron. The marks created on the bottom surface of the clubs will indicate whether the lie is too upright, too flat or just right. Finally, I always measure the size of their hands compared to mine.

Where in the process do most club fitters make mistakes?

Fitters are afraid to change someone too much because of the stereotype that longer clubs are harder to hit successfully. Players with a taller physical stature who have square shoulders and shorter arms many times do not have club lengths which are long enough. They should not be playing with standard, off-the-rack clubs. Overall, for the right-handed golfer, most player's irons are too flat, helping to result in a left-to-right ball flight. This fact is representative of approximately eighty-five percent of the golfing population.

In your opinion, what are your biggest areas of concern in the area of club fitting?

Grips for junior golf clubs are too big. Junior sets need to have more wedges, a thirteen to eighteen degree driver, especially a lob wedge, and a hybrid instead of a three wood. More adults need a twelve to sixteen degree driver. *Almost everyone* should own a lob wedge. The standard lie in irons should be one more degree upright. In the modern game, standard lengths of both men's and women's clubs should be slightly longer than standard. The standard grip on all clubs should be round rather than ribbed. Strong women and young juniors jump into senior or men's clubs too often.

How many degrees of loft should I have on my driver?

Assuming the golf swing and body movements are good, the choice of driver loft depends most importantly on the strength of the player's ball flight and the speed of their swing. Regardless of ability, if only one driver loft were available for all players, it should be twelve degrees.

What does it mean when irons are described as having a cavity back, perimeter weighted style?

This is very similar to the above discussion regarding putter head design. It is the style of iron that allows for the most correction of off-center hits, which are hit off the toe, heel, top or bottom of the club face. The result with the cavity back, perimeter weighted iron will be much more beneficial and forgiving than the old blade club. The blade club had a sweet spot about the size of a dime. The cavity back, perimeter weighted style has a sweet spot somewhere between the size of a quarter or fifty cent piece. In the modern world, all players, regardless of ability, should be using this style of iron. Such clubs blend the visual appeal of the blade style with the corrective features of cavity backed, perimeter weighted irons. There simply is no down side to using these technologically updated irons. So why not make the decision to use them?

What is your opinion concerning hybrids?

During a lesson, probably the last club I want a student to take out of their bag and hit in front of me is a long iron, such as a 3-4-5 iron. These irons are the most difficult golf clubs to hit. In the last few years, manufacturers have developed the hybrid, which is really a blend of the best features of irons and woods. Hybrids are easier to hit, get the ball up in the air, soften the shot, create plenty of power and, in my opinion, are one club stronger than the average iron. Hybrids are good for hitting out of a variety of lies. Are hybrids for everyone? About 98% of golfers can use hybrids. Because shots hit with them are hit high and land softly, hybrids are good when playing into elevated, small greens. Under windy conditions, due to their higher ball flight, hybrids are tough to use. In this situation, when a lower shot is required, it would be easier to hit a knock-down three iron. But that is just my opinion. Hybrids are great for the average golfer.

Why is a golf glove worn?

A glove is worn in order to generate a better grip and a more secure feeling of your upper hand. The usage of a glove is traditional and the grip feels stronger in one's hand. Most tour players use a glove. Remember, the grip is the golfer's only contact with the club! If your grip feels insecure, that it is coming out of your hands, a player has *no chance* of playing good golf! Most people purchase too large of a glove for their hand size. The glove should fit snugly and tightly.

How often should grips be changed?

I am going to answer that question by asking another question. How often have you cleaned your grips in the last year? If the golfer cleans their grips after every round, unless their grip tension is too tight causing undue wear, they should last on average for at least two years. The use of soap is not even necessary. All that is needed is a good golf towel and clean water. On the course, I even wipe off the grip before most shots in order to achieve that tacky feeling. The idea is to clean off the sweat on the grips before it turns into a shiny glaze.

How important for me is it to play with the correct ball?

The more accomplished a player becomes, the more valuable is the selection of the correct ball. Just as important is not using an old ball, such as one which has been used for four rounds. The ball should be new enough so it hasn't gotten damaged in any way. Also, a player should have only *one* type of ball in their golf bag. In this manner, their body gets used to the feel of the specific ball. The feel for the ball must be consistent every time one hits a shot, whether it be drives, irons, wedges, short game shots or putts. For example, a player should never even practice putting with more than one brand type of ball. This practice maximizes one's chance of being a better player.

Do you recommend a four wedge system?

It depends on what type of golfer you are. A beginning golfer probably does not need a four wedge system. Neither would a right-handed golfer with a weak left hand who hits everything left to right with a high trajectory. A player who hits the ball shorter and uses several hybrids would not be a candidate for four wedges. However, a golfer with tremendous length who tends to hook the ball a lot probably needs a four wedge system. So would someone who is becoming a more accomplished player and who is playing better golf courses. The lower handicap, physically strong, competitive player should lean toward the use of the four-wedge system. If the decision is made to use a three-wedge system, one must decide between the choice of a gap and a lob wedge. In this situation, I might recommend the choice of a lob wedge.

What characteristics are important to keep in mind when being fitted for a sand wedge?

This valuable club can be used to help the player perform on the golf course from a wide variety of lies and distances. We need to consider how the physical attributes of the sand wedge club head has an affect on both greenside bunker play and chip-and-run and loft shots off of the turf. The sand wedge can also be used for scoring shots from the fairway.

The reader must first understand several club-fitting terms as they apply to this club. The **sole** is the bottom of the clubhead, similar to that of a shoe. We should already understand that **loft** is the angle in degrees of the face of the club with respect to the shaft. The bottom front edge of the club face is its **leading edge**. The back or rear edge of the sole is its **trailing edge**, which is also the lowest point on the sole of the club. This is the point where the sole makes contact with the ground. **Bounce** is the angle of the sole created between the leading edge and the ground line or trailing edge. Its purpose is to raise the leading edge off of the ground. Sole width can vary greatly. A wide sole brings the leading edge of the wedge higher off of the ground, increasing its bounce effect, but a thin sole keeps the leading edge lower, reducing the bounce effect. **Sole grind** is the process of reshaping the trailing edge from the **heel** to the **toe** of the club head, which allows for an even greater variety of shot possibilities. The width of the sole performs like an airplane wing or skis on water or snow. Should a player open the clubface, this actually increases the club's bounce effect.

While performing a bunker shot, the design of the sand wedge allows the player to enter the club head slightly behind the ball while preventing the leading edge from digging into the sand. As intended, the player is able to more efficiently glide the clubhead through the sand. With shots played off of the turf, either around the green or some distance away from it, club bounce is again an important factor to consider. Bounce can help prevent the golfer from digging the leading edge into the ground. Higher bounce is appropriate for players who have a steeper angle of attack or when the turf is soft. Less bounce is appropriate for players with a shallower, flatter angle of attack and when turf conditions are firm.

The various specification options offered by manufacturers, the need to perform from a wide variety of lies and distances and the need to do so with precision indicates the absolute necessity of undergoing a proper fitting process for this club. Since they are scoring clubs, this should also be true for all of your wedges.

How important to me is shaft flex/stiffness in relationship to student need?

First and foremost, I would say this is one of the more controversial topics in club fitting today. I am not saying shaft flex is not important. It is part of the overall puzzle. But in my opinion, I feel it is overrated by certain people in the golf world! I just don't value this as highly as some people do. It certainly is important to those people who market and advertise club fitting and the selling of new shafts. But it is my belief shaft flex is more about salesmanship than the reality of what it gives you. I personally think the more important consideration is the consistency of shaft flex between the woods, irons and wedges present in the individual player's bag. This factor is more important than having the perfect overall shaft flex. Over time, one's golf swing will adjust to the flex of the clubs they are playing. A sidelight story applies very well here. About twenty-five to thirty years ago, Fred Couples was invited to Tom Watson's house in Kansas City for dinner. While he was there, he visited the basement where Tom stored many clubs. Fred grabbed a three wood he liked and put it into tournament play for about two months. Over this time, everything was great and he hit the club with phenomenal success. Then one day, he happened to take the three wood into the fitting trailer at one of the tour stops to have the stiffness of the shaft evaluated on the flex board. He subsequently found out it was not extra stiff, stiff or even regular. It was a ladies flex. What do you think Couples did? He took the club out of play instantly --- never used it again! Yet it was the most favorite three wood he had ever used up to that point in his life. Exactly what is the lesson to be learned? How strong is one's brain in relation to sports? How much is the value of shaft flex in relationship to one's confidence level? Sometimes either too much or not enough knowledge is hurtful to us. Here is the general rule. The longer a player hits the ball, the more they have to work toward stiffness of shaft. The shorter a player hits the ball, the more they have to work toward a lighter, softer, more flexible shaft.

Do you mind what sort of putter I use? Do you have any suggestions for the *style* or *head design* of putter I should have?

This is a topic which might be of more concern to a low-handicap, advanced player rather than the novice. Putting is the most individualistic part of the game of golf. With that in mind, here are some general thoughts. A player who takes the putter *straight back and straight through* would probably most benefit from the use of a *face-balanced, center-shafted style putter*. If the player has an arcing stroke which is inside-to-square-to-inside, they would be better off with a toe-hang, heel-shafted putter. In my opinion, the latter stroke is the most preferable of the two methods. The average right-handed putter misses putts to the right rather than the left because they take the putter back slightly inside and then stroke the ball toward the hole going through. The first inch of the putt after the putter strikes the ball determines everything about where the ball is going to go.

Should I decide to go through with a putter fitting, what should be some of the additional important considerations to keep in mind?

Again, this information might better suit the more accomplished player who plays in tournaments. Just as with other golf clubs, a player should never accept buying a putter off of the rack. They should at least practice with it for a while and play on the course with it for a few rounds. They should also compare it to another model before buying it. Preferably, each player should carefully go through the proper steps of a putter fitting *process* just as they would for a driver through the wedges. Again, this is because every golfer has an individual body type with proportional differences involving the length of their trunk, legs and arms. The process has a number of steps.

The **length** of the putter allows the player to set up properly to the ball. First, because putter length directly affects both distance and directional control, the putter should be the proper length. This allows for correct posture at setup. The result is a more flowing stroke, which can be more easily repeated over and over again. Since vision is so important, the length of the putter should encourage the *eyes to be either directly over or slightly inside of the target line* and *parallel to the initial target line*. This parallel setup should also be true of the feet and shoulders. It should permit the arms to be comfortable and the elbows to have the proper angular bend.

Just as with irons, one's putter should have the correct settings of both lie and loft! As with all clubs, and as mentioned before, lie and loft are fixed properties, which are built into the manufacture of the club. With respect to the putter, a little review of the concepts of lie and loft might be beneficial here.

Concerning **lie**, *the angle in degrees between the club shaft and ground at address*, the sole of the putter needs to be level with the ground on an even, putting surface. Neither the toe nor the heel should be raised. This is because lie angle affects the initial directional control of a putt, the same as is true with a full shot. If the toe is raised, the lie is too upright, which leads to pulls to the left. In this case, the lie needs to be flattened. On the other hand, if the heel is raised, the lie is too flat, which leads to pushes to the right. In this case, the lie needs to be made more upright.

Loft is *the angle in degrees of the face of the club with respect to the shaft*. Loft of the putter is important because it promotes a rapid, true forward topspin-roll of the ball. Ideally, the player wants the ball to hug the ground, rolling end-over-end. The ideal is to create an absolute minimum of bouncing or skidding. Such a roll increases the likelihood of target line accuracy as well as more predictable distance control on longer, approach putts. Too little loft causes the ball to be driven into the ground and results in bouncing. Too much loft causes the ball to be launched off of the ground and skidding takes place.

For most standard-length putters, the *fixed loft* angle should be in the range of three to four degrees. On the other hand, *dynamic loft* is influenced by what the player does with the putter during the motion of the putting stroke itself, including the forward press. If utilized by the player to initiate the stroke, this move must be taken into account in the fitting process because it effectively reduces the fixed loft. A forward press de-lofts the putter face right from the beginning of the stroke. Thus, the forward press is one factor to consider related to adjusting the final putter loft. In determining the optimal loft, another important factor to consider is the position of the ball at address. Since it impacts loft, this factor also affects the bounce or skid of the ball as it rolls off of the putter face as well as directional and distance control. Should the ball be too far forward in the stance, effective loft is increased and putts are sometimes pulled to the left. Should the ball be too far back in the stance, effective loft is decreased and putts are sometimes pushed to the right. With the arm-lock putter style used by Matt Kuchar, which might gain more acceptance with the ban of the anchored stroke on January 1, 2016, there is no forward press in the stroke. It all depends on where the ball is placed in the stance. Less loft will be required when the ball is placed forward in the stance; more loft when the ball is placed in the middle.

It is well to note that adjustments can be be quite easily made to both of these angles by a qualified club maker. Putter lie can be checked by looking into a mirror while addressing the ball with your putter. Loft can be checked by the use of a dew board, which indicates how the ball is rolling off of the putter face.

Head weight, which affects distance control, is more difficult to determine. Since heavier is generally better, a good range would be somewhere between a high-C and mid-E range on the swingweight scale. In terms of a player's individual personality, they might prefer a putter which has either a heavier or lighter weight. In this regard, green speeds should be a consideration. A putter with a *heavier head weight* might tend to work better when putting on *slower green surfaces*.

A final factor to be thought about in the fitting process is **Moment Of Inertia**. When putting, the goal is to consistently contact the ball in the very center of the putter face. With less skilled players, this does not always happen. Here is where an understanding of Moment Of Inertia becomes important. M.O.I. is the resistance to rotation of the putter head on off-center hits, those where the ball is struck toward either the toe or heel of the putter face. Thus, with a putter with a high M.O.I. rating, the player can maximize their distance and directional control on mishits.

Club Selection
Versus
Style of Shot

Chapter Four
The Driver

The driver is one of the three most important clubs in a player's arsenal. The other two are the lob wedge and the putter. I have had students who do not use a driver but instead use a three wood. I disagree with this philosophy because, in this day and age, the different specifications offered by golf club manufacturers will allow anyone to be fit properly for a driver. If a student will allow me to give them a little bit of information and allow me to fit them correctly for a driver, they will always hit the driver better than the three wood. In all my years playing at all levels, the best and most successful players do drive the ball very well. Twenty-five to thirty years ago, it seemed that successful players were the likes of Ben Crenshaw, Tom Kite, Mike Reid, Calvin Peete, Jack Renner and Curtis Strange. These players were considered short but very straight. Today, it seems most winners are very long. The short and straight theory seems to be gone.

Do you feel, as a good player, that you should maximize the strength that God gave you in driving the golf ball?

I hope you all say yes, because that is how you become a better player. Driving the golf ball is the beginning of almost every hole you play! You want to have the ball in play, but yet you want to maximize the opportunity of your own individual strength. Keep in mind, you can always learn to drive it straight but not everyone can hit it long. When God gives you length off the tee, by all means use it. At the same time, if God gave you less distance combined with greater accuracy off the tee but with a better short game involving feel and trust, do not try to change your style of golf. Whatever deck of cards you were dealt, you need to work on maximizing it. It is hard to change the deck of cards you have been dealt based upon who you are.

What keys are paramount to maximizing one's driving ability and power?

To begin with, the club must **fit** the player in both *length* and *loft*. One's **hands** need to be *relaxed* on the grip. **Setup** to the ball needs to be correct. On the **backswing**, the player's natural body movement (weight) needs to be transferred onto their back foot like either a javelin thrower or baseball pitcher does in their windup. In doing so, the player needs to turn both their chest and hips. A reasonable goal would be to have the ***chest turn 90 degrees*** (twice as far) while the ***hips turn 45 degrees.*** The lower body remains relatively quiet as the upper body coils above it. Continuing the analogy of the javelin thrower or baseball pitcher, *weight* needs to be transferred *naturally* to the front foot on the **downswing.** The club needs to be coming down in the *slot* towards impact, and also needs to be *lagging* for leverage on the downswing prior to ball contact.

If you had to pick the single biggest power producer in the golf swing, what would it be?

The number one power producer is that the club needs to be lagging for leverage on the downswing prior to ball contact. What do I mean by this statement? I am really talking about hinging and unhinging the wrists in order to create this action. The wrists are first hinged and set on the backswing. An angle is created between the left forearm and, by extension, the shaft of the club. This hinging is maximized by holding the grip of the club in the fingers of the right hand rather than the palm. On the downswing, the reverse takes place. The wrists, which had been hinged and cocked to a certain degree during the backswing, now get unhinged at impact. It is this *catapulting effect* of the club head catching up to the hands at impact due to the unhinging of the wrists which creates great power. If the hands never catch up in this manner, the ball will never get airborne. Golfers who have the best timing at the bottom and who produce the best lag are the ones who are going to create the most leverage. They are the players who are going to create the most power.

A student might argue this point by saying, "I release the club too early". As a teacher, I feel this is a cop out to a result. There is no such thing. On the other hand, there are other problems happening, such as coming over the top with a closed club face, a weak left hand, too much tension, and so forth, which would supersede that statement.

Stu Ingraham is currently fifty-four years of age. Physically, I cannot bench press 100 pounds. However, I am still considered very long for my age. Why? I create tremendous angles and generate tremendous hinge. I have got long monkey-arms and big hands. My *timing* is really good. I unhinge and uncock the club at the right time, creating tremendous leverage in the process. This lagging effect is the number one, maximum power producer in golf.

Should you have a total green light and opportunity to maximize your power when a driver is in your hand?

Sometimes! There is a time and place to hit a full throttle driver.

Should a player always, always hit the driver with the thought of full throttle, maximum power?

No! Sometimes producing a shorter shot but getting the ball in play is more important than gaining maximum distance. Golf is not about always hitting a perfect shot. At the end of the day, it is about keeping the ball in front of you, feeling comfortable and shooting a number.

Is there such a thing in golf like a second serve in tennis?

Most definitely, yes! This could mean using a middle to a long iron, a hybrid, a fairway wood or even a maneuvered driver. Here is a story that is a case in point. About fifteen years ago, I was playing in a section event at Deerwood Country Club in Mount Holly, New Jersey. I came to the eighteenth tee with what I thought was the lead. Since there were no scoreboards present, I did not know this for certain. But I was pretty sure this was true. The last hole is a dogleg left-to-right about 380 yards in length. There is a hazard all down the right side and out-of-bounds to the left. The out-of-bounds is pretty far left, but I was not sure how far it was through the fairway at the turn of the dogleg. My assistant pro, playing in the group ahead of me, had hit a pull hook drive out of bounds. However, initially, he did not know he had driven the ball out of play. After searching for his ball and determining it had, in fact, gone out of bounds, he now had to drive back to the tee and hit another ball. Playing one group behind, it was at this point I encountered this situation as I came up to the tee on the eighteenth hole. Based on the knowledge of what had happened to my assistant, the negative thoughts now began to flow for me. How would I react to this situation? I could make it into a negative or turn it into a positive. I decided to play the hole smartly and tee off with a five iron. Because I was so pumped up, the ball probably traveled about 215 yards. I now had approximately 165 yards remaining to the pin and decided to hit a hard eight iron. The ball landed thirty feet from the hole. I two-putted, recorded a 64 for the round and won the section point tournament by one shot. So, what is the moral of the story? Considering the nerves I had in my system, I correctly used what it took to get the ball in play. It is also beneficial to know geographic distances on the course and how far each club can be hit. This a good plug for the use of distance calculating devices in helping to determine club selection, including laying up short of hazards. It is not always about hitting a driver or three-wood on a par four or five hole. I figured par was a good score, which it wound up being, and in the process, I set a new course record. This is how I used a second serve tee shot to my advantage to get the job done.

Should a player have the ability to maneuver the driver right-to-left or left-to-right to accommodate the type of hole they are playing through ball flight?

Most certainly! Here are two examples. The 14th hole at Merion G.C. (East) is a dogleg left, with out-of-bounds and thick rough also to the left, requiring a right-to-left ball flight. On the other hand, the sixth hole at Overbrook G.C. is a dogleg right with out-of-bounds to the left. It requires a left-to-right ball flight.

What are the biggest mistakes golfers make in choosing a driver?

Golfers allow advertisements to dictate their choice of manufacturer. They do not demo the club for a long enough period of time to find out what the correct club is for them. Higher handicap players need to select a driver with more loft. Golfers generally do not investigate fully enough the models of drivers used by tour players. In doing so, they spend the same amount of money on lesser drivers as they would on the tour level driver they should be purchasing. Golfers should be choosing a driver which maximizes their God-given strengths. Everyone is different in this regard. Each individual golfer has certain swing characteristics. One's physical attributes, such as overall height, length of torso and arms, will also play a role in the correct selection of a driver. A higher handicap player, due to improvements in technology, is going to benefit from almost any driver they select. On the other hand, fitting a more accomplished player is going to be more difficult. This level of player should go through a detailed, systematic approach that involves the use of a launch monitor. This technical device collects data on such items as ball and club head speed, launch angle and ball spin rate. Baseline data is first collected on the player's current driver by hitting specially marked balls in front of the launch monitor. The same process is then used in testing various new driver club head-shaft configurations. This experimentation considers factors including shaft type, flex and length, club head loft and desired ball flight and trajectory. All of this takes place under the watchful eye of a trained fitter. The purpose of assembling all of this information is to help recommend the club head-shaft combination that will optimize the performance for that individual golfer. It is like fine-tuning the engine of a racecar.

Can being fit for a driver ever hurt a player?

Sure! People are playing drivers that do not fit them right now. It depends on who is fitting the player and the budget of the person doing the buying.

How high should the golf ball be teed up in using a driver?

The sweet spot on the modern driver is at the top, center of the face of the club. If the player has a normal, standard, rounded swing, they need to tee the ball *higher* than normal so they can contact the ball two-thirds of the way up the center face of the club. Players who use older equipment and over tilters who use a lot of hands need to tee the ball lower.

What are the most important keys when hitting a driver?

The driver swing is the most aggressive in the game of golf. It is the club that produces shots carrying the longest distance. As a result, the player needs to have a green light and swing the club with a pace matching their identity and personality. The player must allow the driver swing to happen and not defend against it. Be on the offensive!

Stu, what are your ingredients in hitting the *second serve tee shot* in golf?

For me, my second serve tee shot is actually an over-the-top, pull-cut. It might be compared to Tiger Wood's stinger, hold on shot. This shot requires creativity. One must *exaggerate* the over-the-top, outside-to-inside path. *Considering knowledge of ball flight laws (chapter 29), the idea is to keep the face of the club head open to the path of the club head.* Do not allow the club to get stuck under plane due to the fear of hooking. Matching the correct grip to the student will help neutralize the club face. In addressing the ball, the player will need to assume an open stance. Due to the shape of the shot, the player needs to aim at the left edge of the fairway. One needs to pick the club up on the backswing. This means taking the club slightly to the outside. The player needs to allow their hands to hold through a bit at impact with a slightly open club face. One needs to get their hands out front of the club head at the impact point. Hitting the shot in this manner will prevent the creation of too much spin on the ball. In *pulling* the club face across the ball, it will not curve too much and will be kept in play. The finish will be low and punchy. Such a shot might be expected to carry approximately 235 yards and then run out to 280 yards. When should a shot such as this be attempted? It depends on the situation. It might be used once or twice a round, such as on a tight, dogleg left-to-right hole where the player does not want to get the ball up in the air and does not want to get stuck under plane creating a big block to the right. Please understand everything that I just described is what I personally do. My method might not apply to each and every golfer who reads this book. However, every golfer should have a second serve tee shot within their arsenal of shots.

Chapter Five
Fairway Woods and Hybrids

Why are hybrids becoming popular?

As the world of golf is changing based on competitions, rounds of golf played and technology, the hybrid club is now introduced as a sellable product. The hybrid is a golf club that combines the best features of long irons and metal woods. The hybrid is a club designed to replace long irons in one's bag.

Do you think the hybrid club overall is a good investment for golfers?

Absolutely! It replaces the two to five-iron in the bag of most golfers. For my average student, the hardest club to hit is either a three metal wood or a two through four-iron. I actually encourage many students who start golf to invest in a hybrid versus a fairway metal wood. The hybrid is more forgiving and thus easier to hit. I always feel the higher the handicap or newer the player, the more valuable the hybrid becomes.

What factors should I consider when hitting a hybrid versus a fairway wood?

One secret to keep in mind with hybrids is ball position and approach. Remember, this is not a fairway wood. I feel the two biggest mistakes golfers make when hitting this club are they stand too far away from the ball and position the ball too far forward at address. When hitting a hybrid, it should be treated like a *six-iron* approach that demands a steeper angle of attack and a more descending blow versus the sweeping motion of a fairway club. This means the ball position should be halfway between the front heel and the middle of the stance.

If your bag has fairway woods in them, make sure the loft of the club matches the strength of your swing. Depending on the player, they might be better off replacing a fairway wood with either a hybrid or a lob wedge. If you decide to use a fairway wood, make sure your ball position is just inside your front foot and be careful with the loft of the club.

What determines whether a player should carry either a hybrid club or a metal three wood?

As I look through and evaluate a bag of equipment, I feel I must address the value of selecting hybrid versus fairway wood clubs in a player's set makeup. If they do carry one or more hybrid club, what loft numbers might they select? The stronger the player and the farther they can hit the ball, I would suggest carrying a three-wood with less loft. Whereas a tour player would carry a three-wood, a weaker player might instead select a more forgiving seven- or nine-wood. Ninety-five percent of the golfers in the world would benefit from substituting a hybrid-club for a three-wood. Make sure the strength of your ball flight dictates not only which fairway clubs and hybrids are in your bag, but also the lofts of these clubs.

Is there any reason why hybrids might be more valuable to golfers than fairway woods?

The length of grass on fairways today is cut much closer and tighter than in the past. A slight mishit with a three wood versus that of a four hybrid can be very different to the average golfer. As a result, the three-wood is losing its value and the hybrid is replacing it. This is because there is a physical difference between the two types of clubs. To begin with, the three-wood has a deeper face. This means the club head is bigger in overall size, there is a greater distance from the bottom to the top of the club face and there is less loft. The height of the three wood face is about the same as or greater than the diameter of the golf ball. Hybrids have just the opposite properties. The overall size of the club head is smaller, the face has a more shallow (smaller) measurement from top to bottom and it has more loft. Hybrids are easier to hit because these properties make it less difficult for the player to get the club head underneath the ball.

Chapter Six
Iron Play

How do you feel about the amount of attention paid to iron play?

Iron play is an area that never seems to get enough attention and emphasis when it comes to evaluating important aspects of the game. The main talk seems to center on driving it far and well, hitting quality wedges and, of course, putting as a means of scoring.

How do you categorize iron play?

Iron play is categorized basically as the use of the three-iron through the pitching wedge. I include the pitching wedge within this category because this club most often matches the three-iron through nine-iron in their set in terms of how it is made. With hybrids involved in the equipment setup of many golfers, the most important iron shots are the 5-6-7 irons in their bag.

Are there any aspects of iron play that you wish to emphasize?

I feel the most important aspects of iron play, which are paramount to success, include *angle of attack*, *lagging the club* and making sure *impact is in the center of the club face* or perhaps *favoring the toe*. The toe is a much better friend than the heel!

Concerning their swing in relation to success in iron play and hitting woods, almost every golfer other than a touring professional seems to fit into one of two categories. One end of the spectrum is a swing that has a shallow approach from the inside. The other extreme has a steeper approach from a little more straight-on or outside.

Can you share several secrets or insights that will assist iron play?

Be aware of being *close enough* to the ball. Distance from the ball is tremendously important and is often a neglected point of emphasis.

Make sure the *grip* is in the *fingers* of the hand rather than in the palm.

Be sure to *cock the club* in order to create an *angle*.

Be sure the *divot* starts *past* the ball, not before.

Learn to *trap the ball* with irons versus "scooping" and lifting the shot. When situated 125 yards from the pin, if you tend to like a lie in the short rough better than a tight lie in a closely mown fairway, then I promise you must be a "scooper". In this case, your swing tends to be better with hybrids, woods and a driver.

Weight needs to be naturally transferred from the *back* foot to the *front* foot. The right foot comes off the ground and up onto the toes, allowing a full, forward turn of the shoulders. Do not hang back on the right side.

Make sure your *arms* finish *folded* over your *shoulder* and *not* extended too high.

What other influences are of importance in iron play?

Know specifically the distance in yards that you hit each iron and the exact yardage to the pin when playing a course. If possible, evaluate the accuracy of yardage markers in the fairway. Of course, carrying a yardage-measuring device is even better in saving time while gaining accurate measurements.

Evaluate the *lie* in terms of hitting a solid shot.

Manage the *wind* conditions.

Know the *firmness* of the greens.

Evaluate the uphill or downhill nature of the lie and shot.

If a bad shot is hit, in relationship to the hole location, evaluate where you want to *miss*.

In closing, as a good player, I feel there are probably thirty-five to forty key shots in a round of golf. Iron play makes up at least one-third of them! This statistic would include wedges to the green.

Chapter Seven
Wedges to the Green

The development of a quality wedge game to the green is a vital part of scoring in golf.

Here is a story that vividly proves my point. A couple of years ago, I was paired with a young man named Jake Gerney, who at that time represented Dupont Country Club, in the fall pro-pro. I did not know Jake personally but knew the week before he had finished runner-up in the Philadelphia Section P.G.A. match play championship. This means he can play! This story is being told because of how good his wedge play was for our team that day. The format was selective drive-alternate shot, which is a difficult type of competition. I happened to drive it really well that day and also putted extremely well. The result was a seven shot victory as we recorded an eight under 63 with ten birdies. The moral of the story and how it relates to this topic is that Jake's wedge play was *awesome*.

The maximum number of wedges that golfers carry is four --- pitching, gap, sand and lob wedges. The most common sequences are either 46, 50, 54 and 58 degrees or 46, 52, 56 and 60 degrees. I mention this progression because I do feel the most underrated club that is _not_ in the bag of most golfers is the lob wedge. The old adage was that you needed to be a good player to use a lob wedge. I totally disagree with this philosophy.

I think a good wedge player needs to be mindful of the following *keys* in order to be successful:

1. The *lower body* needs to be kept "quiet".

2. The *backswing* needs to be about *three-quarters* in length.

3. Enough *angle* needs to be created in order to *"trap"* the ball between the club face and the surface of the ground.

4. The *grip* needs to be *"strong"* enough to cause the club face to *square* at impact.

5. The *ball trajectory* needs to be fairly low with good spin. This means the ball needs to be struck with a descending blow. If you are a "scooper", wedges will not be your friend. During the swing and through impact, the hands should be leading the club head. Ideally, there should be a forward-leaning club shaft.

6. The standard *ball position* for full wedges should be towards the *"middle"* of one's stance. Keep in mind, if the lie is "poor", always tend to play it "back" more in your stance. If the lie is "puffed up" or in short rough, you may play the ball more "forward" in your stance.

7. The following is a teaching secret that might help those players who chase, reach or catch the ball

thin and in the heel when hitting shots. At address, the ball needs to be positioned off the *toe* of the club face. This allows the player to strike the ball more in the center of the club face and helps to avoid contact with the hosel. In truth, with a one hundred yard shot, a ball struck slightly off center on the toe will travel only approximately 5% less than a shot struck solidly in the middle of the club face.

In closing, never choke down on a full wedge unless your feet are *below* the ball (side-hill lie). Always remember, this club can be used to create better scoring and can save a disastrous hole. Good wedge players tend to be good golfers.

How does one play *partial* wedges?

The biggest secret is to take the club back the distance the shot calls for. Before a player decides on how far to take the club back, they need to know how far they hit a full wedge. Partial wedges are all in perspective to one's full swing length. The different *lengths of backswings* should determine the length of yardage the shot requires. Different lengths of backswing might include full, three-quarters and half. On the practice range, the player should investigate the exact distances they can hit each wedge in their bag with these three backswing lengths. The downswing, follow through result is determined by the momentum of the club going through impact. The player must accelerate through and complete the swing to a full finish. There are many times that I have had a shot that I know is 83 yards but which will play more like 65 yards. In this situation, the role of one's *vision* on such non-full shots is just as valuable as knowing the actual distance. This is better known as playing by sight and feel. Yet another way of saying this is that the player is playing the shot with their eyes.

From a good lie, how does one create a wedge shot that quickly checks up on the green?

I would say this is a topic that separates the good player from a decent player. Almost all golfers ask how to create spin. However, the idea with this shot is to generate sufficient but not excessive spin. As I see it, the player needs to do three things to play this shot correctly. It begins with ball selection. One must use a soft, spinning ball. Second, the overall length or distance of the wedge shot needs to be long enough so the ball can be hit hard enough to create some spin. Third, and most importantly, the golfer needs to hinge the club quickly on the backswing and also create a steep enough angle of attack on the downswing in order to trap the ball between the clubface and the turf. Finally, a few additional adjustments need to be considered in order to play the *knockdown* shot. The player might select a club with less loft than the normal yardage calls for, such as a nine iron rather than a wedge. They might play the ball farther back in their stance. They might choke down a bit on the grip rather than play it at its full length. This stiffens the shaft and reduces the distance the ball will travel. Another thought might be to shorten the length of both the backswing and the follow through. Opening up one's stance will help to restrict the backswing and allow weight to transfer naturally to the front foot during the downswing. When played in this manner, the result will be that the ball will come off the clubface on a lower trajectory and check up quickly on the surface of the green. Obviously, all of this must be rehearsed thoroughly on the practice range before being attempted during a meaningful round on the course.

What steps should a player who scoops the ball take in order to improve their wedge shots?

They should consciously try taking the following five steps. First, an effort should be made to move the **ball position** more to the *middle* of their stance. Second, the **club shaft** should be *angled forward* so that the placement of their hands is even with or slightly forward of the club head. Third, at impact, their **weight** should be shifted more on to their *front foot*. Fourth, at impact, in order to make **solid contact** with the ball, one might mentally picture looking *two inches in front of the ball*. This point was emphasized in the last section. Fifth, the **wrists** should be *cocked* or *hinged* very early in the backswing, and the **angle of attack** on the ball during the downswing should be more *steep*.

Because of its importance, I want to spend a bit more time on step four. The *mental image* of looking two inches in front of the ball cannot be discounted. This is important in wet conditions, especially in the Northeast United States in the Spring and Fall, particularly when playing out of the rough. In this instance, a steeper angle of attack is required. This can easily be accomplished by mentally imagining a *coin two inches in front of the ball* and hitting down on it during the swing. The end result will be a shot hit with a descending blow. By striking the ball first, contact will be clean. This same thought can be utilized when chipping and performing sand shots around the green.

Chapter Eight
Around the Greens --- Chipping

A few years ago, I was playing in the second to last group in the final round of the state open at Moselem Springs Golf Club. I came to the ninth hole and hit my second shot short of the green in the rough about ten yards behind a green-side bunker. As I approached the ball, I realized it was going to be a loft-style shot over the bunker which is much more dangerous than a chip-and-run style shot. I then discovered while taking my normal stance that my left heel was touching a sprinkler head, which is an immovable obstruction. After taking my stance and using my fifty-inch putter for measuring purposes, I now dropped the ball into a perfect lie in the fairway, which was my nearest point of relief. Because of the angle and lie, I was then able to hit a chip and run shot. Believe it or not, I knocked it into the hole for a birdie three. Knowing and following the rules along with the knowledge and ability to play shots properly around the green can be a big advantage.

When a player misses a green, what *type* of shot should they choose --- pitching (loft) or chipping (chip-and-run)?

The chip-and-run choice should always be used when possible. When missing a green, the player either has a black or white choice, never gray, in choosing how to hit their next shot. Only use the loft shot when you have to. This example would be having a pin close to the edge with no green to work with or a shot over a hazard or a bunker.

Is there more than one chipping *style*?

There are *two*. In chipping, it is my opinion every golfer is either a scooper or a trapper. A scooper has a shallow, flatter swing creating a wider contact point with the ground. They tend not to hinge at all. The club head gets back to the ball before the hands, utilizing a *scooping* motion with the hands to get the ball airborne. This type of player needs to use a less lofted club. A trapper, on the other hand, has a more hinging, vertical, steep swing creating a narrower contact point between the club head and the ground. The hands get back to the ball or ahead of the ball before the club head, *trapping* the ball cleanly between the ground surface and the club face. They are able to create severe angles. This style player needs to use a more lofted club in relationship to the angles that have been created.

What is hinging?

Hinging is the relationship of cocking the club head back in the backswing. As mentioned in an earlier chapter, the wrists are first hinged and set on the backswing. An angle is created between the left forearm and, by extension, the shaft of the club. In doing so, an angle is created in the right wrist. A vertical angle is created in relationship to the ball and the ground. This, in effect, would always create a steep enough angle of the club head striking the ground, The goal is to make sure we make contact with the golf ball *prior to* striking the ground. This is known as *trapping* the ball.

What club should be used in chipping?

It varies. It depends on considerations such as green speed and the length of the shot and chipping style. Slower greens would require less loft than fast greens, such as a six iron versus a nine iron. How far toward the target do you land the ball on the green? It could be 1/2 of the way or 1/5th of the way. It depends on the speed and firmness of the green, distance to be covered, whether the shot is either uphill or downhill, into or against the wind and so forth. Club selection is also influenced by slope between two tiers. You never want the ball to land anywhere near the slope between the tiers. This would influence the club selection based on the length of the shot. Always remember, no matter what club is selected, the style and approach towards its execution is always the same.

What is the role of the hands in playing the chip-and-run?

Golf is about both hands, not just one hand or the other. I do not think a player hits any chip or bunker shot with a certain hand. Rather, I think it is a combination of both hands. My bigger concern is how the hands are positioned on the golf club. This is key. There are certain fundamentals that need to take place in order to be successful. The ball must be hit solidly. Angle of attack is extremely important. An angle needs to be created where the club head contacts or traps the ball first and then grazes the turf in front of the ball. This requires a steeper, rather than a shallower, flat angle of attack. There are other variables to consider. Are you a handsy or arms player? Handsy players, such as myself, who create a lot of angles and cock the club very quickly, can play the ball farther forward with more weight equally distributed. Arms and shoulders players, who use the bigger muscles, need to play the ball farther back in their stance and forward press more than ever and keep their weight on their front foot towards the hole. Therefore, depending on style, ball position can vary from somewhere between the middle of the stance to the right foot. There is no standard ball position because everyone is a little different. Higher handicaps tend to need to play the ball farther back in their stance. Better players tend to play the ball more forward towards the middle of their stance.

Is length of the backswing related to the length of the chip shot?

It is very similar to putting in this regard. A decision-making procedure is required. Having missed the green, the first decision to be made is whether the ball can be putted. If this is not the case, the next step is to judge the lie. One must also factor in green speed and firmness, slope of the green, wind effect and even the type of ball being used. Once this has been accomplished, one must next settle on the type of short game shot to be attempted around the green --- chip-and-run versus loft. The chip-and-run style should be used whenever possible. If this is the case, the next task is to select a club, based on loft, which will accomplish the goal of striking the ball, lofting the ball high enough and having the ball land on the green. Never land the ball off the green in a chip and run shot, unless it is absolutely necessary. From the spot where the ball landed, the ball will continue to roll toward the hole at a rate of speed that matches the loft of the club. However, there is a factor involved in how far back to swing the club when chipping. This depends on the loft of the club to be used. Quite obviously, if everything were equal, a nine iron would require a longer backswing than a seven iron to have the ball travel a certain distance. *The selection of a landing point on the green is crucial.* One needs to picture an imaginary, specific, small circle on the green where you potentially want the ball to land with the club you have chosen. The golfer then tailors the length of the backswing to have the ball land on the green within this circle so that the ball then rolls the proper distance to the hole. *As with putting, this is like developing the feel of tossing a ball underhanded a certain distance.* The short game cannot be practiced too much. This will become very apparent should you spend any time around the short game practice area at a P.G.A. Tour event!

What clubs might be used for this shot?

One may use a 6 iron all the way up to a lob wedge. The pin position, speed and firmness of the greens, the length of green one has to work with and the weather conditions will all determine what selection to make. *One should think about landing the ball on the green as quickly as possible and then letting the ball run out to the hole.* As with a long approach putt, the goal is to have the chip finish within an imaginary, approximately three-foot circle around the cup that would allow for an easier, makeable next putt. Of course this is just a general statement. *Much depends on the ability level of the golfer.* I say this because it should always be a consideration to plan ahead and try to have the chip finish in the best position in relation to the hole for the next putt. The idea is to build a mental picture of successfully getting the chip either in the hole or close by, and, if possible, on the correct side of the hole.

What strategy would be used with a bare, non-grassy lie with sixty-five feet of green to work with?

One would now play a chip-and-run shot off of the back foot and try to thin the shot.

What would you do if the lie for the chip-and-run is extremely tight and the grass surface is very short, almost like a green?

Select the most lofted club in your bag. Position the ball off of the back foot. Then forward press your hands approximately six inches past the golf ball. The club is now being de-lofted to almost that of an eight or nine iron. Aim an inch in front of the ball thus creating a very steep angle of attack towards impact. Now hit the shot!

Chapter Nine
Around the Greens --- the Loft Shot

This is a very valuable shot around the green.

When missing a green outside of a bunker, when is the lob shot used?

The first two choices are to *putt* or *chip-and-run* the ball. After that, the loft shot is in play. One must use the most lofted club in their bag, which we hope is the lob wedge. This club has somewhere between 58 and 64 degrees of loft. *Everyone should own one!* The object of this shot is to hit the ball high and softly so that the ball lands without creating much roll. This shot is normally used when one has virtually no green to work with, such as being behind a bunker or some such hazard or when one is faced with a very fast downhill shot.

How does the player set up to hit the loft, lob shot?

The ball position is toward the front foot. The amount the club face is opened up depends on one's own strength and the height and length requirements of the shot. Keep in mind, the bounce angle and its effect will be increased the more the club face is opened up! At this point, the player needs to consider the quality of the lie. The better the lie; the shallower the downswing entry to the ball. The poorer the lie, the steeper the entry angle must be. More wrist cock is also needed.

Do you have any *secrets* you want to emphasize in hitting the loft, lob shot?

I have three secrets to share. First, the player needs to try to hit (make contact with) the ball on the toe of the club. Second, the player needs to think about (visualize) hitting about an inch in front of the ball. Third, the player needs to make a fairly big and elongated swing. I find many new players do not make a big enough swing.

What results will these secrets help create?

These secrets will help the player to eliminate both the hosel (shank) shot and a heavier, fat shot. This will help create a softer landing of the ball on the green.

Should the player open up their stance and cut across the ball as some do while playing bunker shots?

Before I give this advice, I would need to see their regular swing. Remember 80 to 85 percent of all golfers come over the top anyway, so this advice would not help them or does not need to be mentioned. Keep in mind, teaching is about the student themselves and their identity. If a player already cuts across the ball, a teacher does not have to promote them cutting across the ball even more in hitting this shot.

At the same time, if a player swings inside-out, has a real strong grip and hits slinging hooks, then this person needs to be encouraged to have a more open stance in order to facilitate opening the face and cutting across the ball.

Is there a final thought in playing this shot which you would like us to consider?

One must commit to making a swing for success and, in their thoughts, always keep on that green light. Mastering this shot requires practice.

What strategy can a golfer use when presented with a muddy lie requiring a *lofted shot over a bunker to a green*?

This is a shot that took me many years to learn and have the trust to attempt. One might come across this scenario in the spring when grass lengths are not consistent and a player gets a bare, thin, muddy lie *behind a bunker*. In this case, one needs to commit to a *fat* style bunker shot requiring the approach of a full swing to have any chance of success. Most people hit this shot fat, so this requires aiming at the very back of the ball. There must be a steep angle of attack, an immediate wrist cock and an aggressive, offensive move through the impact area. The shot I am suggesting will never spin but instead will run out. A major problem for most people is they attempt the shot as if the lie were good. This causes skulls or chunks where the ball finishes half way to the hole. One must *chunk* the ball on purpose and commit to the full, elongated swing. A ***chunk*** is where one actually hits slightly behind the ball and steeply enough to allow the bounce of the club to get deep into the mud and under the ball. On the other hand, a normal swing without commitment to what I have outlined, will cause the bounce of the club to first hit the ground and then bounce into the ball with deceleration. Do <u>not</u> *quit* on the shot! Instead, I emphasize once more, *one must commit to a steep angle of attack and a rather full shot* that, under muddy conditions, gets under the ball. With a packed, hardpan lie, the bounce of the club will result in the ball running out once it hits the green. As a result, it would be impossible to think of stopping the ball near the pin. The player must accept the fact that the ball will run past the pin. As an example of the shot with the muddy lie, I want you to visualize how Phil Mickelson commits to an almost full swing when playing recovery type, loft shots around the green.

Chapter Ten
Greenside Bunker Play

Can a greenside bunker shot and brand new sand create a problem?

About ten or so years ago, Llanerch Country Club in Havertown, Pennsylvania was hosting the Philadelphia Open. A few months earlier, they had completed a major renovation to the course. Part of what they did was to make changes in their bunkers, which included new white, soft, deep sand. My two playing partners were excellent players in the Philadelphia section of the P.G.A.. On the very first hole, we all hit our second shots into the right greenside bunker. It took eight total strokes to get all three balls out of the sand and onto the green. A triple, a double and a bogey later, we all walked to the next tee.

In my opinion, greenside bunker play is the easiest shot in golf. Here is the reason. One does not have to hit a perfect shot to be successful. The insights I am giving you will most probably seem unique and different from what you have been exposed to in the past.

I teach this unique approach due to all of my experiences connected with students through individual instruction, camps and clinics. More than anything, I teach this method because the results are excellent. The shot truly works!

Here is how *most instructors* teach the shot. Get your feet firmly placed in the sand. Aim slightly open to the target. On the backswing, break your wrists quickly. Take the club up and outside the target line. Hit one-and-a-half to two inches behind and cut across the ball.

Adding all of these ingredients together will result in total power outages in a greenside sand shot. My teaching experience over the past thirty-two years indicates approximately 50% do not get out of the bunker, 10% hit off the hosel and 90% finish short of the pin.

One can see this approach is a non-athletic and non-powerful shot that doesn't work!

The next time you are faced with a greenside bunker shot, keep the following thoughts in mind:

1. Be *offensive* (rather than defensive).

2. Do not "shake" your feet in the bunker. This will lower the impact point deeper into the sand in relation to the ball, which raises the possibility of hitting a shot even fatter than normal.

3. Cock the wrists early and create a steep angle of attack on the ball.

4. Do not think about taking the club back *outside* the normal path line. Stronger players can take it a

little outside the line, but weaker players need to have a more standard club path.

5. Set up close to a normal *alignment*.

6. (Insight 1) Position the ball more toward the *toe* of the club face.

7. (Insight 2) Allow your *brain* to visualize/see hitting *one-half inch in front of the ball*.

8. Always use the *most lofted* club in your bag, preferably a 58 or 60 degree L-wedge.

The insight keys of *taking less sand* and *hitting off the toe* will generate far better final result percentages than the traditional method. This approach will take some practice and getting used to. However, I promise you will come to love the bunker shot rather than a bad lie in the rough.

Are you confused about my unique half-inch-in-front-of-the-ball approach toward playing the greenside bunker shot?

You might be a little shocked, confused or even baffled by this approach to playing the greenside bunker shot. Greenside bunker shots are consistently the most poorly played shots by all levels of golfers. Almost ninety percent of their shots take too much sand and are hit fat. I am not trying to get the player to hit in front of the ball. The real theory behind this methodology is to get players to make cleaner contact with the sand at the bottom of the shot. As a result, the downswing is steeper and impact with the sand is able to be made closer to the ball. It is really a *mental approach* toward getting one's brain to accept impacting the sand closer to the ball. This is accomplished by creating a steeper angle of attack and thus taking less sand. The player is now able to commit himself/herself to making a full, offensive swing. Through this theory, it automatically gets him/her to transfer weight to the front foot by impact.

What approach should be taken when encountering a plugged lie?

One must choose the most lofted club in the bag. The ball position should be placed in the middle to back part of the stance. The hands are kept ahead of the clubface. The clubface must be square, neither open nor closed. The backswing needs to have a steep, abrupt takeaway. On the downswing, concentrate on hitting the back edge of the fried egg. This means there is a little bit of space, approximately one inch, between the back of the ball and the edge of the fried egg entry point. Be sure to swing the club offensively and aggressively. This also depends on the individual strength of the golfer. Stick the club in the sand and allow the momentum of the shot to stop where it stops. No follow through is necessary here. The steepness of the lie in the sand will stop the club anyway. Keep in mind, the softer the sand, the shorter the ball will fly through the air; the firmer the sand, the farther it will fly.

What approach should be taken when encountering a long greenside bunker shot?

Much depends on the length of the shot and the type of sand that is present. A twenty-yard shot might require the use of a sand wedge. A short shot to a tight pin might require an L wedge. Soft beach sand might require either a sand wedge or a regular wedge and a shallower approach on the downswing. If the sand is dark, wet, firm and granular, a more lofted club and a steeper angle of attack will be needed to ensure contact is closer to the ball. Keep in mind this latter shot will tend to go farther in distance. Generally speaking, the farther one moves away from the hole, one might progress from L wedge to sand wedge to gap wedge to wedge to 9 iron to 8 iron and so forth in making club selection. The idea is to experiment with this information and learn from the experience. Mastering such shots requires rehearsal and practice. As you might understand, besides determining sand type and length of shot, several additional questions need to be answered before selecting the type of shot to be attempted and the club with which to attempt it. How much does the shot have to carry? Is it an uphill or downhill shot? How will contours in the green effect the shot? How much green is there to work with? What speed are the greens? What are the weather conditions?

On the Green

Chapter Eleven
Putting

What are the most important questions which need to be asked about putting?

There are many times in life that perception destroys reality. Success is destroyed because of perception. The following two examples will tell you that results and reality can supersede perception. If you think you are a bad putter, you probably will be a bad putter. On the other hand, if you think you are a good putter, you probably will be a good putter. Your beliefs will become a self-fulfilling prophecy. The idea is to *believe* in yourself. Are you going to allow critics to dictate your attitude? Are you going to allow perception to smother and influence your confidence and success? Are you going to allow the reality of your success to smother the perception of what people think you can not do? The following two examples will illustrate my point of view.

How important is trust and procedure in putting?

In 1986, I arrived at the Los Angeles Open without a lot of confidence in my *mind* about putting. During a Tuesday practice round, I watched Minnesota native Bill Israelson putt while looking at the hole. I tried it and loved it. I worked Tuesday and Wednesday on it. I woke up really early on Thursday morning and was so scared and insecure about putting that, due to nervousness, both palms of my hands were wet. You would have thought I had dipped my hands in olive oil. I went to the golf course with a morning tee time of 8:50 and still did not know if I should look at the ball or the hole while putting. I teed off on the downhill par five first hole at Riviera Country Club. I hit a good drive, knocked the approach into the right bunker, then blasted out to 3 1/2 feet. I had a dangerous, left-to-right, downhill birdie putt. I stood over the putt and only dreamed that I could have gone through what is called a *procedure*. My procedure was think, think, choke, choke, choke, try to think, choke, bail out, not sure, here we go. Forty-five seconds later, I hit my putt looking at the hole. At the time, Jack Nicklaus used to stand over his putts when he was ready to go for seven to eight seconds and everyone used to say, "Please pull the trigger". It took me *forty-five seconds* to pull the trigger. Low and behold, I hit the putt, missed the next one coming back and forty-five putts later, walked off the eighteenth green shooting eighty-five. Do you think that I believe that routine, relaxation and procedure have any value to the game of putting? I think you just got the answer!

Lee Westwood, Winner of the 2014 Thailand Golf Championship

During a pressure-packed final round, Westwood shot a 67 with 24 putts to win the tournament. After the conclusion of play, an interviewer, looking for a reply, coyly commented to Westwood that "the critics say you can not putt." Clearly, it was a loaded situation. In response, Westwood did not bat an eye and said in a matter of fact way, "Yeah, I never pay much attention to the critics."

If you rated yourself in putting within the Philadelphia P.G.A. section on a scale of 1 to 25 (best), what number would you give yourself?

I would probably give myself an 18. That number, to local amateurs, friends and know-it-alls, would probably be lower. The word on the street is, "If Stu could putt, he would be on tour." But, ask fellow Philadelphia P.G.A. section golf professionals if Stu is a good putter. Most might answer by saying, "He would not be an eight time player of the year in one of the best sections in America if he could not putt." The answer is probably yes. So, is it because I am a better putter than I think? A better player than I think? A better ball striker than I think? I do not know the answer. But what I do know is that I am a timing and strcak putter. I do not know if there are perfect answers to doing physical things correctly. I think it is more about the whole package --- understanding putting, reading greens, understanding the value of ball striking, thinking about where you are in relation to par, evaluating the situation of whether you need or not need to putt and where you have practiced over the past two years (green speeds at Oakmont versus Edgemont). All of those factors are involved when you putt. Putting is so *situational*. The real question is, *"Do you think you are either a good or bad putter?"*

When should the putter be used?

Obviously, we all know, when the ball is on the green, the putter is the chosen club. At what moment does one decide to use the putter even when the ball is not on the green? My feeling is to use the putter if you can. Keep the Texas Wedge in mind! Any time you are in-between chipping and putting, at the end of the day, your overall percentage of success is the highest in choosing to putt the ball.

If you are struggling at putting, the first question you must ask yourself is, "Is the stroke at impact a yip?"

If you determine you are a yip putter, then you might need to try the best bailout in this day and age, the long putter. When the U.S.G.A. and the R&A ruling on anchored putters goes into effect on January 1, 2016, a new and creative approach to their use will need to be implemented. One might also consider using a heavier putter or a belly length putter that anchors to the front forearm. The front shoulder joint then acts as a fulcrum in the stroke and allows for a rocking of the shoulders putting motion. On the other side of the coin, if it is determined that yipping is not your problem, you now need to focus your attention on fundamentals and knowledge.

Suppose it is determined I am a yipper. What might I do fundamentally in order to help solve the problem?

Three such fundamentals come to mind. The first is mastering a grip which takes the hands out of the stroke. The second is the thought of focusing one's eyes on something specific during the stroke in order to prevent the eyes and head from moving during the stroke until well past impact. More attention will be place on this subject later in this chapter. This encourages the player to smoothly swing the putterhead through the ball and helps to prevent the player from becoming excessively "ball bound". The *hit* is taken out of the stroke. The third is to make sure the stroke finishes to the inside on the follow through. This imparts the proper end-over-end spin on the ball and prevents the head of the putter from going to "right field" in the completion of the stroke. Proper ball position is a related consideration in allowing this to happen.

Does eye dominance have anything to do with great putting?

I do not really have an answer about eye dominance other than it affects where the ball should be placed (forward to middle) in ones stance during setup. Eye dominance helps a player visually determine the *ball position* they should take in creating their stance. In addition, a player's brain uses the dominant eye to *aim* properly. When the player addresses the ball, the goal is to be positioned in order *to see the back of the ball at the spot where the putter will impact it during the stroke from behind the ball*. In addition, on the forward stroke, a player's ball position should be *at or just in front of the bottom of the pendulum arc of your putter*. To me, eye *alignment* is way more important than eye dominance. The style of the framework of your ball flight has an incredible influence on how you see your line in relationship to how you align your shot. For example, you are a right-to-left player, you have a four foot, dead straight putt, and I put down a chalk line for you to practice putt and I say hit ten putts. In your brain, it is going to appear as though you are putting to the left edge. It is more eye alignment and the history of your ball flight which will dictate what you see as you look down on the line of a putt. No matter whether it is long shots, sand play, putting or chipping, what I have learned about ball striking and the path of any golf swing is the following. Great putting is based on where both eyes are located in relation to the path. In a nutshell, to be most effective, a player's eyes should be parallel to the intended target line and either directly over that line or slightly inside of it. A putting mirror can be used to determine this.

What about pivoting the shoulders in putting?

In all sports, the most influential part of an athlete's body, in relationship to the brain, is the hands. When a golfer is under pressure, the part of the body that is affected the most is the hands. I will argue that point with anyone! A player's brain dictates motion and feeling in the hands more than any other part of the body. The yips in putting are really about one's brain. Very close to the impact point, the brain supersedes the natural flow of the shoulders and stroke. The stroke is influenced by a hit impulse. The more the player can use his/her shoulders the better off he/she will be because there is no hand movement at the bottom. When is the last time your shoulders had a yip? Do linebackers choke when tackling? Do basketball players choke while dunking the ball? Do boxers choke when punching somebody? When it is that kind of a physical motion, it is not going to happen. But when it is feel, in relationship to one's hands, now it becomes a mental formula which influences results. As with the full swing, the shoulders *pivot* rather than *tilt* around the base of the neck and the spine. Setup posture is important!

How important is the development of routine to putting?

Relaxation and the *procedure* of a routine is probably more important to putting than any other part of the game. A procedure, versus an insecurity, will always succeed. In committing to a procedure, your brain is focusing on something *positive*, not something negative and insecure. You want an outlet of focus. Without a *routine*, the golfer tends to stand over the ball too long, think too much, the body tightens and freezes, the player grabs the putter, the engine does not start, the putter is not taken back very well, the stroke becomes very difficult and, as a result, there are not many well struck putts. Putting seems to take place in a small box in your brain; whereas, full golf shots have mental and physical space with openness.

In utilizing a pivoting of the shoulders methodology, how do you develop great *touch* and *feel* on longer putts?

Developing feel in putting is something everyone should inquire about. Perhaps several thoughts might be helpful. Evaluating the contours and speed of the green along with the line of the putt is important. It is helpful to *visualize* the ball rolling across the surface of the green and *seeing* it disappear into the cup. It is judging the length of the backswing according to the length of the putt. This would be analogous to tossing a ball underhanded a certain distance to a target. It is in understanding that the pace or speed of the forward stroke must match that of the backstroke. No jamming or accelerating is allowed! There must be an understanding of the atmosphere you are dealing with. The *mental aspect* is huge. One must be *positive*.

What are your thoughts about putter fitting (length of shaft, loft, etc.)?

In my heart, I would tell you that it depends very much on where the individual is positioned in terms of their development as a golfer. A person just beginning the game would probably not be concerned with it or want to do it. However, it would be a great idea to consider for a low-handicap, accomplished player who is trying to reach his/her potential. There are many other factors and variables, such as trust and feel, which supersede this issue. Putting is highly *individualistic*. Isao Aoki and Phil Mickelson are two examples of this. In terms of the length of the long putter shaft, the higher I can anchor the putter on my chest, the more I feel the swing and the shoulder movement are related. Putting is a response to scoring, ball striking and length. Where do you hit the golf ball in relation to your next putt? How much do you trust yourself? What do your friends think about your putting? It is a response to society's evaluation of how good a putter you are. I spend time in golf teaching *fundamentals* and getting my students to appreciate the importance of *flow* in their stroke, not the length or style of putter.

What important thoughts you would like to share about putting?

Recognize your *identity* (yips vs. style). The development of *feel* and *speed* is the most important part of putting. *Manage* yourself based on the *situation at hand.* For example, let us say you are even par, have a six foot downhill par putt and you dearly want to run it in. Instead, you knock it past and miss the come-back putt. You proceed to double-bogey that hole and the next hole, shoot 79 and wonder what happened. The thing to remember is *a bogey hurts more than a birdie helps*. It is not about rolling in a perfect putt. It is about *managing* your score and the situation you are in as you play your round. Never try to stereotype your putting ability and/or results into a category due to the influence of friends, competitors and, most importantly, yourself. Once you have accepted and recognized you are a poor putter, the walls will begin to crumble. In general, a golfer cannot *practice* putting enough! I have yet to find anyone who has worked on their putting more than they should. But, if you are putting well, accept it and do not practice too much. Work on other areas of you game.

React to the following statement: "The difference on the P.G.A. Tour is just putting."

Absolutely no it is not! It may appear this is the case because putting is emphasized so much in television coverage of professional tournaments. Remember, on any given Sunday, you are seeing television coverage of those players who are striking the ball and putting the best. And I also think our society stereotypes that all tour players always hit the ball great. It is true putting is the last thing a golfer remembers from playing a hole, the final taste in their mouth. It is the final straw. One player can one-putt from forty feet while another can three-putt to loose a match by one. Is it the final most important thing? Yes it is. However, putting is just part of the puzzle. It is only one of the chapters in the total golf story. If you asked every tour player whether they would rather have confidence hitting the ball or putting, how would they answer? They would most assuredly tell you they would rather be swinging well and hitting it good. You can get lucky while hitting a bad putt --- misread, hit a spike mark --- from six feet and make it. Will this influence your insecurity on the next putt? No! On the other hand, you can not duck-hook a tee shot out of bounds on the first hole and get lucky. How much confidence will you have on the next tee shot? Not much! The next swing will almost never be good because of your insecurity or lack of confidence.

In order to really answer the question, we need to analyze a sampling P.G.A. Tour and LPGA statistics from the 2014 season. The numbers shown in parenthesis represent the overall rankings of the players mentioned on their respective tours in the categories of the game that are listed.

Under more "perfect" conditions than you or I are able to experience, the P.G.A. pros make about 97% of their three foot putts, 75% of their five-foot putts and about 65% of their seven-footers. From ten feet, the likelihood drops below 50%, and beyond that, it really drops off of the cliff to about 25% at 15 feet. Understandably, the percentages, for the average amateur in all of these ranges, are much lower!

The P.G.A. Tour game cannot be reduced to putting alone. In order to illustrate this point farther, let us examine the 2014 statistics of two players with very different styles from the P.G.A. Tour. Both are world-class players, but they do not play the game the same way.

Rory McIlroy was the number one ranked player in the world. He plays a "power" game with a club head speed of 121.5 m.p.h. (7), has an average driving distance of 310.5 yards (3), a driving accuracy of 59.9% (108), a total driving efficiency of 125 (63), a greens in regulation (G.I.R.) of 69.4% (6), a strokes gained putting rating of .273 (41), an overall total strokes gained rating of 2261 (1), a birdie average of 4.57 (1) and a scoring average of 68.82 (1). His ball striking rating was 22 (7) and his all around rank rating in this category was 256 (1). In terms of short game, he had a sand save average of 47.50% (123), a scrambling percentage of 58.5 (88), a total putting rating of 94.3 (12), a putting average per G.I.R. of 1.70 (1), a three-putt avoidance rating of 2.00 (13) and averaged 28.59 putts per round (27). Concerning putting alone, he made 98.28 % of his three-footers (173), 86.97% of his five-footers (18), 71.43 of those between four and eight feet (32) and 30.43% of those between ten and fifteen feet (83).

Matt Kuchar was the number nine ranked player in the world. He plays a more controlled game with a club head speed of 108.9 m.p.h. (155), has an average driving distance of 283.6 yards (136), a driving accuracy of 67.3% (20), a total driving efficiency of 149 (74), a greens in regulation (G.I.R.) of 66.9% (40), a strokes gained putting rating of .458 (15), an overall total strokes gained rating of 1573 (5), a birdie average of 3.82 (18) and a scoring average of 69.4 (5). His ball striking rating was 97 (42) and his all around rank rating in this category was 374 (9). In terms of short game, he had a sand save average of 56.34% (27), a scrambling percentage of 62.4 (12), a total putting rating of 77.3 (7), a putting average per G.I.R. of 1.75 (36), a three-putt avoidance rating of 2.02 (14) and averaged 28.74 putts per round (40). Concerning putting alone, he made 99.75 % of his three-footers (17), 79.03% of his five-footers (113), 72.31% of those between four and eight feet (24) and 32.46% of those between ten and fifteen feet (49).

In comparing these two world-class players, we are really splitting hairs. Rory hits the ball farther, hits more lofted clubs into many greens and thus had a higher rating in all around rank, G.I.R. putting average, total strokes gained, birdie average and scoring average. Matt does not hit the ball as far but is more accurate driving the ball and outranked Rory in total driving efficiency, sand save average, scrambling, strokes gained putting and total putting. It really speaks to the fact that every player, regardless of their ability, needs to be aware of their identity and then play to their strengths. Strengths and weaknesses need to be identified. As a result of this self-examination, time then needs to be spent on parts of one's game that need improvement rather than just pounding balls on the range. Despite their obvious differences, Rory and Matt do have something in common. They both have great short games. The statistics bear this out!

Considering the LPGA, Stacy Lewis is one of the most impressive players on the woman's circuit. In 2014, she registered three victories, had eighteen top ten's and rose to third in the Rolex Women's World Rankings. Stacy's average driving distance was 258.88 yards (15) and her driving accuracy in hitting fairways was 79% (24). Her sand save average was 47% (45). She hit 76% (5) of the greens in regulation, had a putts per G.I.R. average of 1.751 (2) strokes, averaged 29.63 (24) putts per round and had a scoring average of 69.532 (1). She was ranked number one in rounds under par (85), birdies (460) and sub-par holes (468). She was ranked number two in putts per G.I.R. (1.751) and total rounds played (109) and number three in rounds in the 60's (50). As evidenced by these numbers, Stacy most certainly has a terrific "all-around" game.

Statistics help to reveal a player's identity. As already mentioned, all players need to realize they have both strengths (advantages) and weaknesses (disadvantages) with respect to the identity of their own individual game. Sand saves, chipping and putting are interconnected. The longest driver who has a high G.I.R. ranking might not be ranked statistically as the best putter. However, with close scrutiny, statistics do reveal parts of a player's game that need improvement.

The answer seems to lie in getting the ball inside of ten feet, and better yet, five feet. It is true that improved ball striking can get the ball closer to the hole. However the tour leader in greens in regulation percentage every year is only in the low seventies. Do the math! Seventy-one percent of eighteen holes is 12.78 greens in regulation per round. That means 5.22 greens per round are missed. Remember, these are the best players in the world. The full-swing power game is only part of the equation. That means the real answer to the initial question is that putting is certainly important, but so are wedges inside of one hundred yards as well as the many short game shots played around the green, including chip-and-run, loft and sand shots. This is the area of the game where players of all levels can improve their scores by getting the ball inside five feet of the hole. Of course, all of this is supported and influenced by the importance of both course management and the mind game.

Should one try to be perfect while putting?

It is just the *opposite*. The golfer should avoid getting over jammed mentally with trying to make a perfect stroke and a perfect putt. One should allow their *natural* reaction, feel and procedure to take over. The more the player tries to aim, think, and make a perfect putt, the more jammed their brain gets. It does not go naturally any more. The player should think in terms of words such as *flow*, *calmness*, *relaxation* and *mellowness*. Putting is a tremendously *brain-related* activity.

Is length of the stroke related to rolling a putt a certain distance?

Absolutely! As with chipping, this is like developing the *feel* of tossing a ball underhanded a certain distance to a target.

How do you marry the concept of rocking your shoulders and having the brain thought of tossing a ball underhanded a certain distance to a target?

People seem to be able to toss a ball the proper distance with just a ball in their hand. But, you put a club in their hands and ask them to do the same thing and they are not even close to being able to accomplish the same task. To me, a lot of this has to do with the black-white syndrome. "My first putt finished either too short or long." The player then says, "I have got to make sure the next putt either gets there or does not go too far. I have got to *hit* the ball either harder or softer." One's brain in putting needs to have more of an *in-between, grey approach,* not purely one which is either black or white. Not full throttle. Not defensive, non-throttle. Most of the time, that is the case. That is what is called feel, insight and procedure --- looking, feeling and doing. This is where it might be important to think about *rolling* rather than hitting the ball. It is important to realize as golfers we all have the same thinking and problem-related insecurities. Each of us just handles it differently. It is all about our brain thinking in a negative way. It is not the fact I did not think I could do it physically. My brain focused on negative insecurities instead of focusing on *positive self talk* which emphasizes where I have been successful in the same situation in the past.

What can be done to prevent being ball bound in putting?

The golfer cannot stare at the ball for too long of a period of time. When this happens, one cannot proceed. The player gets frozen, has no flow and has no offense. Whatever it takes, the golfer must do something *unique* to get himself out of being ball bound and frozen. It is about creating percentages and angles that influence impact. One must be *natural, calm, relaxed, flowing* and *moving*!

As the golfer looks down at the ball with their eyes, what do they focus on?

Every *individual* is different in this regard. There probably is not an exact or perfect answer to this question. There certainly is no right or wrong answer. The thought is to anchor the eyes and head from moving during the stroke until past impact. The player wants to get the putter backstroke motion going the required distance for the putt at hand and then accelerate through the ball, not quitting at the ball. What you do choose to do will help prevent you from being "ball bound." In order to accomplish the required steadiness, players do different things. Some players focus on a spot on the back of the ball, such as a specific dimple. Others focus on a spot in front of the ball. Some, especially on short putts, wait until they hear the sound of the ball hitting the bottom of the cup. Alternative approaches have the player look at the line, look at the stroke or even look at the hole. Still others focus on nothing in particular! Positive putters tend to have their own *routine* and do not stray from it. Negative putters seem to be always searching for an answer. In my opinion, the brain is attached to the individual player's insecurities. The mind is way stronger than any physical thing or swing key we can do. The player needs to experiment and find out what works for them, first on the practice putting green and then on the course during rounds. It is a process that involves searching by trial and error.

What is your mindset in terms of starting the engine? When you pull the trigger, where is your brain?

I hope you do not think about starting the engine. Just do it! The player cannot be searching for an answer here. Thoughts must focus on such words such as trust, relaxation, confidence, success and procedure. Just get it done! There must also be management based upon the situation being faced. The idea is not to over-analyze pulling the trigger. In some cases, players might even consider *avoidance* of the matter as an answer to the question.

Why is a golfer's practice stroke so different from when they are actually putting the ball?

The player has no negative thoughts while taking a practice stroke. As soon as the ball is ready to be hit, the human mind changes. The changes are influenced by aiming incorrectly, nerves, over thinking, worrying about your stroke and, lastly, the mental impact point while the ball is being struck. This is why the development of a routine is so important.

How should the backstroke compare to the forward stroke in putting?

I do not care if you take the putter back a little inside or outside on the backstroke. You have got to go opposite in your follow through in relation to how you took it back. What you cannot do is take the putter outside and then try to take it down the line toward the hole on the follow through. You can take it back outside and then back to inside and let it cut across the ball. Or go inside to outside -- continue to make that motion. Or go inside, to square, to inside. Most players do not know where they took their putter in the backstroke. Eighty percent of golfers miss more right than left. Why? Here is what you cannot do. *It is that they are trying to take their follow through to the hole!* It is too hard mechanically to take the putter straight back and then straight through to the hole. It is not a natural move. It is the same thing with the golf swing. Putting is just a miniature golf swing along the ground. That is all it is. As long as you do the same all of the time, it is alright. **When I putt the best, I putt slightly inside, to square, slightly back to inside.** In this approach, the follow through must match the backstroke. When I putt badly, I take the putter back slightly inside, to square, *to the hole or even to the right of the hole and high.* Now I am all over the place --- right, left. What good is the hole? The only good thing about the hole is it is a target. It is a starting (ending) point. After a starting point in putting procedure, one must almost let go of that point (the hole) in your brain or you will tend to follow through to that point. The natural putting stroke does not go to a point. It goes back across as a *natural* maneuver through impact that actually goes left of that point. When a player is putting well, they do not even think about it. It would be like hitting a full four iron and trying to follow through straight out to the target and the club would go over your head over your right shoulder and never cross over your left shoulder. A golf swing is not a Ferris wheel. Because you are standing beside the ball, it is a circle on an angle. While putting, the brain of a golfer tends to go toward a Ferris wheel, straight back/straight through mentality, not a natural slightly inside-slightly square-slightly back to inside path. There is not a shot in golf that should be straight back/straight through. Do this and you are jammed up and trying to *push* the ball to the target. You want to stroke the ball and allow it to *roll* and *tumble* to the target.

What makes for a successful and confident putter?

Protect par by always considering the percentages of outcome or result.
Sometimes it is better to be defensive (and have the ball finish close to the hole).
The goal of every putt is not necessarily that it be made.
There is at time and a place to go for a putt versus a percentage putt.
Trust in success.

Putt *naturally* without overanalyzing where the stroke is going.

Allow the positives to supersede the negatives.

The stroke should be a miniature golf swing.

The putting stroke finish needs to be natural (completed).

Commit to the path of the stroke going *slightly* to the left (inside) past impact .

Line up to the intended line and then eliminate (forget about) the hole.

Backstroke distance always determines the length of the putt.

Give attention to rhythm and tempo.

Speed control and attention to pace should be the paramount, final thought (more attention to distance than line).

Putting is not black or white but shades of grey

Roll the ball

Perhaps focus on a spot directly in front of the ball or on a dimple on the back os the ball during the stroke!

Swing the putter

Relax

Just go play!

Confidence

Remain quiet

Eyes over or just inside the ball

Neutral clubface

Soft grip pressure

Allow the putter to do the work

Soften

Smooth

Flow

See the ball go into the hole.

Keep the putter above the grass.

Aim properly.

Accept every putt once it has been completed.

Commit to the same pace of stroke every time.

What should be avoided?

An early three-putt

A three-putt bogey hurts more than a one-putt birdie helps

Too much tension

Getting caught up in the "line to the hole"

Over thinking

Over staring at the ball

Pushing the putter down into the green

Worrying about results

Recoil on the follow-through

Lines in putting (for some golfers)

Defending a miss on a certain side because of prior misses

Allowing a putting attempt that rolls too far or short in one direction to influence the next stroke in the opposite direction

Overreaction to negative past history of thoughts

Hitting the ball

Getting stuck inside on the backswing

Inside-out stroke disease

Brain focus on the hole; follow through to the hole

Insecurity

Jamming

Scarring connected to results

Anxiety

Tightness

Sweating

Nervousness

Chapter Twelve
The Long Putter

This method will remain legal until January 1, 2016

In June of 1990, my life changed when I switched to a long putter.
It was such a unique change in style and approach that *I was able to succeed enough to survive.* I was able to start over again!

Who is the right person to decide to try the long putter?

The individual golfer needs to assess their historical performance and personality. If you are the type of person who uses feel in golf and have no problems with insecurities and confidence, then I would recommend the use of a short putter. With the short putter, the player can feel more with their hands. On the other hand, if you are the type of individual who tends to use too much hands at impact and has insecurities about putting, then the long putter will give you a bailout to the hand influence at impact. The type of person using a long putter is using more of a shoulder motion, has an anchor to the chest and is using a longer, heavier putter head with a longer, stiffer shaft.

Is there a downside to using the long putter?

Four thoughts need to be considered here. First, the golfer probably has already stereotyped themself as a failure in putting because they are investigating a long putter. Second, players who use the long putter tend to struggle with feel in long distance putting. Third, in anchoring the putter to one's chest and pivoting one's shoulders to putt the ball longer distances, it is sometimes difficult to control the backswing pendulum movement. It is sometimes difficult to match the *feel* in swinging the putter to the distance one is trying to putt. Fourth, traveling with a long putter is not easy to do.

Is the long putter the perfect answer to being a great putter?

No! Here is a better question. **Is the long putter an option to get through the insecurity and the potential yips where you can no longer perform with the short putter?** The answer is yes! **Do I know any players who are phenomenal long putters?** No! **Do I know a lot of successful players who use long putters or know they are out there?** Yes! **Do I think these players are the best in the world?** Probably not. But remember, before they switched to the long putter, they were in a category of insecurity and lack of confidence with the short putter. Their confidence was so low that, for them to succeed in the best way possible, they would have to use the long putter. The long putter is really more of an answer to bailing out of a failure than it is the perfect answer. But many golfers love golf enough that this alternative is a great "bailout" to keep them from quitting the game. If more were known about the proper fundamentals of long putting, and players could become "great putters" by using this method, would they actually choose the long putter over that of the traditional short putter? The answer would probably be yes. However, I do not believe there are enough differences between the long and short putter for this to happen.

If you were coaching and teaching a young junior to become a good player early on, would you ever start them with a long putter?

No! It is my opinion they should experiment with the conventional method first. This is especially true since the long putter is going to be banned on January 1, 2016. The arm-lock putter might prove to be a viable, future putter style choice because the grip end can be anchored to the forearm, thus reducing hand manipulation in the stroke.

What part of the game of golf is potentially the most insecure as a result of a failure?

It is the yips of putting. That is the most powerful negative result in the game of golf. The bailout to that problem is the long putter or the belly putter.

Did you conquer that insecurity?

Yes --- by switching to the long putter!

What are the individual, physical things you can do with the long putter that would help you to become a better putter?

The only physical thing using the long putter takes away is the feel of overactive hands at impact. One must make sure the length of putter shaft and the lie and loft of the putter head matches their height and posture. The remaining thoughts that a golfer should have are important no matter what style of putting they select. These would include alignment, ball position and path of the putter head. Are they swinging the putter? Is the proper spin being placed on the ball? Is your brain thinking hit or roll? Grip style and arms setup are very individualistic. Grip pressure should be light.

What suggestions do you have concerning how to start the putting stroke with the long putter?

Golf is not a reactionary sport. The ball just sits there almost daring to be hit. As with full shots, it is damaging to begin a putting stroke from a dead stop or static position. When the golfer freezes over the ball, forget it! The idea is to create a *flowing* motion, where whatever you do is actually the *beginning of the backstroke*. With the short, conventional putter, some players get their stroke *rhythmically* started with a forward press of the hands. Since the butt end of the grip is anchored to the chest, this *motion* is not possible with the long putter. Another motion must be substituted in its place.

I might answer this question by suggesting something I did to start my stroke on an occasion where I really putted phenomenally. *My brain went to the **top corners of my shoulders** where I began my* *stroke.* I did not even know I was taking the putter back. I putted with <u>no</u> manipulation of hands. There was <u>no</u> pushing, <u>no</u> dragging, <u>no</u> inside or outside, and <u>no</u> too far back. There was a *natural* flow of the shoulders. Other players who use the long putter might initiate the stroke by gently **tapping the putting surface a few times with the blade of the putter**. Some might tap their feet or wiggle their toes. Whatever you do, the idea is to get the *brain* to avoid conflict and focus on the *positive*. One must develop procedure, patience, relaxation and trust. The idea is to avoid the roadblocks that create that lack of motion. This will prevent the five-and-one-half inches of matter between the player's ears, the brain, from entertaining and processing negative thoughts. Negative thoughts will be blocked!

Here is another thought to consider. Should there be any *pinching between the thumb and forefinger of the lower, right hand*? I feel the thumb and forefinger can prove to be over influential to the stroke. If you feel these two fingers are becoming over active, I would instead recommend a *slight application of pressure with the **pinkie finger*** to begin the stroke. This simply helps to get the putter started in motion without freezing. This is another example of a positive smothering a negative.

How should the length of the long putter be determined?

The length of the long putter should match the height of one's body. This is a rather general rule statement to make and should be accompanied with some experimentation on the individual golfer's part. For golfers around 5', 8" in height, the length of the putter should be approximately 48". For golfers around 6', 1" in height, the length of the putter should be approximately 50". For golfers around 6', 6" in height, the length of the putter should be approximately 52". The use of a putting mirror might be a good tool in answering this question. When in the correct posture, the eyes should be directly over or slightly inside the ball and initial target line.

How should the long putter be anchored to one's body?

It should be anchored against the chest without movement. For the right-handed golfer, the top of the grip is held in the palm of the left hand. There is no forward press in the use of the long putter. The anchoring, pendulum point should not move from its centered position. The stroke is fairly similar to a normal, long swing.

Fundamentally, is there any difference between the short and long putter in setup?

No! There are no real differences between the two styles. There are actually many similarities with respect to ball position, eyes over the ball, weight distribution, parallel setup, etc..

What is the biggest tradeoff between using the long and the traditional, short putter?

The hands definitely have more *feel* in the short putter than in the long putter. Players who use short putters tend to have more feel for distance in their putting. They tend to be stronger in approach putting.

On the other hand, the advantage of the long putter is that it eliminates the excessive use of the hands, generating more confidence in holing shorter putts. Long putters are heavier than traditional, short putters. In terms of judging distance, longer length putts require a longer stroke. Building the proper momentum is important. The length of whatever backswing is taken should match that of the corresponding forward swing. Personally, how do I judge whether a student of mine either can or cannot putt? What do I look for? First and foremost, I look at the impact point of their stroke and their natural follow through and release. Second, I look for their distance control. If they have both, I know they are overall a good putter.

What is your preference in the style of right hand grip?

The selection of the style of the right hand grip is a very individual thing. Over the course of my career, I have experimented with many styles, traditional standard - forefinger down the shaft, claw (saw) and so forth. My preference is the claw grip because it allows me to stroke the putter more in tune with the *swing path* of a normal golf shot or chip rather than on a line toward a target.

Here is how the claw grip is formed. The grip lies between the fore and middle fingers of my right hand. The thumb is positioned on top of the grip. The shaft rests against the palm of my right hand. As mentioned before, grip pressure should be very light. The *shoulders* dictate the path of the putter, eliminating the fingers in the hit. With this shoulder dominated stroke, I do not have a target oriented thought. The advantage of the claw grip is that I am *naturally* able to swing the putter slightly to the inside on the backstroke, back to square at impact and slightly to the inside on the follow through. Other grip styles mentioned above are too much in the fingers and are too target-oriented. Line oriented thoughts get the brain to direct the hands toward the target. These grip styles allow the hands to take over in the stroke. On the other hand, my grip philosophy actually tries to *take the hands out of the stroke* with the long putter. I am not allowing the brain/fingers to dictate the movement of the putter. I am allowing the anchor point on the chest and the pendulum motion of the shoulders to dictate the stroke with the long putter. This eliminates the feeling of the hands to make impact.

How much time do you spend practicing putting?

Over the years, it seems the more time I spent practice putting, the worse my putting became. I finally came to the conclusion I was thinking way too much about how to do it rather than simply doing it. The more dedication I put into my insecurity, the more I worried about it. I emphasized it too much. When a person is insecure about something, it is difficult to be successful with it. In one sense, I do not want to tell someone not to practice putting. But, what I am saying is if you are an individual who is a worrier, who is insecure about their putting, then *avoidance* can be a great answer. For me, I have been able to succeed through avoidance and lack of thought. Would I recommend this approach to my students? Absolutely not! Avoidance is simply a choice certain players might have in combating an insecurity. Most people feel that through dedication and hard work, they will get better. I agree with that. But if you are a person who is insecure about something, such as putting, and worry too much about it, then practicing and working at it can actually hinder results. Practice helps a player to convince themself that they can perform a certain skill better in golf. Once again, it is important to understand the strongest influence upon performance in all sports is one's *brain*. The individual golfer has got to know themself and realize what type of person they are.

Chapter Thirteen
Putting Word Association

Read over the bold print phrase. Cover up the information printed directly below it. React by saying what immediately comes to mind. Does your response agree or disagree with what is listed? Discuss!

Roll **of the ball**

Continues to tumble; wants to get to the hole; feeling it

Hit **the ball**

Explosion; sudden doing; almost only with the hands; club head travels faster on the forward stroke than the backstroke

Length of stroke

Based on the length of putt; feel of distance; same backward and forward stroke

Weight distribution

Natural to standing over the ball; not something one thinks about

Putter loft

Not too lofted so the ball lifts at impact; too little loft causes bouncing

Anchor to the Body

Snug as you can get it; with no movement; the whole goal; where on the chest? Right under one's chin

Backstroke path

Naturally; slightly inside; as if you did that with no brain attached (does not do anything special), if the shoulders took it back, would naturally go to the inside

Feel

Combination of relaxation and confidence

Backstroke equals forward stroke pace

Absolutely yes; fairly similar; avoid hit impulse; clock pendulum; no deceleration; avoid too short of a follow-through

Equivalent of the forward press (motion)

Natural maneuver; gets the stroke started for certain people; cannot do so with the long putter or the arm-lock; to start the putter, ***my brain went to top corners of my shoulders***; I did not even know I was taking the putter back; putted phenomenally; <u>no</u> manipulation of hands; <u>no</u> pushing, <u>no</u> dragging, <u>no</u> inside or outside, <u>not</u> too far back, there was a shoulder flow

Tapping the putter

Getting oneself into go; starting the engine; into a procedure; getting away from locking down; a natural happening

Chapter Fourteen
Putting Article

Knowledge plus **results** builds **confidence** and confidence builds **relaxation**.

Why is putting such an important part of the game?

Putting makes up 35-50% of the total number of strokes during a typical round of golf. Putting serves as the greatest equalizer between the power hitter and the finesse player. The very first P.G.A. Tour cut I ever made was at the 1986 Doral Open. My Saturday morning pairing was with Ben Crenshaw, who is still considered to be one of the all-time greatest putters. In that round, Ben hit ten greens in regulation and shot 71. I hit fifteen greens in regulation and shot 77. You can now realize why he stayed on tour and I am a teaching professional.

What traits are important in developing feel?

Just as feel is important in the full swing, so it is especially vital in successful putting. The mechanics of grip, setup and stroke vary among great putters, but all have a superb sense of feel on the greens. In order to sharpen feel on the greens, one must develop the same traits as in the full swing: a clear sense of *pace* in the stroke, great *patience* and a *reaction to the target*. Incorporating these traits will help a player make more putts and will help promote emotional equilibrium when they miss a putt. ***Knowledge*** plus ***results*** builds ***confidence*** and confidence builds ***relaxation***.

Since putting is so individualistic, what grip styles are there to choose from?

The player has quite a variety from which to choose, starting with the *overlap*, *interlock* or *ten-finger* grip styles, one of which they will probably use for the full swing. *These are all right-hand (for a right-handed golfer) dominant, power-producing grips.* But, since the velocity required in hitting a putt is so low, several other variations are possible. *Here, the aim is to make the left hand (for a right-handed golfer) most dominant.* Such grips would include the *reverse overlap*, *split-handed*, *cross-handed*, *left-handed*, *finger-down-the-shaft*, and *hands-overlapped* to name a few. There are other exotic styles, as well as the grips used for the side-saddle and the extended-putter-length technique, which I have used since 1990.

What is the most common among all grip choices?

This would be the *reverse overlap*, which puts the entire right hand on the grip and brings the two hands quite close together so as to work better as one unit. Among the others, the advantage of cross-handed and split-handed is that the left wrist is less likely to collapse in the forward stroke. All of the grips mentioned are viable options that may be recommended by the professional, particularly if the conventional reverse style is not effective or comfortable.

In terms of setup, what are the elements of putting technique supported by a majority of great putters?

One's **eye line** is *directly over or slightly inside of the ball and the initial target line.*

One's **eye line and shoulders** are *parallel to the initial target line.*

Set the **club face** *square to the intended target line.*

Correct *positioning of the **ball** in relationship to the dominant eye.*

Keep **body motion** *limited.*

Use an *accelerating stroke.*

Be *comfortable.*

Make *solid contact* by striking the ball with the "sweet spot" of the putter.

How would you describe the stroke?

I like the putting stroke to be like the swinging of the pendulum of a grandfather clock. The stroke is done with the arms and shoulders. It is a two-sided action, with the left hand and arm dominating, while the right hand rests lightly on the club and stabilizes the stroke. The golfer should feel they are using a "one-lever" system, stroking through the ball with the left wrist stabilized and the left hand and arm remaining in line. One of the main causes of poor putting is deceleration on the forward stroke because the left forearm does not keep moving. *Stabilizing the left wrist overcomes that problem.* Concerning the conventional stroke, the left wrist may be allowed to hinge slightly on the backswing for a longer putt, but it must be firm and "unbroken" on the forward swing. This is the optimal type stroke, but there have been some successful "wristy" style putters. Most times, these players are "handsy" in their long game, which tends to lead to more wrist hinge in their putting stroke.

Why is attitude so important concerning putting?

There is no skill in golf where lack of confidence demonstrates itself so dramatically as in putting. Good putting starts with a *positive* attitude, and that attitude is, **"I can putt"**. Any golfer who has experienced the special feeling that a particular putt was going to drop, even before it was hit, and then makes it happen, gets the sensation that one can literally *"will the ball into the hole"*. What is happening, of course, is that a *positive attitude is freeing up the player* and allowing them to make his/her best stroke. This markedly increases the chance for success. On the other end of the spectrum is the feeling, "there is no way I am going to make this putt". Such an attitude can cause dire consequences, especially on short putts.

Do you have any concluding thoughts on putting?

Putting is obviously a vital part of the score and therefore, most certainly, an important part of the game. If a player does not putt well, they do not play well --- period! Yet, of the hundreds of thousands of lessons given worldwide every year, how many were on putting? There are no statistics, but anyone close to the game knows that the percentage is ridiculously low considering the importance of putting to scoring. Is it because the student shows little interest in putting? Is putting instruction not promoted enough by us, the professionals? Does putting seem so simple that lessons are considered unnecessary? Is it that there is a *lack of agreement* on the true fundamentals of putting? It may be these factors as well as others, but whatever the reason, *players need to be encouraged to spend a greater percentage of practice time on putting.* It is the fastest way to improve a player's score. As we all know, it is the last taste in one's mouth when a round is finished. When an individual first starts the game of golf, no matter what the age, I feel it is extremely valuable for them to conquer putting as soon as possible. In my forty-six years of being around the game, I almost always have found that good players seem to be good putters and poor putters always seem to struggle. Keeping this in mind, one can see putting results tend to stay with the player throughout his/her golf career. I have always found that when individuals themselves know they are and are recognized by their peers and competitors as successful putters, it tends to stay with them forever. On the other hand, people who are recognized as failures in putting never seem to get out of that category. This tends to lead to lack of confidence and putting insecurities.

Chapter Fifteen
The New Approach to Putting

Do you understand the identity of the putting stroke?

Let the results dictate the future.

Here is my reasoning. I began to develop and believe in this new approach as a result of playing in forty P.G.A. Tour events and nine major championships. Over this time, I watched the putting strokes of other professionals. I studied the flow of the stroke, its path and the spin placed on the ball. I really started to understand physically what makes for a successful putter. From a teaching standpoint, while observing a student during a lesson, I can see what is happening physically. The mental side of a player is more difficult to evaluate, although results tend to dictate this aspect. Once developed, I began to teach my method to all of my students, regardless of their level of play. A really good example comes from a lesson I had with two young boys, ages six and nine. I always begin a lesson on the putting green with four or five footers. Each boy attempted about ten such putts without making a single one. A few putts finished four feet past the hole. After showing them this "new technique" I had been teaching, one boy then made six out of ten and the other made seven. It was like, "Whoa"! I asked them, "Did that feel different?" They couldn't believe it. As young boys new to golf, they did not have any prior experience with the game. There was no negative baggage developed over years due to not seeing the ball go into the hole. They did not understand golf or relate to good, bad or indifferent results. What I taught them was so unique that their brains went directly toward what I had taught them instead of toward something else. That brings me to this point. I think one of the secrets of putting is to get a *key,* which eliminates jamming and the mental negatives which enter the brain. This is huge. An evaluation must be made. Is the key a fake, or is it something physical that yields positive results? That is where I found this new approach or technique to be so successful. Students, especially those who have been playing for a while, need to be broken of the insecurities developed due to missing putts. Sports are about blending athleticism, the right physical approach and controlling the mind.

What is the new putting approach or technique? Can you explain it?

It is taking a regular golf swing and making it *miniature*. What does this mean? You tell me. When a golfer takes the club back in a full swing, does the club go straight back or does it go slightly inside? The shoulders and hips turn/rotate/pivot, the ball is hit, the club comes back inside over the left shoulder and it is a golf swing. It is the same motion with a driver, fairway woods, irons, wedges, chips, sand shots and so forth. Then why should a putt be any different? The shoulders naturally *pivot* --- they do not rock or tilt --- around a central point. In my opinion, our society has stereotyped the brain to have us think the putting stroke should be straight-back-and-through to a target line. And I totally, one hundred percent disagree with this statement. The best players in the world do not even know where the stroke goes. They do it *naturally* with _no brain_ attached. The putter does not go back inside and straight through, but instead *slightly* to the inside on both the backstroke and follow through, especially on fast greens. Here is the absolute key. *If the brain is not attached, and that is exactly what is desired, the stroke goes inside-to-square-to-inside on the backstroke to follow through. This is inside and to the left after impact. Without manipulation, the face of the putter remains square to the arc as the putter head moves throughout the stroke.* Knowing the best players do this, the positive results are proper spin on the ball, softness, feel and speed control. The same ball flight laws that apply to the full swing are also true for putting. The spin generated on the ball is the same. While golf shots spin through the air, putts spin on the grass of the green.

With all of this in mind, I have included a list of nine positives I have noticed about this putting approach.

1. The player's brain is able to **get away from the target**. *The **hole** does not dictate where the follow through goes.* If the golf ball is the biggest negative influence in hitting full shots for the regular amateur player, then the hole is the biggest negative for such a player in putting. When a player allows the hole to have tremendous influence on their brain, then they get away from the athleticism, natural movement and flow of the putting stroke. We are too much attached to the hole.

2. Without brain attachment, **the follow through becomes a miniature golf swing**. Post impact, *the forward swing of the putter naturally goes inside and to the left relative to the target.*

3. The **thought of the backstroke** is eliminated. For me personally, one of the biggest putting negatives I have had to fight throughout my entire career has been brain attachment to the backstroke.

4. The **on-off switch related to speed** is turned off. On the first hole of a round, how many times have you left an approach putt four feet short, only to knock a similar putt on the second hole five feet past the hole? It happens a lot. It is called the on-off switch to speed. My putting approach eliminates that!

5. Fascinatingly, and perhaps most importantly, it creates **incredible and correct *spin* on the golf ball**. Without it really happening, it almost seems as if there is slice spin. In reality, positive *topspin* is created. The ball is able to hug the ground and hold its line more effectively. This is a *physical* issue. Putts are struck much more solidly. On the other hand, an inside-to-out putter head path, which finishes high and to the right, has negative results. Such putts will be contacted on the heel of the putter and are usually thin and not solidly struck. In comparison, the result of a full swing shot struck with an inside-to-out path might result in a shallow impact shank that is thin or heeled.

6. As long as the **face of the putter is kept square to the swing arc, the amount the stroke finishes to the inside and to the left (of the intended target line) through impact is not important**. The idea is to avoid maneuvering the putter face closed or holding it open. This too is a problem that I have faced all throughout my life. In this case, the brain would be concentrating on one of two avoidance approaches. First, afraid of missing the putt low, the player blocks it right. Second, afraid of blocking the putt right, the player decelerates and hooks left. Because the theory I am teaching has the brain

attached to a natural through swing, which moves inside and to the left, none of these scenarios ever come into play. The player is not worrying about where the ball goes. Instead, the brain is attached to a swing key where the follow through goes inside and to the left of the target line. The remainder will take care of itself. The ball goes into the hole. The idea is to avoid getting defeated by one's fears.

7. There is a tremendous **flow to the stroke versus a "hit impulse"**. Here is what hit impulse means. Sometimes, just before impact, the brain "explodes" through impact. *There is an impact explosion of nerves.* In this situation, among many thoughts, the player might be unsure of speed. *Due to past history and fears, there is jamming, flipping, holding on and release.* My theory eliminates all of that. *The brain is not attached to these negatives.* Instead, the player is swinging, flowing and keying going inside and left.

8. It eliminates the *opposite* **syndrome** in putting. What might this be? Here is an example. Suppose a player has a straight five-foot putt on the first hole. The player proceeds to pull it left. On the next hole, they have the same type of putt. Now the brain says, "I do not want to miss the putt left," so they hold onto it and miss it right. This is a *mental* issue. The positive *"do this"* of the stroke key concerning the follow through moving inside and to the left eliminates all of this.

9. It helps to **counterbalance a sloping putt**. What does this mean? Players sometimes putt a curving putt based on a fear of missing it one way or the other. On a downhill right-to-left, six-foot putt, which breaks the width of a cup, the fear is missing it low, so they block it. Or they fear missing it high, so the stroke decelerates. When the player makes a proper stroke, the ball rolls as it should. In this case, the ball is less likely to dive underneath the hole than with a stroke that goes toward the hole with deceleration. My theory smothers the impact explosion of nerves.

Can you list a few players to watch on the P.G.A. Tour whose strokes represent what you are teaching?

Watch Ernie Els, Billy Mayfair, Ian Poulter and/or Jimmy Walker concerning what I am attempting to teach, not Tom Watson's inside-out, heel leading the toe, block (last hole of the British Open several years ago) to the right follow through. Billy Mayfair represents the most *exaggerated* example because his follow through goes rather noticeably left and inside of the target line. If a student does not get it at all, I might share Mayfair's stroke with him/her. Ernie Els is the player who perhaps most identifies with the concept I am trying to teach. His stroke is a little less exaggerated and more middle-of-the-road. Ian Poulter is probably the most ideal because his putting stroke arc moves only slightly to the inside on the back-stroke and slightly to the inside on the follow through. It might be said that Poulter's approach is rather conservative in nature. Jimmy Walker is an example of a current P.G.A. star who demonstrates a very reliable and natural inside-to-square-to-inside stroke worthy of note. The whole key in teaching is to find out (get to know) what the student needs to hear and how it will be accepted. Watching video of these players' strokes would go a long way towards confirming this in your mind's eye.

How is the natural swing arc created which results in the putter face being kept square to the arc as it finishes to the inside and left of the target line?

You might have seen Chi Chi Rodriguez perform a demonstration related to swing arc and the square position of the clubface to that arc. As mentioned above, this demonstration holds true for *all golf shots*. With a club on the ground and held in a fixed place at the club head end, he pivoted the club around in an arc and struck a ball, which was also on the ground. In this case, the club shaft represented the club or putter face. The result was that the ball rolled straight out from the club shaft while the club shaft pivoted and swung on around to the left in a circle. As previously mentioned, this demonstration applies to putting as well, *as long as the ball is properly positioned in the stance and the club or putter face is square to the swing arc.* Remember what has been said about the influence of eye dominance concerning ball position. As a point of information, the ball cannot be positioned either too far forward or too far back, which would create pushes or pulls respectively. This also illustrates that there should be a *center point* or *fulcrum* to the putting stroke. This will allow the face of the putter to be kept square to the swing arc as it finishes to the inside and to the left of the intended target line through impact. A good image would be the pendulum of a clock, which swings from a central pivot point. For a conventional, traditional Steve Stricker putting style, where the arms and shoulders form a triangle, this fulcrum point is somewhere in the center of the chest. For the Matt Kuchar arm-lock method, it is at the left shoulder socket. Think about how this information impacts ball position.

What grip style should be used?

I do not really think it matters. My thought is that the approach, which I have outlined above, is more difficult to do with a cross-handed grip. My one concern with this grip is that the cross-handed style tends to result in the player holding on through impact toward the target or even a little bit to right field. It is basically a release blocking style. I do not know if this is actually true. It is only my opinion. One would have to experiment with this grip style. If a player came to me using a cross-handed style and was putting great, I would simply leave them alone with what they were doing.

In your new approach to putting, do you view it as a shoulder's-dominated stroke?

In a perfect world, the answer is probably yes. It is probably more shoulders and arms than hands. The hands are the maneuvering part of the body and are one of the most influential things to life. If one's hands are taken out of the golf "equation", there are great issues. But, to me, as a "feel" player, I do not think that is such a big issue. It is more of an issue of who you are. What exactly is your golf *identity*? What comes most *naturally* to the player? In my case, I have monkey arms and big hands. I have always been a hands-type player, so I am probably going to use more hands in chipping and putting than a guy who is say five feet eight inches tall, 220 pounds and is solid as a rock. He is probably going to be more arms and shoulders-dominant as both a ball-striker and a putter. I would let that be determined by the player's build and personality. It is up to each individual player to figure out his/her identity and go from there.

Looking either from above the player looking down or down the line from in back of the ball, and speaking three-dimensionally, what do you see in the motion of the great putting stroke?

Please keep in mind this is a *three-dimensional* concept. As examples, I am thinking about professional players such as the previously mentioned Ian Poulter or Jimmy Walker. It largely depends on the observer's vantage point in examining what they actually do. The first view of the putter head motion is from above the player's head looking down. The same motion can be seen from down the line, either toward the perspective target or back from it. Upon careful inspection, the observer will be able to see the putter head moving in an arc. The fulcrum is the center of the chest. The putter face remains square to the swing arc throughout. *Relative to the **arc**, the stroke is slightly-to-the-inside-to-square-to-slightly-inside*. From another vantage point, yet another putter head motion can be detected. *Relative to the **ground**, the club head comes up off the ground on the back stroke, moves back down to the ball at impact and then sweeps up off the ground into the follow through.* This putter head motion relative to the ground can most easily be seen from a face-on view of the player during the stroke. These are natural motions and not forced or contrived ones. In order to fully convince yourself of what I have just described, you probably will have to actually look at video of Poulter and Walker performing their strokes. It is amazing what can actually be seen through the power of observation!

What I have just described is really no different from a full shot. However, in teaching most students, especially those who come from shallow inside and finish too high and to the right, I might say one cannot follow through too low and to the inside and left. Teaching is about the percentages of what people do, not about what exactly should be done. In order to correct the inaccuracies of what society teaches, I have to instruct just the opposite, possibly in exaggeration. The learner needs to hear the opposite of his/her scarring. I am not teaching the perfect approach. Here, however, is what I am concerned with. What does the student need to hear in order for them to improve his/her game? I am trying to break the student away from the target-oriented nature of teaching putting. I need to share a simple putting key with my students with the hope of creating a through swing which will pivot to the inside and left after impact and impart the proper spin on the ball.

Insights and Secrets

Chapter Sixteen
Keep Your Head Down

What is the most common excuse golfers and observers use when someone hits a poor golf shot?

It is the statement, "Keep your head down!" I am sure you have heard it before. There are people who do not even play golf who have heard that comment. Next to "fore", it is probably the most common phrase in all of golf.

As a professional golfer, why is it the most harmful advice anyone could give you?

It is one of the major reason golfers have problems hitting the ball. This may be a bit shocking, so allow me to explain. Have you ever observed other professional athletes, such a those who play baseball, hockey, tennis and of course golf, who use an object to hit a ball? As soon as these athletes make contact with the ball, their heads immediately look up in the direction where the ball is going. They do not keep their heads positioned where the ball was at impact. In my years of experience with professional golfers, I have yet to see one of them keep his/her head down where it was at impact. Several great examples of this would be Annika Sorenstam, David Duval and, most recently, Inbee Park. But yet, every time a golfer misses a shot or two, their husband, wife, friend or partner will say, "You did not keep your head down!"

What problems will be created by keeping your head down?

Bad lower backs are created because one's spine is being twisted by following this advice. Keep in mind there are two parts to the spinal column. There is the lower portion called the *lumbar* spine. The upper portion is called the *thoracic* spine. The latter is designed to rotate while the former is not. When a player's head stays down on the follow through of a golf swing, his/her spine is being twisted, not turned. The more a player focuses on fitness and flexibility, the more efficiently his/her thoracic spine will function while playing golf.

This improper advice will cause the golfer to **become too *ball-conscious*.** Being too ball-conscious will result in stiffness in the arms and legs, poor posture, hitting on top of the ball, hitting behind the ball, lack of a small shallow divot and failure to line up to the target. The golfer cannot follow through in a folded position when his/her head is still down at the ball.

There will be a **lack of *weight transfer*.** The golfer's weight will stay on his/her right foot causing inconsistent hits. If your weight never shifts to your front side before impact, you will never be able to hit down through the ball as you should for a good golf shot. Remember, during a golf swing, two things are happening rather simultaneously. The *arms are swinging*, but the *body is also turning* at the same time. In improperly keeping the head down, the arms will swing, but the body will *not complete turning or pivoting*. In fact, as a worst-case scenario, the body may never be involved at all. At any rate, one of the most important components of the swing will not be happening as it should. The player will be unable to finish his/her swing into a balanced finish.

It will **create a "*shank*"** which is making contact with the ball on the hosel of the club. Most golfers who have problems shanking the ball are those who are too ball conscious with that head down syndrome.

There will be a **lack of *finish***. If your head is still down on the follow through, it is almost impossible for your swing to continue with a full circle.

If I am now convinced of the incorrectness of the head down advice, what should I think about when I attempt a golf shot?

When you set up to the ball, keep in mind my basic philosophy. Relax and be as *natural* as you possibly can. When you swing the golf club, allow your club, arms, hands, legs and weight do whatever they want to do. Keeping this philosophy in mind, *your head will naturally come up when you make contact with the ball*. Most golfer's problems arise because they try to do something special, such as keeping the front arm straight, make a big shoulder turn, drag the club back and, of course, keep the head down.

In your opinion, what would happen if such thoughts were erased from a golfer's mind?

They would be able just to relax and swing the club *naturally*. I am convinced golf would be easier and more rewarding. Of course, good technique is important and that can be taught, but **relaxation** and **calmness** at play is paramount. The mental note is to attempt to take a more uncluttered, relaxed approach to the game.

Why do so many golfers try to keep their heads down?

The reason why is because moms, dads, friends, opponents, partners and even wise guys driving past the golf course have told us to do so. In summary, I hope you are now convinced there are terrible negative results in the syndrome of "keeping the head down."

Chapter Seventeen
The Value of the Golf Ball to the Golfer

In 1984, I was playing in a 36-hole J.C. Goosie Mini-tour event in Orlando, Florida when I witnessed a very unfortunate event involving a golf ball. A player, whose name escapes me now, was playing the 18th hole with a one-shot lead on the final day. He proceeded to drive his ball into the adjacent first fairway. He was playing a Titleist 1 without any special identification markings. Another player, also playing a Titleist 1, had driven his ball into the fairway of the first hole. As the players approached each other, they realized there were two identical balls sitting side-by-side. What was worse, neither ball had been personally marked for identification. There was no way of identifying who owned which ball. The playing partners in each group were right there to witness the situation. The player who was finishing up and leading the tournament said, "I think this is my ball, but I'm not sure. Who cares! I will just choose one". He proceeded to finish the eighteenth hole, recording a par. His playing partner called over a rules official and explained what had happened in the first fairway. In his haste, the offending player signed an incorrect scorecard for a lower score and was disqualified. The mistake had cost him $4,500. He was devastated! This is a shocking example of why the golf ball is so important to a golfer.

What is the basic, bottom line importance of the golf ball?

The golf ball is the object that goes into the hole, which creates a resulting score, that helps define who we are as a golfer. Baseball, football, basketball, soccer, field hockey, bowling and tennis all use a ball to determine a score. The stationary golf ball controls the result in golf.

What does the ball do for the golfer during setup? What is the greatest negative of the ball for a beginning golfer?

It helps determine the proper distance a player should measure from the ball, their posture, where in their stance the ball is positioned and alignment.

What is most important about the personal selection of a ball?

The most obvious factor is its cost. There are a wide range of choices here depending on its quality and durability. I suppose we could say much depends on the ability of the player. Another factor is length versus feel. Harder balls might produce more distance for the beginner while softer balls will produce better feel for a variety of shots played around the greens.

How many brands and types of balls should a player carry in their bag?

There should only be *one brand and type* of ball in a player's bag at any one time, especially if you are a tournament player competing under the one ball rule. This should be an obvious answer because each individual player needs to become accustomed to how a particular ball will perform during practice or in either casual or tournament play. In order to develop feel, a player always needs to practice putting and chipping with the same ball they use when playing a round. Use of one ball is especially important during tournament play where the "one ball rule" is usually in effect!

How important is ball flight in the game of golf?

From a teaching aspect, both the instructor and the student need to be aware of ball flight when giving and taking lessons. It is the number one thing a student needs to understand in order to advance as a player. The student needs to be aware of the cause and effect relationship between club head path and face angle as they relate to ball flight. How and why is the ball spinning and curving? What is the height of its trajectory? What distance does it travel. What is the angle of attack during the swing? If a student can be educated to understand these things, they will go a long way towards becoming their own best teacher. It is important to point out here that the quality of the ball is also an important consideration in all of this.

How important is rolling of the ball in putting? What causes the ball to roll properly on the green?

It is valuable to understand that the factors causing spin of the ball on the grass of the green are almost identical to the factors causing the spin of the ball in the air. The ball reacts to the putter face in the same way. There is both hook and slice spin. *Club face angle* and *club path* have a tremendous influence on the way the ball spins on the grass. It is best to have the putter face moving on an inside-to-square-to inside path, just as with the full swing, rather than straight-back-and-through to the target or out to right field. The ultimate spin causes the ball to tumble end-over-end moving forward.

As it relates to the ball, why is it important to study the lie of the ball during a round?

The ball will react a certain way depending on how the ball lies in grass, dirt or sand. Off of dirt, the ball will probably not travel extra yardage. Out of the rough, the ball might go right or left. It might also come out softly and short or as a flier traveling too long of a distance. Whether the ball being played is hard or soft is also a factor.

How important is it for the player to identify his/her golf ball in every round of golf?

This is very, very important! It doesn't matter how you identify your personal golf ball through your initials, a logo, an imprint or magic marker dot or drawings. Be sure the mark is permanent and that it will not disappear in the ball washer. The bottom line is the ball must be personally marked for identification. If you open my golf bag any day of the year, how many types of balls do you think you will see? Only one. There should be only one brand of ball in your bag at one time and it must always be marked for identification purposes.

Chapter Eighteen
The Reason for Missing a Golf Shot

No matter what the ability level --- professional or duffer --- all golfers miss shots. This is part of the game. Unfortunately, our brain tends to absorb the negative results and future shots become difficult. Many golfers do not know how to handle this situation. Such golfers need to ask themselves several questions in order to have any chance of improving their next shot. Toxic negativity must be placed aside. It all begins with genuinely absorbing good information and understanding it. The better a player can *understand* and then *utilize* the **fundamentals**, the more effective they will be. Once a player has the **knowledge** and **ability** to categorize their mistakes, as well as understand the cause and effect principals of the game, they will then be able to see improvement. The individual will then have the capability of "fixing" mistakes during a round and be able successfully to move on with confidence to the next shot. This also applies while hitting balls in practice.

Why do Tour players take additional practice swings after missing a shot during a competitive round?

They are *wiping out that bad previous swing* and attempting to correct the mistake they made. They are erasing that bad thought and substituting it with a positive one. Their next shot can then be attempted with the correct mindset. Once again, this shows the powerful influence of the *brain* on playing the game of golf.

Here are several questions to help begin the thought process.

1. Was the shot missed because of **fears**, **grip**, **setup** or just by making a plain old **bad swing**?

2. By what **part of the club face** was the ball struck (toe, heel, bottom or was the ball hit "fat")?

3. Was the missed shot a bad hook or slice? If that is the case, does the player understand **ball flight laws** in relation to that last shot? How was curvature of the shot influenced by the relationship between the club head *path* and *face angle*?

In the case of answering this last question, it is important to note there are **nine possible ball flight patterns**. Ball flight depends on the relationship between two important factors. *Club head face angle* is responsible for approximately 85% of the initial, ball takeoff direction. *Club head swing path* is the other important factor. Both create just as much spin. Sidespin of the ball is created by the face and path going in different directions. The greater the "gap" (difference) between face and path, the more sidespin is created and the more the ball curves. The ball does not know the location of the target line. It is a matter of physics. Straight shots happen when the path and club face are going in the *same* direction. *Slices* and *fades* occur when the club face is *open to* the path creating a *clockwise* spin. *Hooks* and *draws* occur when the club face is *closed to* the path creating a *counterclockwise* spin. The greater the differential between the two variables, the greater the slice or hook is generated respectively. It can be likened to the intermeshing of the teeth of gears in a machine. Golfers armed with an understanding of this knowledge can go a long way toward fixing their golf swings.

Now it's time for a little test about your understanding of cause and effect and its relationship concerning club head path and face angle!

What about the situation for a right-handed golfer where the ball starts right and then slices further to the right?

In this case, the swing path of the club head was too much inside-out and the club face was open to the club head path. This might indicate a grip position that is too weak.

What about the situation for a right-handed golfer where the ball starts left and then curves further left?

In this case, the swing path of the club head was too much outside-in (better known as "over the top) with a closed club head face to the path. This might indicate a grip position that is too strong.

Be sure to read over chapter twenty-nine covering ball flight laws for a more in-depth discussion of this subject!

Answering these kinds of questions will help any level of golfer understand and improve their ball striking without advice from a P.G.A. professional. This might be the ultimate goal in taking lessons from a qualified teacher!

Politicians, co-workers, family members and friends may lie to you. The flight of a golf ball will always tell the truth.

Chapter Nineteen
Misconceptions

A lot of practice always creates positive feelings and confidence.

Practice is always the answer to overcome insecurities.

A practice round on a strange course will always help you.

Uphill putts are always preferable over downhill putts.

Situational pressure is always greater and harder than expectancy pressure.

The older and more experienced you are, the less nervous you become.

Because he has won a major, Mark Brooks is a better player than Sergio Garcia, Luke Donald and Lee Westwood.

Keeping your head down is a good thing.

Your swing speed should be easy and slow.

An upright swing is better than a flat golf swing.

Longer length golf clubs are always harder to hit than standard.

Never leave a putt short.

A birdie helps you more than a bogey hurts.

Always use a driver when you can.

Make sure your weight gets to the front foot on a driver swing.

I have not played for two months; I know I will play badly.

The more I concentrate on the ball, the better the results.

I should go through my entire swing thought checklist before I hit a shot.

One must hit down to hit a good iron shot.

One should always drag the club low on the takeaway.

Always hit a lot of balls before a competitive round.

Watch televised lessons offered on the Golf Channel and you will definitely get better.

Always compare your swing to that of a tour player and you will improve.

Chapter Twenty
Driving Range Comments That Hurt You

As a golf professional and teacher over the past forty years, I have found that almost every student comes to me with the following erroneous thoughts. I hear these comments, statements and expressions all of the time. Where did they originate? Perhaps they came from a family member or a friend at the golf club or at the driving range.

Keep your head down.

Keep your head still.

Keep your eye on the ball.

Make sure you see the club hit the ball.

Do not sway.

Transfer your weight and use your legs.

Keep your front arm straight and firm.

Take the club straight back and straight through.

Extend your arms.

Make sure you swing slow and easy.

Finish real high on the follow-through.

Bottom line, I never want my students to have any of these thoughts!
Just remember, every golfer is different. We all need to find out what information and swing keys match up to our own identity. Certain golf information can either hurt or help you.

Chapter Twenty-one
Secrets in Golf You Have Never Heard

Explain the short game penny theory!

In your mind, *imagine* a penny located somewhere between a half-inch to an inch in front of and to the inside edge of the ball. The goal is to imagine creating an angle of attack with one's club head so that the club head lands on top of that penny while performing the shot. *In actuality, this does not really happen!* However, with this theory, the player is *mentally* creating a steeper rather than a shallower angle into the ball. A shallow, flatter angle into the ball leads to either one or the other of the following poor results. The first such scenario would be hitting behind the ball, commonly called a fat or a chunk. The second would be not striking the ground at all, instead striking the ball at its equator that results in a thinned shot or a skull.

This mental secret or insight can be used by all players whenever playing a variety of greenside shots. If you are a physically strong, good player, use your legs properly and already cock the club enough, this theory might not be of concern because you are already doing what needs to be done. On the other hand, this information might be of great value to the average player who does not do enough of what I have just described.

This theory is applicable to all greenside sand shots, chip-and-run and loft shots. However, although the concept is the same for all of them, the manner of execution is different for bunker shots versus chip-and-run and loft shots. It has to do with ball contact. Allow me to explain.

While playing a greenside bunker shot, rather than striking the ball first, the idea is to enter the sand with the club head slightly behind the ball. When playing such a greenside bunker shot, the average player might "shake their feet into the sand" too deeply and thus lower their body too much in relationship to the ball. They might not use their legs enough or inadequately cock their wrists. They probably also have been told to hit an inch-and-a-half to two inches behind the ball, which means they are actually hitting three inches behind the ball. My secret formula gets the average golfer to have the club head enter the sand closer to the ball than in the past. By using the penny theory of *imagining* to hit a half-inch to an inch in front of and to the inside edge of the ball, it automatically gets one's body moving more forward toward the ball and the target.

We should also consider how the physical characteristics of the club head of the sand wedge could have an affect on bunker play. These characteristics were already covered in the chapter three section having to do with properly fitting the sand wedge. Allow me to reiterate! The characteristics of importance include the **sole** and its width, the **bounce** angle and the **leading** and **trailing edges** of the club face. Bounce lifts the leading edge of the club face off of the ground. You might remember that a wide sole also brings the leading edge of the wedge higher off of the ground, increasing its bounce effect, but a thin sole keeps the leading edge lower, reducing the bounce effect. Should a player open the club face, this actually increases the club's bounce effect. Exactly then, you might ask, how do these characteristics influence the entry point of the club head in the sand? My answer has to do with the amount of bounce, the width of the sole and the position of the trailing edge. Should the trailing edge make contact with the sand before the leading edge, the player would then be hitting even farther behind the ball. An even worse chunk would be the result.

The same theory also applies to greenside chip-and-run and loft shots where the club head actually makes contact with the ball. I want you to understand that although the shots are different in terms of ball contact, the brain theory and idea behind them is the same.

The bottom line is that this theory improves one's percentage of moving the impact point *closer* to the ball for all greenside short-game shots. The special secret is to get the golfer to create an angle of attack where the club head is striking closer to the ball at impact than it was in the past. The golfer's short game will improve because the proper angles will have been created in order to hit these shots.

What should I consider in playing a standard, green-side bunker shot?

In supplying an answer, I am repeating what I had to say about the penny theory from the last question. I am consistent in teaching this sand method to all players regardless of their skill level. Thus, without exception, there are a few key points to be made for each and every player. First, I want every golfer to create a certain steepness of *angle* of the club head coming up from the ball in the backswing. The more a player hinges or cocks the wrist angle and the club, the steeper the angle becomes and the more he/she can catch the club head closer to the ball. Second, I want to see more of the toe of the club *hit the golf ball.* In the player's brain, they should think about hitting a half-inch to an inch in front of and to the inside edge of the ball. In the mind's eye, the idea is to *imagine* creating the impact point to be closer and more in front of the ball than it has ever been before. This *concept* is totally opposite from most instruction --- get your feet dug into the sand, keep a stiff leading arm, open up the face, take it outside and cut across the ball and hit two inches in back of the ball. However, my suggestion is as follows. The more angle the player can create, he/she will be able to produce a club head strike with the sand closer to the ball at impact than it has ever been in the past. The golfer will be much more successful in playing such a shot. I have found this approach has worked very well in my teaching over the past thirty-three years.

Can speed in putting be categorized?

In the golfer's brain, every putt should be divided into one of six, speed categories: ultimate fast, fast, medium fast, medium, medium slow and slow. For example, suppose a golfer has the following putt on the first hole. It is eighteen feet in length, uphill, into the wind, into the grain and the greens have not yet been cut. How does one approach the speed of the putt? If the golfer never considers the speed category of the putt, they will never be successful in completing it. Feel for distance must be understood. In the above scenario, without considering speed, the golfer might hit their first putt

93

halfway to the hole. Before attempting such a putt, the golfer should have used the above-listed speed information to label this attempt in the slow category. On the next such putt, with the opposite conditions and without similarly categorizing speed, they might hit the ball ten feet past. Such golfers might say to themselves they need to hit their putts either harder or softer. This is called the black and white syndrome. They have no gray in their thoughts. *When it comes to putting, successful golfers need gray in their thoughts!* Golfers need to *feel the distance* in their putts. The mentality should be that of tossing a ball underhanded a certain distance. One needs to have look, feel and do. To summarize my thoughts, every putt should be judged into a speed category.

How do I attack that horrific lie around the green?

Typical spring, green side lies have the golfer confronted with a situation where grasses grow unevenly. Picture a clump of long grass surrounding the ball while the remaining grasses are short. In addition, the situation might require one to have to pitch over a bunker to a downhill pin position where the ball is going to keep rolling. The answer in playing such a shot is to commit oneself to hitting a "bunker style shot" on grass. This requires both a mental and a physical adjustment the golfer might not be used to. Instead, they are used to trying to hit the shot with perfect backswing distance and contact point. Realistically, there is simply too much grass above the ball to hit the shot solidly. In attempting this approach, a fat shot will be the real result. The shot needs to be chunked on purpose. The chunk shot is a shot that is struck behind and underneath the bottom of the ball that is obviously in the ground and as deep as the bounce of the player's wedge will allow.

What club always needs to be in your bag? Hybrid? Driver? Putter? Wedge?

The putter comes in first, the driver comes in second and the lob wedge comes in third. Everyone should consider owning a lob wedge! This is especially true for players who carry the maximum number of fourteen clubs. Ranging between 58 and 64 degrees, it would be the most lofted club in your golf bag. Most players carry a sand wedge, which has a loft between 54 and 56 degrees. The L wedge would be one of the most invaluable clubs in your iron set makeup. At the minimum, it probably would come into play eight times per round. The lob wedge is used on most shots from the distance of maximum power to a shot that may only carry two to four feet. If your shot around the green does not call for a chip and run type shot, then the lob wedge should be used. A misconception is that a lob wedge is only for advanced or really good players. Actually, the higher the handicap, the more valuable this club becomes.

What is the secret to hitting out of <u>heavy</u> rough?

The golfer must first make an evaluation of what is being faced. What is the type of grass? Is it long in length, thick, sparse, dry, wet or some combination of this? In other words, the player must first categorize the lie. Is it feasible to hit a normal shot with normal swing and distance? Is it so thick and heavy that you cannot commit to the desired result? For example, one might face a 170 yard shot with a lie which is extremely thick and the ball rests down in a hole. The player is going to have to select a more lofted club in order to dig down and play the shot. However, what about the lie where there are two-and-a-half inches of rough and the ball is only half-way down? The top of the ball is even with the grass and perhaps 35% down below the surface. The average golfer will attempt to dive down after the ball. They tend to come in too shallow and hit below the ball catching too much rough. The ball might only travel 80 to 100 out of a possible 170 yards. This is a mistake! The secret to dealing with such an average lie in the rough is to try to offensively and aggressively "thin" the ball without getting too steep. This means catching the "belly" or middle of the ball with the club head. So, in review, if the rough is super thick, one needs to get steep. On the other hand, with an average lie, one needs to get fairly level and shallow with the swing.

What should be one's strategy in hitting a trouble shot?

Golfers need to be creative, aggressive and firm. Whenever possible, they need to be thinking more offensively, visualizing a "green light" mentality and gambling a bit. When they miss the fairway, most people are way too conservative and just chip out. Instead, whenever possible, they should think about creatively advancing and *maneuvering* the ball down the fairway to get as close to the green as possible. This might mean hitting either a low or high shot, one that bends left to right or right to left or some combination of these four possibilities. Perhaps the resulting shot might even end up on the fringe of the green or in a green-side bunker. The dangers of hitting the ball into a lake or stream have to be taken into account. However, the idea behind this sort of strategy is to <u>not</u> waste a shot, but rather to have a chance at saving par. If the requirement is to draw or hook the shot out of trouble, you normally need to use less club (more loft) and de-loft it. If you choose to cut or slice the ball, the correct choice would be to use more club (less loft). This is because such a shot opens the face and there is a non-release of one's hands, which creates loft at impact.

Why is the toe of the club the golfer's best friend?

The toe is one of the most valuable parts of a golf club. This is true with the driver, irons and wedges and even the putter, but especially when considering the short game. Why? A successful shot has *never* been hit on the heel or hosel. The hosel is a very dangerous part of the club. The resulting shot is commonly called a "shank." If a player ever gets into the "shank disease", they will simply understand why the toe of the club will be their best friend. Out of frustration, hitting such shots causes many people to simply quit the game. You might ask, what about striking the ball in the middle of the face? One would not need a teacher if they were able to consistently obtain this result! The problem is that golfers miss many shots. The thing to remember is the opposite of the heel of the club is the toe. Golfers need to learn to miss shots more on the toe than the heel. Shots can be missed on the toe, but not the heel. For example, suppose one is attempting a sixty foot chip-and-run with an eight iron. In actually playing the shot, if the ball is struck one-half of an inch off-center towards the toe rather than on the center of the club face, tests show this shot will spin less and travel only eighteen to twenty inches shorter than the perfectly struck chip. Such a shot will matter much less than a shank. A shot played off the toe might wind up on the middle of the club face, whereas a shot played off of the center could wind up on the very damaging hosel. Let me mention one final thought. If you are a player who tends to hit most shots in the center or slightly on the toe of the club, then this theory is not needed in your game. The bottom line is the toe is better than the heel.

Approach to Cerebral Improvement

Chapter Twenty-two
Knowing Your Own Identity and Having Realistic Goals

Golf is by far the most mind-oriented sport there is. It takes talent, skill, trust and the effective management of one's emotions to be successful. There must be a game plan in place. One must do an *honest* assessment of these factors and compare them to actual results.

As golfers, we all want to be better. We dream of special goals such as making a hole-in-one, breaking one hundred, winning a club championship and playing inside the ropes in a P.G.A. Tour event.

What if the player simply lacks the ability to reach their goals? This is a roadblock to fulfilling their dreams. Such self-discovery can destroy one's confidence, build insecurity and cause a loss of trust. Sometimes, in frustration, a player might even quit the game.

Golfers need to take a serious "look in the mirror" and understand who they really are. Some golfers think too highly of themselves. Others do not give themselves enough credit. I love it when golfers set **goals** for themselves and create a **game plan** for success. This might include such steps as setting a target score, taking lessons from a qualified instructor or even just practicing the correct way with the proper thoughts.

This is what I did years ago. Back in 1977, when I was a senior at Cedar Crest High School, I set some goals for myself. I set out to win the Lebanon-Lancaster league championship, the District Three championship and the state Pennsylvania Interscholastic Athletic Association championship. In the end, I won all three, winning the state tournament by seven strokes. This success earned me a three-quarters scholarship to East Tennessee State University in the fall of 1978.

In my years of teaching, I have seen just the opposite situation occur. During his senior year of high school, prior to going to college, one of my junior students attempted to qualify for the U.S.G.A. Junior Amateur. If you watched this young man during a few of his lessons, you would have been impressed with the action of his swing and ball flight. It took a two-round score of 147 to qualify for this national event. My student shot rounds of 95 and 102 to miss by 50 strokes. This is a prime example of someone who did not belong in a national tournament qualifier. His expectations obviously needed to become more realistic. This is an example of how one's confidence can be destroyed with these types of results. Playing tournaments for experience is paramount. However, choosing those within one's ability level is tremendously important.

A similar example occurred with a junior player headed to college with the intent of playing intercollegiate golf. Both of his parents, neither of whom played golf, thought their son was a great player. During the pressure of competition, when the "flags are up" and the nerves are raw, he could not break eighty. So, when he tried to qualify for the team, you can guess the results. He did not make the cut. Expectancy pressure can sometimes be greater than situational pressure.

It is frequently difficult to live up to expectations. Golfers have much to learn from their experiences. What is learned from competing in interscholastic, high school matches, in local, lower-level junior tournaments and in club events is a great barometer in self-assessing one's true abilities. If a golfer cannot consistently shoot even par from the back tees at their own home course, it is unrealistic to think he/she could successfully qualify for a national-level event held at an unfamiliar course.

This is a topic that has always caused me some concern. It is very difficult to instruct/teach individuals who have no true assessment of their *inner* selves (personality, competitive nature, nerves, etc.), their golfing ability and where their games are headed.

I am not a fan of continually using cameras, television and computers in instruction. I am, however, in favor of using this technology if the student wants to do so. If video is used in teaching, my suggestion is initially to video the first five or so swings of the student during his/her initial lesson with me. Then, after several lessons, his/her swing can be put on video again. By comparing the "before and after" results, the student will be able to better appreciate the instructional differences/changes which have been made in areas such as setup, grip, distance from the ball, swing path, power and ball flight.

Many students I teach think, after one or two great shots, that all shots should produce the same results. Unfortunately, the blend of their poor golf knowledge, unrealistic expectations and their fear of a bad shot poisons their perspective. In their eyes, their scores seem to remain the same rather than show improvement. Unrealistic scoring goals are never met and disappointment sets in.

As their teacher/coach, I need continually to remind them to keep a realistic perspective of their scoring results as compared to their individual expectations.

As a former tour player who has played in nine majors, I try very hard to help these players understand who they really are when comparing true golf ability with actual results.

I have taught every level of golfer from a 3-year-old to a 91-year-old, to a blind player, to a tour player. I have found all golfers need to understand their real level of ability. The key lies in not categorizing failure based on unrealistic goals and expectations. I have seen many golfers destroyed when results are compared to unrealistic expectations.

All golfers need to understand and appreciate a good shot and feel good about the results. They should not allow the inconsistency of their poor shots to supersede that good feeling. Appreciating the *process* of improvement is extremely important. This process involves developing a game plan and setting goals. Should the instructor interview a student at the beginning of their first lesson in order to assess their goals and expectations? This depends on the individual student, the goals he/she has set, the amount of time he/she is willing to commit, how much of a financial investment he/she is willing to make and how much progress he/she desires to make.

Chapter Twenty-three
Warming Up Versus Practice

Practicing the sport an athlete is involved in and serious about is obviously something which needs to be done. However, there is a right and wrong *way* to practice. There is also a wrong and a right *time* to practice. One of the greatest examples of this happened to a junior golfer who I taught for a few years. Prior to the tournament, this player took two lessons, simulated several competitive rounds on the practice range and played regular rounds over a twenty-three-day period of time. He then arrived at the course just outside of Philadelphia (French Creek) to attempt to qualify for the Pennsylvania state amateur. His confidence was at its highest level. Prior to teeing off, he hit a lot of balls. With three balls remaining, he hit two duck hooks and finished off by shanking a wedge. He then proceeded to shoot 83 and miss the cut by three strokes. It took about two minutes to destroy the confidence he had built up over the past twenty-three days. This is a great example where warming or loosening up is much better than hitting seventy-five balls to a target allowing the results to dictate your security towards an important, meaningful round of golf.

I feel golf involves the brain as much as any sport in the world. Since it is an individual sport, this is especially true. There is no one to pass the ball to if and when things begin to go wrong. It is all about you. Golfers have a lot of time between shots that allows the mind to influence the course of events. The ball is either teed up or on the ground waiting --- almost daring --- to be hit. Other sports, such as baseball, tennis, football, hockey and soccer are quick and reactionary.

The best golfers practice the game when needed. After shooting a 64 in the first round of the Canadian Open, a player will probably not be hitting balls for two hours on the range. Instead, they might go fly-fishing or to the mall to watch a movie. Should you be playing along side a coastline and there are decent waves, how about surfing?

On the other hand, after shooting a 75, a player might hit balls or work for a few hours on some other aspect of their game that caused a problem. Any time a golfer is insecure about a certain part of their game; that is when it is time to practice. This does _not_ mean ten minutes before a competitive round.

My routine prior to a competitive round is to arrive at the course early enough to first get a feel for the greens. Then I only warm up by hitting ten to fifteen practice balls with either a seven or a nine iron. I have _no_ target in mind. The last thing a player needs to leave the driving range with is a negative insecurity about a shot they just hit in a practice session.

Keep in mind, there is a time simply to warm up and a time to practice in order to gain confidence in what you are doing. Be careful in your choice! The negatives in a player's mind can be incredibly influential and can supersede the positives. In this world today, negatives always seem to be brought to the forefront, exposed, advertised, and emphasized.

If a pre-round warm-up is not a time to "practice", what should the session look like? What are its ingredients?

As I have mentioned many times in this book, it depends totally on the psychological makeup and personality of each, *individual* player! A player should not be in the position of "trying to figure it out" while warming up to play in an event. This should have been worked out ahead of time. Instead, here are some suggestions for warm-up. At one end of the spectrum is the free-wheeling player who arrives only a few minutes before his/her tee time, hits a few balls, runs a few putts and is ready to go, like myself, Stu Ingraham. On the other end of the spectrum is the organized, analytical player who arrives an hour or more before his/her tee time in order to get ready. Then there are those players in the middle of the spectrum who are some combination of those players at each end of the curve. Player A works his/her way through the whole bag from wedges to the driver. Player B hits a certain number of balls with several selected clubs. Player C hits focused shots to selected targets while player D has no targets at all in mind. Player E always finds it necessary to work out and stretch before even going to the range. Player F budgets his/her time by the minute. Player G has no routine at all. Player H needs to start their warm-up time at the putting green. Player I always finds some time to hit greenside chips, loft shots and sand shots. Player J needs some quiet time before the start of the round. All players run a few final putts right before beginning play. The bottom line is you have to experiment and see what works for you and then design your personal warm-up routine!

If I have only twenty minutes to practice full shots, what should I do?

In this situation, I believe the best club to practice with would be a 6-iron. This club generates confidence, is somewhat forgiving, but still shows the results of good and bad swings.

What different kinds of practice do you recommend?

I am suggesting two separate approaches to practice. One approach is to work on areas of weakness, such as shanking the ball. In this situation, a player needs to work getting out of the shanks, which means working on wedges. A second approach would be to evaluate one's overall game. This would call for the creation of a pie chart based on the percentage of shots hit during an average round of golf. Each individual pie chart would be broken down based on scoring ability. Percentages would indicate nine different kinds of shots made during a typical round. The resulting percentages would indicate current strengths and weaknesses and would thus help the player budget appropriate future practice time.

Most people do not do either. They do not look at themselves and who they really are as a golfer. Instead, they randomly hit a few clubs and most probably overemphasize the driver. They have no game plan and neglect the short game, which is half of the game.

No matter what one's identity is as a golfer, the area where we *all* have the greatest opportunity to be equal is in the short game, especially putting. Even players who shoot 100 can practice the correct things and become as good a putter as a great player. Because it involves strength, that is not the case in driving. Everyone is not physically capable of hitting the ball long distances! Adding eighty-five to a hundred yards to one's drives is unrealistic. Thus, players need to figure out what their limitations are and identify who they are as a golfer. Within their range of strength and ability, they can work on certain areas within their game in order to lower their scores. Based on the results indicated in the pie chart, they can figure out what areas they can realistically improve through knowledge and dedication.

Especially for a better player, what different practice routines should I use?

A player should not go to the practice range and just beat balls. One suggestion would be to go through all of the clubs in the bag, starting with the wedge, and eventually progress to the driver. A second possibility would be to simulate playing a round of golf on your own or some other course. You might pretend you are playing under tournament conditions. Be sure to simulate targets of varying distances on the practice range which would match up to actual shots on the course. Hit one shot at a time. The only thing missing would be the actual hazards or out of bounds stakes on the real course. Another version would be to practice either like Jack Nicklaus did in his heyday under the tutelage of Jack Grout or like Tiger Woods does today. In so doing, work on a pre-shot routine for *each shot* hit on the range. Do not rapidly hit one shot after the other "machine gun" style. This pre-shot process will be covered in much more detail in chapter twenty-seven. Tiger works on fades, straight shots and draws with all of his clubs. He hits shots with high, medium and low trajectories. The idea is to be creative in ball-striking, such as might be needed to hit a low wedge to a green requiring a slight draw. Still another practice session might center around the short game. Again, hit one shot at a time changing locations each time. This is a good way to practice chipping, bunker play and putting without hitting shot after shot to the same target. This simulates being out on the course and paying attention to each shot as it is played.

Would you please elaborate on the use of the pie chart in evaluating a player's game?

There are two major divisions, long and short game, and nine overall categories within each **pie chart**. The long game includes the driver, fairway woods and hybrids, long irons (4-5-6), short irons (7-8-9), and wedges (pitching, gap, sand and lob). The short game includes the putter, chip and run, and green-side loft and sand shots.

Remember, the percentage of types of shots to be practiced indicated in the pie charts is based on ability and score. The breakdown is very situational. For example, the high-handicap player who shoots 100 is going to have a lower putting percentage (38 putts for 38%) in their round for total score than a low-handicap player (30 putts for 43%) who shoots 70 even though the former had more total putts during the round. The pie chart for a 15-handicap player who drives the ball very long will not be the same as a player who shoots 85 and drives the ball 185 yards off the tee. On top of this, there are many other factors to consider concerning the individual percentages within the pie chart. Some of these factors would include the length a player can hit the golf ball, equipment makeup, weather and overall length, difficulty and condition of the golf course. One player might have several hybrids rather than a 3 and 4 iron. It might be the other way around for another player. While one player might carry four wedges, another might carry only two or three. The pie chart is only one of the steps in the process towards deciding how to deal with both strengths and weaknesses. Based on one's individual player identity, the goal is to determine how a player should be budgeting his/her practice time in order to visit all nine parts of the game and to turn weaknesses into strengths.

In order to take this a step further, examine the *two pie charts found on the next few pages*. The first one represents a low-handicap player who would average in the low 70's and the other represents a high-handicap player who shoots 100. Whereas the percentage breakdown for both the low and high-handicap player might be 45% for the long game and 55% for the short game, the differences show up in several of the nine sub-groups. There might be subtle differences in use of the driver. During a typical round of golf, a low-handicap player might use a driver only 10 times and a 3-wood four times on the par four and five holes. A high-handicap player might use the driver fifteen or more times on the eighteen holes of the round. The high-handicap player would most probably use their fairway wood or hybrids more in approaching the greens on such holes. As mentioned before, because they are not hitting the ball as close to the pin as a low-handicap player, the higher-handicap player probably would have more total putts in their round. Since they are missing more greens per round than the low-handicap player, they would have higher percentages of use for chip and run, loft and sand shots. The percentages in the long to mid irons, short irons and wedges would remain fairly similar for both types of players.

What is the purpose of doing all of this? In the end, the individual golfer would be much more able to evaluate whether he/she is using their practice time effectively and wisely. Most players go to the range and hit a few of their clubs and their driver for most of the time they are there. In fact, they might use the majority of their time to hit their driver. On the other hand, how many players work their way through their bag from wedges to driver? How many use the short game pitching, chipping and putting areas? In considering the pie chart results, players of all levels should be spending much more of their time on the short game rather than no time at all. This is what the best players in the world do in comparison to the average person who simply goes to the driving range and pounds out balls.

Is there any other way of evaluating my strengths and weaknesses over a sample of several rounds?

Absolutely! In fact, these charts should be utilized as a starting point in order to build the pie charts mentioned above. They are definitely an important part in the process of identifying who you are as a golfer and then building a game-improvement plan. If the player is attentive to the information that is able to be gained by their use, **charts** can be extremely effective game analysis tools. The player will be able to answer the following two questions. What are my strengths? What are my weaknesses? Three examples of such charts are found at the end of this chapter. They are briefly explained below.

P.G.A. Tour players are beginning to use this sort of data collection in order to help improve their games. If the best players in the world are doing this, why should the rest of us golfers not make use of this kind of analysis as well!

A great way to analyze one's personal game is by actually compiling statistics while playing. A friend of mine, and also a student, John McLaughlin, charts each individual round he plays based on different categories. This chart is entitled the **John McLaughlin Composite Performance Chart**. He enters the data from each round into a program on his computer. He then divides the total numbers in each category by the total number of rounds played. In this way, John can calculate the per-round average for each category and then determine areas of weakness in his game that require improvement. By honestly analyzing results, a player can seek assistance and create a game plan to become a better player.

The following suggestion would allow an ambitious player to design a rather in-depth analysis tool in order to evaluate his/her game. Such a player could create a personal spread-sheet on his/her home or laptop computer based on the nine parts of the game featured in the pie charts. Data could be quickly collected **(see the In-round Data Collection Worksheet)** in these areas during or following an individual round and then be entered into the spreadsheet. After ten rounds or so, an overall picture of the various parts of his/her game would begin to take form. This information could then be used in order to create the player's own, personal pie chart. As time passes by, more and more data would be able to be collected and the statistics could be continually updated and examined. Weaknesses could be pin-pointed and solutions to the problem areas would be identified, applied and worked on. Progress in game improvement could be plotted. The idea would be to "monitor and adjust" to changing circumstances. The player would then be able to properly balance their time between improving weaknesses and maintaining strengths.

A similar approach would be to use the **Composite Shot Ball-Flight Chart**. This chart can be used effectively in order to keep track of in-round, ball-flight patterns for all types of shots, especially those from the tee and approaches to the green from the fairway, rough and sand. After a chart has been completed, a right-handed player might be able to answer the question, "Is my ball-flight pattern predominantly right-to-left (draw/hook), straight or left-to-right (fade/slice)?" Solutions to these types of problems are covered in chapter twenty-nine. The player could also see if they are consistently over- or under-clubbing shots through their club selection.

Should a player want a simpler version of the nine-part evaluation tool mentioned above, he/she could make use of the **Composite Shot Scorecard**. This scorecard can be used while playing a nine- or eighteen-hole round in order to collect important statistical information in several, selected areas. This individual round data can then be transferred to a multi-round, self-designed, computer-driven spreadsheet chart like the one used by John McLaughlin in order to build a more complete and accurate picture of what takes place for the player over a several-week or season-long time period. This is what both the L.P.G.A. and P.G.A. Tour does for their players. I share statistics like this in chapter eleven for Rory McIlroy, Matt Kuchar and Stacy Lewis. The data could then be used in order to analyze several important factors and answer important questions. How many greens were hit in regulation (G.I.R.)?

Do I need to learn more about hitting my driver, irons and wedges? Do I need to improve my sand play, my shots around the green and/or my putting?

Each chart is a little different than the others. One chart might appeal to a certain golfer more than another. As I have mentioned, it all depends on the *individual,* their goals and the amount of work they are willing to put into the game. The information drawn from these three charts, compiled individually or separately, is yet another solid way of determining a player's golf *identity.* Once these statistics have been compiled, a picture begins to build about a player's true identity as a golfer. Personal weaknesses and strengths in their game can be identified. A personal pie chart could be created for the individual player. In the end, the information gained will allow the golfer and possibly an instructor to focus on what needs to be addressed while taking a lesson. Fully considering the player's *true* personal physical limitations and/or positive abilities, a game improvement and maintenance plan can be created. Areas of weakness within the nine key parts of the game that need to be worked on are identified. Solutions to these problems can be determined which then will need attention on the practice range. Thus, based on player performance on the golf course, this game plan will be revealed in the form of the pie charts mentioned above.

Here is the bottom line. Identify your greatest weakness, gain the proper knowledge to fix it and then spend practice time working on it and perfecting the skill. However, at the same time, continue to work on *all* of the nine areas represented in the pie chart. Questions will arise necessitating new learning and additional solutions and refinements. Keep going around the *cycle* of the pie chart on a continual basis and be sure to give attention to all of the areas, especially the one or two you normally run from. Over time, the level of the water of your game will be raised and all of the boats will float higher!

In-round Data Collection Worksheet

Course_____

Player_____ **Date**_____

As you play your round, use line "hash marks" { ⁄⁄⁄⁄ } in order to keep track of the shots you take in each of the following nine categories and plug the totals into the personal computer spreadsheet you have designed following the round. Results compiled over time will help you to create an accurate practice time budget pie chart.

Long Game:

1. Driver:

2. Fairway wood/Hybrid:

3. Long irons (4-5-6):

4. Short irons (7-8-9):

5. Wedges (pitching, gap, sand & lob):

Short Game:

6. Putter:

7. Chip & run:

8. Loft:

9. Sand:

Practice Time Budget (Low Handicap)

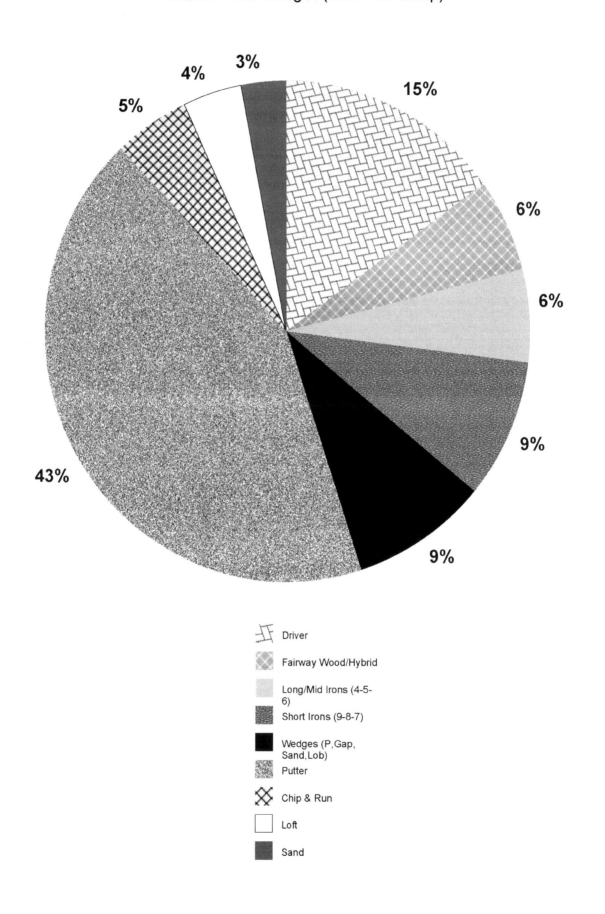

Legend:
- Driver
- Fairway Wood/Hybrid
- Long/Mid Irons (4-5-6)
- Short Irons (9-8-7)
- Wedges (P, Gap, Sand, Lob)
- Putter
- Chip & Run
- Loft
- Sand

Practice Time Budget (High Handicap)

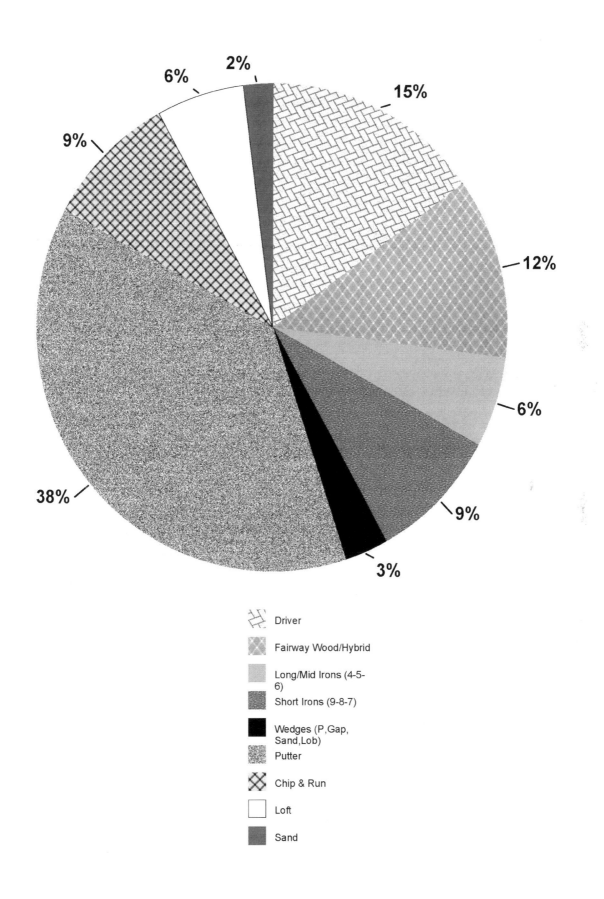

Date	Golf Course	Yardage	Par	3 Putt Greens	Poor Full (long) Shots	Poor Bunker Shots	Poor Tee Shot	Missed Short Game Shots	Gross Score	Total Shots Thrown Away	Best Possible Score	Realistic Final Score (1/2 Col. "K")
3/23/14	Dunedin (FL)	5412	72	1	1	0	4	7	94	13	81	87
3/24/14	Cove Cay (FL)	5483	71	2	0	0	2	3	80	7	73	77
3/25/14	Bardmoor (FL)	5782	72	2	2	0	3	4	92	11	81	87
3/26/14	Westchase (FL)	6033	72	2	2	1	2	7	97	14	83	90
4/6/14	McCullough's	5700	71	3	3	2	3	2	95	13	82	89
4/8/14	Merion West	5733	70	1	0	0	2	4	85	7	78	82
4/15/14	Merion West	5733	70	1	1	1	1	0	85	4	81	83
4/21/14	Ballamor	5932	72	6	0	0	1	5	96	12	84	90
4/28/14	Renault Winery	5748	72	2	0	1	1	0	82	4	78	80
5/4/14	McCullough's	5700	71	4	3	0	1	1	87	9	78	83
5/6/14	Merion West	5733	70	1	0	1	1	4	86	7	79	83
5/16/14	Harbor Pines	5438	72	1	1	2	0	1	81	5	76	79
5/18/14	Twisted Dune	5777	72	2	0	2	0	0	86	4	82	84
5/24/14	Harbor Pines	5438	72	2	4	0	3	2	86	11	75	82
5/26/14	Renault Winery	5748	72	3	2	4	2	3	99	14	85	92
6/29/14	McCullough's	5700	71	3	2	0	0	1	85	6	79	82
7/1/14	Greate Bay	5517	70	2	2	1	1	2	89	8	81	85
7/13/14	McCullough's	5700	71	1	1	0	1	4	89	7	82	86
7/15/14	Merion West	5733	70	2	1	1	3	1	84	8	76	80
7/20/14	Renault Winery	5748	72	1	2	0	0	1	80	4	76	78
7/27/14	McCullough's	5700	71	0	1	1	0	3	88	5	83	86
8/3/14	Blue Heron Pines	5824	72	0	0	2	2	0	89	4	85	87
8/5/14	Hidden Creek	6133	71	4	1	0	2	2	98	9	89	94
8/8/14	Sea Oaks	6030	72	3	2	1	3	3	92	12	80	86
8/17/14	McCullough's	5700	71	1	1	2	0	2	86	6	80	83
8/24/14	Blue Heron Pines	5824	72	0	1	3	1	4	88	9	79	84
8/26/14	Merion West	5733	70	1	2	1	1	1	87	6	81	84
8/31/14	Renault Winery	5748	72	1	4	6	2	8	104	21	83	94
9/3/14	Merion West	5733	70	1	2	0	0	2	85	5	80	83
9/7/14	Blue Heron Pines	5824	72	0	2	2	1	3	88	8	80	84
9/9/14	Merion West	5733	70	0	2	1	1	2	88	6	82	85
	Totals (31 rds.)			53	45	35	44	82	2751	259	2492	2629
	Averages (31 rds.)			1.71	1.45	1.13	1.42	2.65	88.74	8.35	80.39	85

John McLaughlin Composite Performance Chart (2014)

110

Composite Shot Ball-Flight Chart

As you play an eighteen hole round of golf, take the time to *plot the locations* of where your full shots finally come to rest from the tee, fairway and/or rough. *Circled numbers* indicate the **hole played**. Write down the **circled number locations** where the ball comes to rest on the below graphs, which represent par 5, 4 and 3 holes played. It might also be helpful to write down the **club** that was used next to that circled number location. This process will help the player to identify his/her tendencies related to their round. Should you have a teacher, these patterns and tendencies will aid them in your instruction.

Par 5's   Par 4's

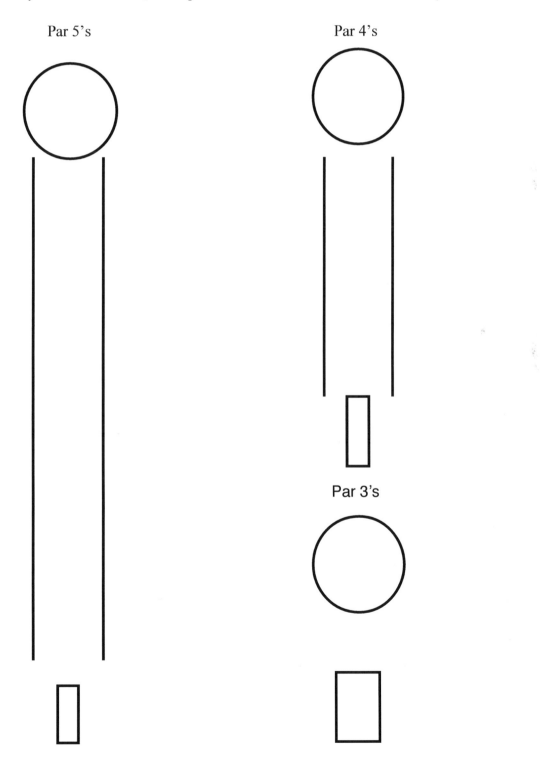

Par 3's

Composite Shot Scorecard

Golf Course_____Date_____Score_____

As you play an eighteen-hole round of golf, take the time to complete the following statistical survey. Use line "hash marks" { ⫽⫽⫽ } as you play and add up totals at the end of the round.

Hole #	Par	Fairways Hit	G.I.R.	Sand Save	Chip/Pitch Up & Down	Putts
1						
2						
3						
4						
5						
6						
7						
8						
9						
10						
11						
12						
13						
14						
15						
16						
17						
18						
Totals		/14	/18	/	/	

Chapter Twenty-four
Practice Rounds and Habits

In this day and age, we sometimes do not have the opportunity to play a practice round prior to a big tournament or event. It might not be allowed at the facility where the event is to be held. You might not have time due to a busy work schedule. It simply might or might not be an advantage to do so.

Is it vital to play a practice round before a big tournament?

It depends on the type of person you are as well as the difficulty of the course to be played. Some people, such as myself, do not mind going blind to a strange course. As long as I have a yardage book or have knowledge about layup-type of holes on the course, it should not matter. Others allow the negatives to be found at the course to affect them mentally. They might compare the tournament to the practice round. It is important to note that course conditions, such as speed of greens, weather and tee and pin placements are all variables that might be very different on tournament day. In addition, practice rounds seem to take forever. Unfortunately, our society tends to remember the negatives of past history rather than future positives. Earlier, when I talked about the particular course and facility, I was referring to such factors as out-of-bounds, hazards, sloping greens and blind shots. If these are present, a practice round *can* definitely be a real asset. Due to elevation change, do the yardages actually play as true yardages? Are yardages well marked? Are pin charts available? Do you know exactly where the tee markers and pin placements will be set on tournament day? Are you aware of green depths? These are all factors that will determine whether a practice round is needed!

Here is a tip for all of you technology buffs. One can easily go to the Internet and use Google Earth to locate a G.P.S. satellite view of the course you are about to play. This application will not only help you view the routing and hazards from above, but will also help you judge on-course distances. Notes can be taken covering various holes and maps can even be printed out. A course management plan can be created before the round.

What are important habits to go over during practice rounds?

a. Know where the locker room, pro shop, practice short game area, practice driving range, practice putting green and staging area are at the facility where you are playing.
b. Find out if the course has a yardage book. It will be a valuable source of much information, such as depths of greens and carries to and/or over hazards.
c. Know where the first and tenth tees are located.
d. Find out if you can play alone versus groups of three or four.
e. Find out if you can hit more than one shot into the green.
f. Find out the expected pace of play for the round.
g. If possible, experiment with hitting at least two separate clubs off certain par fours and fives, but especially on par threes.

h. If distance range-finders are not going to be allowed during the tournament, find out if yardages marked on sprinkler heads are measured to the center or front of greens.

i. If possible, talk to the professional staff or on-site rules officials about special rules, conditions or special tees that might be used.

j. Find out if the greens hold normal iron shots.

k. Find out if the greens have a lot of grain in them.

l. Examine each green to determine if there is a particular section of the green that the ball rolls toward, such as a valley, mountain, highway or body of water. If possible, map each green complex for sections and slopes. While you are there, be sure to run practice putts at several potential hole locations. Although the greens might be cut down more closely on tournament day, this kind of inspection might also give you some idea about green speeds and the way putts will break around the hole. In this way, during the tournament round, when you are approaching the green and figuring yardage, you will know how to attack the pin position. Find out where water drains off of each green.

m. Be sure to test the type of sand conditions that exist on the course.

n. Be aware of hidden hazards.

o. Look for different spray paint/colored dots indicating pin positions on the greens for the various days of the tournament. Determine where these hole positions are in relation to the center of the green and nearby green slopes. Tee marker positions for the various rounds will also be indicated by spray paint colors. This is why it is advisable to plan a practice round for *later in the afternoon* of the day before the first round when the tournament staff is setting up the course.

p. This was already mentioned, but as much as possible, hit putts around the marked hole locations.

q. Ask the professional staff what normal prevailing winds exist at the course.

r. Ask the professional staff about what disaster holes, if any, exist from previous tournaments held at the course.

s. Attempt various chips and putts around the greens.

t. Do roll practice putts on the practice green if the green speeds and conditions *match* those of the actual greens on the course. However, *do not* roll putts on the practice green if the green speeds and conditions are *different* from those on the course.

u. Try to envision a target winning score for the tournament and/or a score that will get you through the cut line.

v. If you hit a poor shot (into a hazard, out of bounds, lost ball in a bad area, etc.) during the practice round, always hit another shot in order to create a positive thought on that hole.

w. Never keep score during a practice round.

Try not to put too much pressure on yourself concerning the practice round. I find too many people try to treat practice and tournament rounds the same. Do not get into the trap of saying, "I have not practiced much or played a practice round so this justifies why I am going to play poorly." Such thinking is a surefire setup for failure. Keep my philosophy in mind. One can still play good tournament golf without prior practice or despite not having played a practice round in order to see the course beforehand.

Chapter Twenty-five
Course Management

Course management is an area of the game most golfers are never taught. A player can receive coaching concerning this aspect of the game, but ultimately, it must be learned through the player's own experiences over many rounds, through competition and over many years of playing the game. Unfortunately, many professionals and coaches do not have the time to spend with their students and players on the golf course. This chapter covers the thought process which lies behind several course management decisions a player might typically face during a round. The details of how to execute these shots have already been covered in prior chapters.

What basic decisions need to be made at the teeing ground?

Position the golf ball on the opposite side of the tee versus your normal curvature of the ball flight. For example, right-handers who draw should position themselves on the left-hand side of the teeing ground. Pick the most level spot. Always attempt to tee the ball where the grain of the grass is growing towards the target; never against. If the shot calls for a driver, hit it with an offensive thought. If there is a little bit of insecurity about the tee shot, you might consider attempting a second serve tee shot using a three wood, hybrid or long iron. All tee shots on par fours and fives do not always need a driver. A driver might still be used, but it might be hit in a different way. Such options include choking down on the shaft, hitting a cut shot or even hitting a lower trajectory, partial shot which travels closer to the ground. On a par three, be sure there is not high grass or a clump of grass behind your ball.

If you hit a tee shot which you think might be lost or out of bounds, should you hit another golf ball?

Always! It not only saves time, but just as importantly, it also gives you an opportunity to hit a free practice shot. Remember, by rule, you must indicate you are hitting a provisional and inform your competitors of the identity of the ball (number different from the previous shot along with personal markings).

If the tee shot enters a water hazard, should you hit another ball?

No! Always walk down to the hazard first and proceed from there. You might save a lot of yardage from where you would have dropped to the hazard. In doing so, you might shorten the distance of your next shot.

What basic decisions need to be made once my ball finds either the fairway or the rough?

First and foremost, identify your ball. Be ready to hit the shot when you are away.

The next decision is to judge whether the lie is normal enough to play a regular shot? If so, select a club based on the normal distance you can hit a shot of that remaining distance. Due to slope of stance, length of grass, up- or downhill nature of the shot, we now need to manage the shot. The player needs to monitor and adjust according to the situation. Should the lie be poor or in thick grass, the player now needs to select a longer club with less loft because the ball will not carry as far in the process.

Before beginning a round, one must consider how far the ball is likely to carry on that particular day. Weather-related factors that will affect carry include heaviness of the air (humidity), temperature, wind direction and altitude. Be sure to manage the round based on pin positions and the dangers lurking around the green complexes. This is an important consideration should you miss the green. Also, how are you feeling physically and/or emotionally on that day? Are you stiff or loose? Are you nervous or pumped up? These are all factors to consider in playing the game.

Is there anything else I should consider in planning a shot from the rough on either side of the hole on a tree-lined course?

Yes! Don't forget to look "up." See if there are any overhanging tree limbs that will affect the shot. Also, are there any trees between where your ball lies and the hole location on the green? All of these considerations will affect trajectory (high, medium or low) of the upcoming shot along with shot type (cut fade or knockdown) and club selection.

What necessary items should I have in my bag during a tournament round?

Before stepping to the first tee, be sure to have the following items available in your golf bag: money, at least one towel, a golf glove, golf tees, coin markers, a tool to fix ball marks in the greens, enough golf balls with your personal mark to get you through the round, spare pencils, a yardage book, a pin chart, a yardage measuring device if allowed, snack items and an umbrella if the conditions dictate. Make sure you have your golf shoes. Check all of these items well ahead of time!

If I miss the green on an approach shot and the ball is in a grassy area, what must I decide?

Once again, identify your ball and check out the lie. The lie and how much green there is to work with will help to determine whether the shot selection will be chip-and-run or loft. The precise details on how to play these shots are covered in prior chapters.

If I miss an approach shot and the ball is in a greenside bunker, what must I decide?

The player must now consider the length of the shot, the quality of the lie and whether the sand is soft or hard, wet or dry. If the lie is really bad, the player might need to consider playing a percentage shot away from the pin and take their "lumps."

If I miss the green on an approach shot, should I putt or chip the ball?

My rule of thumb is always to putt the ball when possible! Several factors again come into play. Much depends on the lie and the quality of the fringe surface over which the ball will roll or have to carry. How tight is the lie? What type of grass are we dealing with? Keep in mind, a hundred putts rolled over shortly mown grass will always finish nearer the hole on an overall average than the same number of chip shots.

Do you have a few insights to help me manage my putting?

Try to be a little conservative and gentle at the beginning of the round. An early three-putt can be very damaging. Be sure to consider the percentages. Be conscious of feeling the speed early in the round. Pick your moments when to be aggressive. Allow yourself to get into a rhythm with your stroke. A three-putt bogey hurts way more than a birdie helps you.

As the current leader, how can I continue my momentum, close the deal and win the tournament?

Be sure to keep hydrated and bring along a small snack to eat. This will help you to keep up your energy level. On a dry day, keep a towel half-wet. It should never be wet on a rainy day. Use new balls as often as needed. When you are playing well, keep using the same ball. Always have an idea how well your opponents are playing. Never allow a past shot to affect future ones.

Remain in a one-shot-at-a-time, in-the-present mindset. Let the process take over! As just mentioned, never allow a particular shot to destroy a round because it appears to be a turning point in that round. Keep playing and continue to be persistent. Only allow yourself to analyze such a shot after the round is over. Post-round is the first time to evaluate what might have gone wrong. Was it physical or mental? If it was the latter, what exactly was going on between the ears when the shot was hit?

While competing in the 2014 Open at Hoylake --- which he won --- Rory McIlroy shared he had two words that he continually thought about on-course during the four rounds. When pressed by the media about sharing this information, he said he would do so after the tournament was over, which he did. What exactly were these two words? The first word was ***process***. The idea was to "stay in the moment" and "play one shot at a time." The second word was ***spot***. When putting, roll the ball over a selected spot in front of the ball on the chosen target line between the ball and the hole. In both cases, commit to the shot and do not worry about results. While playing the course, these two words allowed Rory to stay calm, remain focused, be patient and make good decisions. In doing so, he was able to block out the negatives. This speaks to all golfers that knowing their *identity* is important and that one needs to find out through experience what works for them. This is what worked for Rory at that point in time. Your identity might lead you to something else.

At the 2015 Abu Dhabi HSBC Classic, Martin Kaymer, winner of the 2014 U.S. Open, had a ten-shot lead on his nearest pursuer early in the final round. He proceeded to bogey, double-bogey and triple-bogey three of the remaining holes to shoot 75. Previously unheralded and eventual winner, Gary Stal, shot a seven under par 65 to win by two strokes.

In early 2015, Jimmy Walker was tied with Hideki Matsuyama entering the final round of the Hyundai Tournament of Champions. Patrick Reed was two strokes back. From the fourteenth hole on, Walker played rather cautiously and was one over par on that segment of the round. Reed, on the other hand, holed-out an unlikely eagle from the fairway on the same hole Walker bogeyed, had two more birdies and a bogey to play the same five holes at three under. Walker lost to Reed in a playoff. One week later, Walker shot a final round 63 to win the Sony Open by nine shots, playing the first seven holes at even par and the remaining eleven holes in seven under. He obviously learned from his experience the week before. He never let up the second time around!

No one can say with certainty what had happened in the minds of each of these players. What exactly had they been thinking during the various segments of playing their rounds? What challenges had they incurred? If you have played enough tournament golf, you too probably have had to deal with somewhat similar situations. Several questions come to mind. How can I benefit from their experiences? How might I handle myself mentally? There probably are not any simple, exact answers. However, try to keep a few of the following, *positive* "do" statements in mind. *Do* be strong in your mental approach. *Do* continue to focus and concentrate. *Do* remain in the moment, the here and now. *Do* relish being there and being presented with the challenge at hand. *Do* realize your real competition is yourself; that the only person you can control is you. *Do* have the self-discipline to manage your fears and emotions around the situation by staying committed to the process of carrying out your self-created pre-shot routine. *Do* have a course management plan in mind. *Do* remain aggressive when you can, but be cautious when the percentages are not in your favor. *Do* keep playing the game. *Do* remember the factors that have gotten you here and have driven your success. *Do* believe in yourself and play within your abilities. *Do* be yourself. *Do* remember you are in a position to win the tournament because of your positive mental approach. Close out the deal by keeping the momentum going, having a positive mindset and enjoying the ride.

After forty-six years of playing golf, I feel I am still learning about the game. How, you might ask, is this happening? Over time, I have continued to learn and benefit from both off- and on-the-course situations I have been through. This has happened as a result of both good and bad decisions I have made and by learning to manage my game more efficiently. These experiences will continue to help me as I move onward in my career. Hopefully, they will assist you as well to be a better and more proficient player. At this time, I am certain of one thing. All of these factors must be processed through one place, and that is the *mind*.

Chapter Twenty-six
Dealing with Negative Demons

Is too much knowledge a dangerous thing?

Sometimes, with too much knowledge, the wavelengths start crashing in your brain. This is a case of knowing too much! For example, let us say you are playing a golf course you know all too well. If you know all the negatives about a course and all of the places to which you do not want to hit the ball, at what moment does your brain begin to focus on the negative? This is knowledge and history at work versus knowing nothing and just swinging. *Using knowledge the right way is the greatest asset in golf.* Allowing too much knowledge to cross over the wavelengths is a negative. In some cases, playing a practice round is a negative. Hitting too many golf balls before a competitive round, especially if you hit some poor shots you did not like, takes you down that negative road. The best players in the world are not necessarily the most knowledgeable or talented. They are the ones who do not allow the negative demons into their formula while they are participating at a high level. The 156 guys who tee it up in a P.G.A. Tour event all have the physical ability to shoot four 67's and win the golf tournament. What stops them from shooting a winning score are the negative demons and insecurities which get inside their system when the "flags are up" and they are pulling the trigger. The greatest players in the world continue to focus their minds on the positives as often as possible. The top twenty-five players all hit the ball pretty similar to each other. One might be a bit longer, another a bit better at bunker play and another a bit better at putting. We are only talking about a small difference. *What separates the most successful tour players at any given time is that they can block out the negative demons that enter their system while they play.* They have learned, through experience, to know and trust in what they are doing. They focus totally on the *task at hand* and block out all of the rest. It seems too simplistic, but that is what it all comes down to. A tour player understands these expressions.

What life choices can you make to smother the negatives from entering your system?

Good golf shot! Good support team! Happiness! Going fishing, to the mall or the movies while you are under pressure at the event so you do not think about the game so much. There are all kinds of factors that will help influence your thinking or non-thinking that will help. Good players might not hit a lot of balls during a tournament when they are playing well. Others might be just the reverse because they are supposed to and that is just who they are as a player. I am a little bit different in this regard. It is good to get away from the game. This is what allows someone who has been away from the game for two-and-a-half months to play well the next time out. If you say to yourself, "I do not expect too much of myself today; I am going to play badly", that is just what you will do. Congratulations! You are going to play bad. You just told yourself you are going to do so. It becomes a self-fulfilling prophecy! If you want to choose that negative thought, it will most probably happen. I am just the opposite. I try to have zero negative thoughts in this sort of situation! For example, when I was growing up, the last thing I wanted to do was three-putt the eighteenth green before I played a competitive round the next day. If I did, that idea stuck with me. You do not want to allow this to take place. Unfortunately, we live today in a very negative world. How many times do you see great hero stories reported today on television or in the newspapers? Not very often. As a society, we tend to let the negatives supersede the positives. On the other hand, the bottom line is that the best athletes in the world, when playing at their highest level, do not allow this to happen to themselves. This is the main quality that separates the greatest professional athletes from just another athlete.

How would you define being mentally in the *zone?*

It is a place in which the *professional* athlete always wants to be. In fact, being in the right *mental* zone in golf is an area we *all* want to get into. It is an area that is fun, relaxing, confident, aggressive and positive. These good things are all mixed together in order to create an atmosphere that produces a tremendous result in one's golf game. When this is happening, the player is <u>not</u> thinking about score and end result. When players are in the zone, they are able to stay in the moment, focus totally on the task at hand, stick to their game plan and play one shot at a time. They are able to block out all of the distractions going on in the world around them. They are trying to downplay and avoid overanalyzing the situation they are in. Someone in the zone is probably ahead of their normal comfort level. They are relaxed, enjoying the situation and going along for the ride. There is a feeling of softness and relaxation and being on autopilot.

How does a golfer stay there?

The reason a player feels so good is because none of the negative demons have been allowed to enter their world. Everything the player has dreamed about is happening. They are maximizing their ability. One's scoring is at its highest level. The player tends to want to keep on going. If a person can continue to do that, and the best players in the world get in the zone more frequently than others, they simply enjoy the ride and accept it. No matter what our ability level as a golfer, we all get into our own positive, accomplishment zone of value. The problem is, something triggers us out of it. *The player starts thinking improper thoughts, ones they should not have.* Brain interference enters their world and hinders them. As I see it, there are three main reasons for this to happen. First, the scoring situation the player is in is not within their level of comfort. Second, the player starts to allow some sort of negative demon to enter their brain. Third, the player begins to say to himself/herself that soon something not so good is going to happen to me. People tend to get off track and begin to go in a bad direction. They do not want to accept the position they are in because they envision it being too good for them! They probably are afraid to be there because it is an uncomfortable world in which they are not used to being placed. *They get away from their **pre-shot routine**, **course management game plan** and true goal of playing good golf and shooting a good score.*

What is the value of developing a swing key?

The physical swing key itself does not really help. However, the swing key, whatever it may be, allows the golfer to smother or supersede the negatives that come from insecurity. That is what the formula is all about. In thinking of the swing key, the golfer is able to hit a few good shots and thus skyrocket their confidence and relaxation. Even if the swing itself is not perfect, no matter who they are, if a person is relaxed and confident enough, they can still be successful in hitting shots. It does not mean they will hit a perfect shot each and every time, but one that is acceptable within their own, personal boundaries. The eight to ten most common swing commandments the public hears as far as swing keys go are the worst they could hear --- keep the left arm straight, drag the club, keep the head down, keep the head still, make sure to transfer weight from the back to the front foot, and so forth. The beginning golfer will not get any better because the information they are getting is not even close to what they should be thinking about. At most, perhaps only one percent of such golfers have the *correct swing keys* on their mind. In my opinion, the better golfer you are, the more you need whatever it takes to get the insecurities away from your system. The best players in the world are the ones who are on autopilot and are aware of procedure, relaxation and calmness and have a true game plan at hand.

How do understanding swing keys relate to your teaching philosophy? Is a swing theory, style or system approach important to every student?

Swing keys are important thoughts the golfer needs to be thinking about that will help them make corrections and improve. Swing keys relate to a thought of doing something specific during the swing. Most times that is not the case. You might inquire, what are the correct swing keys? Since *every individual in the game of golf is different,* it depends on such factors as their history, knowledge, equipment, build, flexibility, personality and ball flight. Swing keys must match the player's *needs*. But the most important part is the player's golf *identity*. As a P.G.A. professional, when a student first comes to me, I cannot automatically tell them what they should be thinking about. Only after I meet them, watch their ball flight and get to know who they are, can I give them several things to think about which they can work on over a period of time. No doubt, there are going to be some things that a player always needs to watch. However, in my opinion, there is not a standard swing key everyone should be thinking about. This is why general magazine articles (example: suggesting a transfer of weight from the back to the front foot) about golf can be very misleading. This is so because much of the information they hear or read about does not meet their individual needs as golfers. Such articles, rather than being helpful, can instead be very damaging and harmful. Teaching golf is not about a certain swing system, approach, theory or style. A theory or system cannot supersede a person's individualism. Everyone is so different that they cannot possibly be taught in the same way. Instead, instruction is about communicating to each and every individual student *specific, corrective information that they need to hear.* It must exactly match their identity - who they are as a golfer. Their individual situation needs to be maximized. Adjustments need to be made based on the "deck of cards" they come with. The goal is to have them understand what they are doing wrong and then educate them to feel the opposite of the cause of their major problem. That is what my philosophy of golf instruction is all about.

Stu, as a golf teacher, what statement can you make which is very critical to every student you teach?

I try to answer two basic questions. Does the individual student's current *grip* match their needs at the time I am teaching them? Is their *setup* good enough to move forward? Correct grip and setup are two areas of concern which physically need to be matched to each individual student I teach. If this foundation is not in place, then moving forward with the communication of swing mechanics information becomes useless.

What are the three worst diseases a player could have in the game of golf?

Fats or Chunks:

There are only two shots in the game where the *club head does not make contact with the ball first*. They are the bunker and the chunk lob shots around the green. However, when making a *full golf swing* and in attempting to hit the ball properly, the first point of contact with the club head should be the back of the ball, not the ground. Improperly striking the ground first on a full shot is something a player who is considered to be a "scooper" might do. In an attempt to "scoop" the ball off of the ground, the unhinging of the wrists takes place prematurely. This type of player allows the head of the club to catch up to the hands a little too early, the head of the club bottoms out and they hit the ball "fat." This so-called and improper "casting of the club head" or throwing of the hands too early can take place when hitting both woods and irons off of the turf or even when chipping.

Beyond this, the shanks and yips are the absolute worst diseases one can get. I will attempt to explain what they are, how they develop and what one needs to do to try to get rid of them.

Shanks:

It is a shot that is hit off of the hosel of an iron, which normally shoots dead right or, if the problem is real bad, dribbles straight ahead. I feel most shanks are caused by swinging too much from inside to out through impact. Once in a while, the miscue is caused as a result of the player excessively swinging "over the top." The first type of player to have this problem generally has too strong of a grip and tends to either hook the ball too much or fears doing so. Here are several helpful insights that may help you to prevent a shank. Aim one inch inside the ball. If you need to do so, place a tee or a coin at that exact spot as an instructional aid. Make sure you fold your club (left arm and elbow) through impact to the chest right away. Get your head up much quicker at impact. Grip the club much lighter.

Yips:

This is a slang term that represents impact explosion or train wreck when the brain triggers a movement or jamming of the hands a fraction before impact. It may creep into any shot, but the two most prevalent (major) areas this disease affects are putting and chipping. I am not sure if anyone truly knows where the yips come from. The following is an insight that may help. It seems to be tied to an insecurity a player feels. People think and worry about it way too much. In some cases, avoidance and ignorance might even be better than practice. Practice is easy when the flags are not up. Sometimes, the yips are caused by poor mechanics. One must try to determine if the cause is bad mechanics or plain insecurity. Also, do not allow friends or society to continue to influence your mind about this apparent weakness. The more time that goes by without a fix, the deeper and worse the problem becomes. Lastly, do whatever it takes to not think about this problem. Change equipment, style of shot and/or grip. Try to use a swing or motion thought to supersede your impact brain explosion.

Chapter Twenty-seven
The Power of Visualization and Creating a Personalized Pre-Shot Routine

Why, you ask, might I as a golfer ever consider incorporating **visualization** and a **pre-shot routine** into my game? I am not convinced these two concepts would make a difference for me. I do not see the sense in it. It seems like a waste of time!

Have you ever allowed score or outside distractions to influence your golf? Here are several examples of what I mean. Perhaps you needed a par or two to break eighty for the first time, and you became rattled. It is the final round of the club championship, and you have a two-stroke lead. As you step up onto the first tee to hit your first shot of the day, you notice quite a crowd has formed. You suddenly realize you do not have a clue how to handle the situation. In a practice round leading up to an important tournament, you hit one out of bounds on the 10th tee. You are playing the first tournament round today and are getting ready to tee off on a similar hole. You notice those white out of bounds stakes are out there to the left! Later on in the round, you are getting ready to hit an approach shot to a green heavily guarded by bunkers and a pond. You are faced with a pressure pitch over a hazard to a pin located in the right center of the green. At the end of the round, you have a medium-length, slick downhill putt to a pin on the eighteenth green with a one-stroke lead. What might you do in each of these situations? If you can identify with any one of these scenarios, which I am sure you can, then here is a possible solution for you.

We have all been there at one time or another! We need something to help us block out or eliminate the negative demons and thoughts that confront us in these situations. We tend to dwell on the negative rather than the positive. Society has burdened us with many negatives that tend to supersede the *positive steps* we should be taking to solve a problem. No less of a golfer than the great Jack Nicklaus used to begin each year under the watchful eye of his teacher, Jack Grout, by going over all of the fundamental basics of the game. On the practice range, Jack would not mindlessly pound ball after ball like most of us. Instead, he would slowly and methodically go through his *visualization and pre-shot routine with each and every ball*. He would *imagine* he was on the course in a tournament round getting ready to hit an important shot. If attention to this *process* is good enough for perhaps the greatest golfer of all time, such a *procedure* should also be good enough for the rest of us. Why not pay attention to *visualization* and the development of a *pre-shot routine*?

What exactly is preventing you from being better than you are? Is visualization and a pre-shot routine one of the ingredients lacking from your game? If this is so, what is stopping you from using this *process*? In fact, what is the reason we all do not do this? In the next few pages, I am going to share with you a common sense, step-by-step approach for dealing with the negative demons that influence us. Once it becomes part of us, we should then use this one-shot-at-a-time process for each and every shot we encounter. It is a positive method of keeping the *mind in the present*. Since it is such a *repetitive* process, in an ideal sense, all of the pieces must be put together into a seamless flow of events that should be performed the same way every time a shot is attempted.

When considering cause and effect, which came first, the "chicken or the egg"? It is an age-old question that has baffled scientists and philosophers throughout the ages. Common sense and recent brain research seems to confirm it was the egg. Put simply, the reason comes down to the fact that genetic material does not change during an animal's lifetime. Therefore, the first bird that evolved into what we would today call a chicken, probably in prehistoric times, must have first existed as an embryo inside an egg. The living organism inside the eggshell would have had the same DNA as the chicken into which it would develop.

That brings us to the golf question concerning the consistency of ball-striking. Which came first, knowledge of the correct swing technique or confidence in creating the correct shot shape and trajectory and knowing which direction the ball is going? I think we can safely say at this time it is the *knowledge of the correct swing technique* which is the most important consideration. A successful golfer must master the correct individual *swing mechanics* for them. One must also add in a working *knowledge of ball-flight laws*. Once the ball begins to fly in a predictable direction on a regular basis, with the desired shape and trajectory, great confidence then develops. The two factors --- swing technique (mechanics) and confidence --- then begin to merge with and feed off of each other! You first gain the information you need to know about swing mechanics, you then work at it and proactively put it into practice and apply it on the range and eventually the skill internally becomes part of you. New experiences in the game lead to more questions. In a never-ending cyclical fashion, as already indicated with the nine-part practice time budget pie charts, the player keeps revisiting these three areas over and over again, perhaps picking up something new, refining and improving the skill each time. As with the practice time budget pie charts, these three areas of learning need to be kept in balance. Hopefully, you can see this kind of approach can be very advantageous in learning the tremendously creative sport of golf. Continual trips around the cycle enable you to become a changed golfer. In a manner of speaking, you might be able to become one with the game. In a physical sense, you can eventually be equipped to be on automatic pilot. Now all you need is the *mental* piece!

Golf is about managing one's misses. Out of a *reliable* **physical technique** comes **predictability of ball flight**. Once this has been accomplished with some regularity, the player now begins to **believe** in their **capabilities** and **confidence** grows. They begin to experience **success** with their game. On top of this, if they develop and incorporate a solid, individualized visualized **pre-shot routine**, the player will be able to avoid thinking too much and instead be able to concentrate on performing the task at hand! When the routine is put into practice, the player is now able to greatly narrow the focus to what needs to be accomplished. They will have the ability to block out surrounding mental negative distractions and extraneous thoughts. It is an approach that is truly a positive and trustful. The player discovers the challenge of winning the inner conflict with themself can be won. A fearless swing can be the result.

I can not emphasize enough the importance of developing and consistently performing this visual pre-shot routine. For all of the above-mentioned reasons, this chapter might be the most practical and valuable one in the book. Players who win on the P.G.A. Tour tend to be those who have developed the *self-discipline* necessary to implement and stick with such a routine under all conditions for each and every shot. They are able to play with a **quiet mind** and have a greater chance of getting into and remaining in the **zone**.

We are now going to go through a guided visualization exercise connected with striking the golf ball for any full shot in a round of golf. Later on, we will do the same for a greenside shot as well as a putt. As a reader, you need to put yourself in the place of the golfer I am going to describe for you. As mentioned above, please understand, the correct swing mechanics for you as an *individual* must be identified and worked on ahead of time and mastered on the practice range. Through repetition, proven swing habits are turned over to the autopilot of the subconscious mind. The practice range is where the player needs to put in all of the hard work necessary to gain the knowledge to perfect the various parts of the game that help to produce lower scores. However, once on the course, a player needs to leave the technical part behind. The physical part of the game needs to be put aside. The focus must now be placed on the *mental* side. The pre-shot routine will help us take our game from the practice area to the golf course. In this section, we will be covering how to give yourself the best chance of hitting consistently good shots once you have reached a reasonable amount of proficiency in striking the ball. We are meeting you where you are at the present time in your golfing career. In your "mind's eye", you are going to *picture yourself successfully making the shot before it actually happens*. It is déjà vu all over again!

Visualization is an inner, positive approach to successfully completing any body motion. *Vision* is the trigger mechanism that positively allows us to see the ball traveling through the air towards the intended target. In the process, everything intentionally slows down, and the player is able to focus and concentrate on striking the ball. We are able to see the ball curving through the air with the intended trajectory toward the desired target. Visualization, when combined with a pre-shot routine, allows us to eliminate all the outside, negative thoughts and distractions and instead concentrate and focus on the task at hand. The process helps us to remove anxiety and instead promote a quiet, relaxed state of mind. Because the eyes lead the muscles, visualization helps the brain to direct the muscles of the body to perform correctly. In doing so, golfers must develop a step-by-step personalized routine for striking the ball where they *relax* and get lost in the same process every time.

The pre-shot, visualization routine described below is only an example. Keep in mind, it works the best when you can design and individualize one for your personal use. This will take some preparation, thought and creativity on your part. Once created, the visualization and pre-shot routine initially needs to be worked on and perfected at the practice range. Then it needs to be taken to the course and implemented there. As all of this takes place, and positive results are accomplished, belief and confidence in what you are doing will develop. Only then will you have true ownership of the process as it becomes a deeply ingrained part of your game.

Before going into the visualization, here are some key phrases and thoughts to keep in mind related to the pre-shot routine. As I have already stated, it is up to each individual golfer to examine the information and then *create their own routine that works for them*. Be sure to incorporate these thoughts based on your own personal preferences. Since a personal routine has individual idiosyncrasies, no two routines will be exactly the same.

Orderly checklist
Ritual; routine
Calms the mind
Accomplished quickly and methodically
Allows one to gather thoughts
Promotes focus on the upcoming shot
Generates a positive feeling about the shot at hand
Preparation for success
Repetition; same steps each time
Steps in the process blend together; continuity and consistency
Visualize; see clearly in your mind's eye
Elapsed time for the process is within seconds for each shot
Target rather than trouble oriented
Make a decision how to play the shot, commit and then let go
Trust the plan
The mind has great control over the body
Focus upon what you want to happen
Block out or eliminate negative influences and distractions
Practice your tailored routine on the range and in front of a mirror
Judge the lie to determine whether it is a uphill, downhill or side-hill. Is the ball resting in the fairway or is it in the rough? If in the rough, is it sitting up in the grass, or has it sunk down deeply?
Is the wind across, helping with or hurting against?
What trouble exists around the green? Where can I afford to wind up if I miss my target?
The target must be specific, such as a branch in a tree or the edge of a trap when hitting from the tee of a par four or five. In the case of a par three or a fairway shot, it must be either the flagstick or a specific location on the green.

It might sound rather weird, but the visualization process will encourage you to heighten the awareness of your senses of sight, touch, smell, sound and taste. Being aware of one's surroundings is important to the success of hitting any shot. The particular situation faced might be on the tee, in the fairway, in the rough, in the sand or even in the trees. I will walk you through a step-by-step example of a typical pre-shot routine. Let us get started!

Approach Shot to the Green:

I am playing at a place that is close to my heart, Indian Valley Country Club in Telford, Pennsylvania. This also happens to be the home course of my co-author, Bob Ockenfuss. Having played in the pro-member at Indian Valley for many years, I am very familiar with the layout. What will be described is the start to finish, step-by-step visualization and pre-shot process I would walk through in playing the first hole at this facility. This sample is only for one hole, but this same process would apply to individual shots as they would occur on any hole I might play. I am suggesting it should be the same case for you any time you tee it up! The steps in the process should be taken without delay. Planning for your shot should be taking place while your playing partners are performing theirs. See if you can *picture* what I will describe in your mind!

The first hole at Indian Valley Country Club is a medium length par four with a second shot over a creek to a small green. It is a beautiful early summer morning in late June. The blue sky is dotted with white, puffy clouds. The warming rays of the sun create a yellowish-orange hue on their underneath surfaces. Temperatures are in the high seventies. Everything is green. Birds can be heard chirping in the trees. The grass is coated with a glistening dew. One can smell the fragrance of the flowers, the freshly mown grass and the earthiness of the soil. A slight breeze rustles the leaves on the trees. All in all, it is a picture perfect beginning to another great day of golf.

I have just hit a nice second serve, low-cut drive of about 275 yards into the middle of the fairway. As I walk up to my ball, I begin to analyze my second shot. I feel the ground below my feet and sense the lie is flat. Although the grass is short, the lie is not exceptionally tight. I grab a few blades of grass and throw them into the air in order to judge the effect of the wind. As I face toward the green, the blades of grass float gently above and past my head and back over my shoulders. I sense a gentle breeze is blowing into my face. I further observe the flag on the flagstick is fluttering towards me. I use my yardage calculation device and determine the distance to the pin is exactly 125 yards. Furthermore, I notice the flagstick is located at the front, left portion of the green. It is a slightly downhill shot over water to a green that has a severely sloping false front. I do not want the resulting shot to finish either short into the false front or left and thus short side myself. These both would be difficult up-and-downs. I keep the contours and the speed of the green in mind. The safe bet is to take enough club and finish a bit past and to the right of the flagstick into the middle of the green. From there, I will have about a ten-foot, slightly downhill putt. A birdie is a possibility, but par is the worst that should happen. I must know exactly how far I hit each club in my bag ahead of time. Knowing I hit a sand wedge 118 yards and a gap wedge 127 yards under normal, windless conditions, I determine my club selection for this shot will be a gap wedge. My plan is to attempt to hit a lower trajectory, partial punch with less spin rather than a full shot in order to keep the ball under the wind. I must be disciplined, clear and decisive in my decision-making. I fully commit to the chosen shot.

Once the club-selection process has been completed, it is now time to aim at the target. I stand behind the ball and draw a line between myself, the ball and the target. I might extend my club in front of me in order to accomplish this. The target I choose must be specific and small. In this case, it is a spot in the middle of the green ten feet to the right of and behind the flagstick. Since the target is far away, I select an intermediate target a short distance in front of the ball on the same line between the ball and the target. This time it is a discoloration in the grass. When standing beside the ball, it is easier to align myself to a nearby target than a distant one.

Considering the playing conditions, I now visualize in my mind's eye the shot style I want to hit. Due to my playing style, I must also feel the shot in my body! I picture a fade, draw or straight shot. Do I want a low, medium or high ball-flight trajectory? I finally see the ball flying through the air towards the target with the desired shape and trajectory. I might even recall a similar great shot from the past that had a great result. I see the ball land softly beyond the flagstick and quickly check up. I am picturing the shot in my mind before it happens.

I pull the fifty-degree gap wedge from my golf bag! It is time to take some practice swings. This can be done either behind the ball or to the side of it. My style is to take my swings to the side of the ball. The idea is to meaningfully mimic the swing I want to make. I am actually rehearsing my mechanics to hit the desired fade, draw or straight shot. On this occasion, my choice is a slight draw. I am developing a feel for the intended shot, especially in my grip.

A swing trigger allows me to gain total concentration and have everything come into focus. Some players may accomplish this by tugging upon their shirt sleeve or pants or by clapping their hands. My method is to close my golf glove with the Velcro strap. Once this has been successfully accomplished, all of my conscious thinking is finished at this point. I am now on *autopilot*!

At this point, some players might choose to use a cleansing breath in order to help rid their body of tension. In doing so, they would inhale deeply through their nose with the aid of their diaphragm. They would then exhale fully through their mouth.

After I have settled all of this in my mind, I approach the ball from my original location behind the ball to one beside it. As I step to the ball in this manner, I simultaneously grip the club appropriately for the type of shot I want to make. I can feel the familiar texture of the grip in my fingers.

As I step to the ball, I observe the target with my eyes. My style is to place my right foot first and follow it with my left foot. My first goal in doing this is to correctly measure myself the proper distance from the ball. This will help me assume correct posture, alignment and ball position between my feet. I adjust the club face perpendicularly to the initial ball takeoff direction I want to have. I shuffle my feet in order to attain proper alignment, width of my stance and ball position. As this happens, my eyes shift back and forth to the target two times. I constantly remain in motion.

I must be able to develop a way of getting my swing into motion. Jack Nicklaus, being left-eye dominant, turned his head to the right. Gary Player kicked in his right knee. My technique is to waggle the club head twice, a slight, almost imperceptible push forward and then a rebound one-piece takeaway off of that.

It is important to keep the number of target looks and waggles consistent.

Since the whole thing is a process, if interrupted for some reason, I must begin all over again.

Everything seems to slow down as I see myself make my rhythmic back and through circular, inside-to-square-to-inside swinging motion. I hear the club face make the familiar, solid "clicking" sound as the ball is compressed. Once the shot has been executed, I hold my finish in balance. I do this so I might observe the ball in flight and evaluate the feel of the swing that has produced the result. The ball flight tells me everything I need to know. If it is a good shot, I absorb it like a sponge for future reference. If it is poor, I wipe it away with an additional practice swing and return the offending club to my golf bag. Whatever the final result may be, my goal is to accept the outcome of the shot.

On this occasion, the ball comes off of the club face perfectly as planned and rises gradually into the air. It curves gently from right to left. The trajectory is slightly lower due to the partial swing I have made. I see the ball land softly on the green just beyond the flagstick and take one hop before checking up and coming to a stop. This intended amount of spin did not allow the ball to rocket back off of the green. As it comes to rest, I see the white ball contrasted against the green putting surface resting approximately ten feet above and to the right of the flagstick. The outcome of the shot has taken place exactly as I had planned. A successful shot has been completed. Just like that, it is off to my next shot

It might seem to have taken longer, but the entire process probably lasted only a minute or so. My goal is to have the pre-shot process take the same amount of time from start to finish on each and every shot. Be assured, you will get better at the process once you create your own, personalized routine and then work at it repeatedly. It might seem like wasted effort, but the reward through added attention to detail will definitely be lower scores.

Short Shots Routine

A pre-shot routine should not be confined to only full shots. Each part of the game should have one. Again, each player has to go about creating their own, individual routine. Please refer to chapters eight and nine as a refresher on how to execute either a chip and run or a loft shot. Here then is a brief guided visualization related to short shots.

As I approach the green and my ball somewhere near it, I begin to visually analyze my situation. I soak up all of my surroundings. I attempt to understand how the circumstances dictate how I need to play the shot. Will I be playing a chip-and-run or a loft shot? In planning what to do, I ask myself several questions. What particular lie do I have? What is the grain like surrounding the ball? How much green do I have to work with? Is the hole location close to the edge of the putting surface with little green with which to work? Is there a hazard or bunker in my way? What is the exact distance of the flagstick across the green from where my ball lies? How fast are the green speeds? Is the shot up, down or side hill? What are the contours of the green like? Are there various levels to the green? What is the slope of the putting surface around the flagstick? How about the grain of the grass on the green surface? Will wind influence the shot? How far must I carry the ball to the *exact spot* where it must land on the green? How much break must I play to have the ball finish either in or near the hole? If the ball does not go into the hole, from where do I want to play my next shot?

All of this will dictate both the style of shot I choose to play and my club selection. After weighing all of the factors, I make my final decision. This time it will be a chip-and-run shot with an eight iron. I begin by standing behind the ball much as I do for full shots. I form a positive picture in my mind how to play the shot. I see the exact spot where I want the ball to land on the green and then have the ball roll to the hole. I then walk beside the ball and take a few practice swings in order to get a proper feel for the shot. In doing so, I rehearse the length of my swing. When ready, I set my feet to the ball in a similar fashion as for a full shot, working on distance from the ball, alignment and ball position. I hit the shot and see the ball roll into the hole.

Putting Routine

The pre-shot routine in putting is very similar to the one used for short shots. Almost the same factors must be weighed before I stroke the ball. If necessary, please refer to chapters eleven through fifteen related to thoughts on putting.

As I approach the green and see where my ball is located, I again begin to visually analyze my situation. I say this because there is much to learn before even reaching the green. I use my eyes to read the green. There are many factors to consider. I might begin by bending down to mark my ball and, in doing so, attempt to view the surface from a vantage point lower to the ground. In a like manner, I might observe the surface on a line from in back of the ball toward the hole and also from the other side of the cup looking back the other way. I evaluate the *slope* or *contour* of the green and try to take note of where water might drain off the surface at its lowest point of elevation. Most greens are sloped from back to front, but it might be different in this case. Do I face an up, down or side-hill putt? I attempt to get even more feedback on slope and *firmness* of the putting surface as I walk across the green. In doing so, I try to sense the angle of slope with my feet and also judge the amount of *moisture* which is present in the ground. *Grain* indicates which direction the blades of grass are growing. A "shiny" appearance indicates the grain is running away (down grain) from me, while a "dark" appearance means I am going against the grain. I examine the edges of the cup I will be putting towards. A rough, worn edge indicates the down grain side toward which the grain is running. The opposite sharp, up grain side is the direction from which the grass is growing. Downhill, down grain putts will be faster and will not have to be stroked as firmly. Uphill putts against the grain will be slower and need to be stroked with more force. I also closely inspect the area around the cup. What lurks just behind the hole? How careful do I need to be in judging *speed*? What will happen during the last few feet of the intended line as the ball slows down and finally comes to rest? Will the ball continue to roll out or come to an abrupt halt? A few final factors might come into play as my decision-making process winds to an end. Are there mountains or bodies of water nearby? Is wind a factor? Putts tend to break away from mountains and towards water. If the sun is setting, where is it in relation to the hole? Blades of grass would sometimes be growing toward the sun at the end of the day. Only the stream in front of the green is a factor this morning. Based on all of these observations, I attempt to place the putt into one of the six speed categories mentioned in chapter twenty-one. Should my ball be located closest to the hole, I attempt to accomplish all of this evaluation while other players are putting. If others are first to putt, I might observe their results before it is my time to play. I might be able to pick up something I missed!

At some time during the process, especially if the putt has some length to it, I might walk off the distance of the putt and count the number of steps I have taken. This will help me further judge the pace of the stroke. I must consider two factors, speed and direction. Speed is more important because most three-putts are caused by either rolling the ball too short of or too far past the hole.

I evaluate my putt from all sides. I might make a final attempt to visualize the speed and break from behind the ball --- down the line of the putt. In doing so, I trace the path of the ball rolling to the hole. I might also find it helpful to again estimate the roll of the ball from behind the hole, especially on downhill putts. In this manner, I am able to envision the ball rolling to the hole on a certain path with the correct amount of speed and break. Another estimation on break is possible by standing to the side and below the line of the putt in order to get even more detailed feedback. From the side I can much more accurately evaluate speed and break. From this vantage point I am able to estimate the apex (high point) of the roll of the ball on a breaking putt. My goal is to have the ball roll over this point as it curves toward the hole. Since this is a breaking putt, I will not want my initial target line to be starting at the apex point, but instead *above* it.

On longer putts, I might divide the green into sections in order to evaluate the surface over which I will be rolling my ball. I picture the path the ball must take necessary to finish near the hole. My eyes trace each part of this path, fully appreciating each turn and the speed as the ball rolls over and over.

As I mentioned before, if other golfers putt before it is my turn, I need to be keenly observant and learn from them. In order to keep up the correct pace of play, I need to complete as many of these observations and calculations as possible while first approaching the green. My *mind*, like a computer, is quickly sizing up all of this information in rapid succession. Much of the process can be wrapped up while the other players in the group are finishing out the hole.

Having completed the evaluation and planning, I now move on to actually performing the shot. I stand behind the ball, replace it on the green and fine tune my aim. Some players might use a colored marking stripe drawn on the ball to line up with the projected target. In my case, I do not do this. In fact, it seems to change all of the time during my various rounds of golf. I prefer to see the ball rolling with perfect speed into a certain part of the hole, especially on breaking putts. *Before* I make the stroke, in my mind's eye, I positively see the ball roll into the hole. My goal is to keep the same, orderly routine and take the same amount of time for each and every putt. I now stand beside the ball and make two practice strokes. I look at the hole one last time, draw my eyes back toward the ball and then go! My eyes remain looking at the spot where they had focused. I stroke the ball confidently and hold my finish at the end without recoil. This enables me to evaluate my effort. I hear the sound of the ball making contact with the bottom of the cup.

Much decision-making has taken place leading up to my turn. When it becomes time for me to putt, the time frame to complete the final process has been only slightly in excess of thirty seconds. The goal is for me to repeat the exact same steps and take the same amount of elapsed time each and every time I putt.

Chapter Twenty-eight
The Golfer's Approach to Utilizing Brain Research

Padraig Harrington, commenting after his 2015 playoff victory at the Honda Classic at the P.G.A. National Golf Club, said, "I really do believe in myself. I think I have found that *mental edge* I had been lacking over the past number of years. I hope to stick with that going forward and consistently be contending."

Since the mind is so powerful in golf, as co-authors, we recently decided to look into studies about the brain and how it might apply to golf instruction. I have found that much brain research has been done over the past ten years, much of it having to do with education and learning. It has been found that our brains have *the ability to act and react in ever-changing ways*. It has to do with the ability of the brain to reorganize or transform itself. For example, when a player makes a ***change*** to their swing, their brain creates new connections or pathways between neurons, called synapses, to record that swing change. An electrical or chemical signal is passed from one neuron to another. The brain gets rewired and transformed. When a new skill is ***accepted*** and ***practiced repeatedly***, the brain will increase the strength of the synapses and make a stronger connection. New pathways are established and old ones are weakened and gradually disappear. This is why repetition is so important in learning golf motor skills. Repeating the same motion over and over again leads to the action known as "muscle memory."

Such changes in the brain are dependent on the experiences we have. In this way, changes take place in our brains in response to how we use them on a daily basis. When a person is inflexibly stuck in a habit of mind or habit of doing, it is important to ask the question, "What might I do differently?" By doing this, if they are willing to do so, a person can change their ordinary way of thinking by trying something new. It is so easy to get stuck in a certain way of thinking and being because it is safe and comfortable. Yet when we stretch ourselves, we create opportunities for possibilities and good outcomes! In order to improve, a player must commit to change and growth. This is true when running a business, managing a family or when playing golf. It is "thinking outside of the box." For example, a golfer might ask, "Should I accept what my instructor is telling me to do in my lessons?" In another sense, they might also pose another question. "What might I consider doing differently tonight between rounds to keep my mind straight that will allow me to increase my chances of performing on a higher level on the course tomorrow?"

Brain Stretching Exercises:

We have done some thinking about these findings and have come up with some interesting thoughts. The idea is to be ***flexible*** in what you do in your daily life. This is true about what you do during the week at work or over the weekend. In order to get you started, here are a few small suggestions about tasks you can do *differently* that might help expand the creativity of your brain. Sometimes just altering *our normal routine* can break up the hesitancy in our minds to try something new. Here is a list of creative "exercises" to consider.

1. Drive either to or from work or the course taking a different route than the usual one.

2. In walking from point A to point B at work, travel a totally different route than you would usually take. If you normally take an elevator, this time walk the stairs.

3. If you normally eat at a fast-food restaurant! Maybe live on the edge next time by packing your own lunch.

4. If you have constantly checked e-mail while on past vacations, do not check it at all on the next one.

5. Instead of drinking iced tea, lemonade or soda, drink water infused with oranges or cucumbers

6. Rather than doing the same exercises each and every time you work out at the gym, vary them between differing programs of strength, flexibility and cardiovascular fitness. Perhaps add in yoga.

7. If you normally walk inside on the treadmill and listen to music on your I-Pod, walk outside this time and use all of your senses in order to "smell the roses!"

8. If you normally add sugar or a creamer to your coffee or tea, do not add any next time. As you drink the new concoction, can you appreciate a different taste or smell?

9. Instead of watching television, read a book or try completing a Sudoku or crossword puzzle.

10. Rather than sleeping late on Saturday, wake up early and get started on the completion of a household project you have been putting off.

11. Rather than checking the time by using a smart phone, use your wristwatch.

Focus Factors to Consider in Keeping One's Mind Right for Golf

Map out a **plan** for golf improvement. Setting realistic **goals** will increase the probability of success and reaching one's potential. This allows us to reach outside of our comfort zone in order to accomplish something we might not have previously expected to be possible.

In taking lessons, ask yourself several important questions. Do I actually want to change in order to get better? Can I actually identify, see and accept what needs to be changed? Can I identify what is going on with my current swing without getting defensive about it? Based on what I am learning through instruction and positive results achieved, am I able to develop a plan for success which is different from what I have been doing? Can I continue to "think outside of the box" and stay with the program?

"Competitive golf is played mainly on a five-and-a-half-inch course, the space between your ears."
Bobby Jones

Earning success is a **process**.

Life is all about making **choices**. Focus on the power of **positive** thinking.

"Earn the right to be proud and confident." John Wooden

Have *positive* **"self-talk" conversations** with yourself while playing on the golf course. Our reaction to situations is a *choice* --- glass half full or empty. Keep reminding yourself, "I <u>can</u> do this!"

Believe in yourself and your **method of play**. Find a swing that works for you and spend time *perfecting* it.

Focus on the **glass being "half-full"** rather than "half-empty"!

Experiencing **success** will help a player to *relax*.

When competing, just **"want to be there"** and *enjoy* **the activity**. Embrace difficult situations.

Physical and **mental exercise** plus attention to **nutrition** and **flexibility** is good for the brain because it helps to create new neuron connections.

While **practicing on the range**, one can work on technique by hitting several shots with the same club. On the other hand, in the same environment, it might be more helpful to recreate this same swing under match or tournament playing conditions. This might be accomplished by either "playing a round" at the practice range or by now and then throwing in a shot with a totally different club. Alternately attempt to create draws and fades. Simulate playing the first hole of either your home course or another course where that hole gives you trouble. Practice specific shots you are likely to encounter on the course. By incorporating visualization and a pre-shot routine, all of these scenarios would creatively simulate on-course situations. The player would avoid the mindless activity of merely beating balls, which is totally unlike hitting shots during a round. Work on the *tempo* (pace) and *rhythm* of the swing. Always practice with a *purpose*. It is best to place a *limit* on practice time in order to maintain mental focus.

Purposeful and **perfect practice** makes *permanent*.

Football, baseball and tennis are all **reactionary sports**. Players are reacting to a stimulus. On the other hand, since the golf ball lies on the ground just waiting to be hit, golf might be referred to as a **non-reactionary sport**. Basketball is a little of both. Shooting a jump shot from the floor is reactionary during the flow of the game. The player has to adjust to the defense being played by the other team. Alternately, shooting a free throw from the foul line is non-reactionary because defense is not being played against the free throw shooter. The distance of the shot is always the same. Although the shot must be attempted within a ten-second time frame, free throw shooting is somewhat similar to hitting a golf shot. The player has to initiate the action. Both are target-related. Both *should* incorporate a pre-shot routine. By perfecting a pre-shot routine and by using visualization, golf can be made into more of a reactionary sport. Focus is narrowed and improved shot consistency is produced as a result of going through the process and hitting each shot within the same time frame.

"Success is 10% inspiration and 90% perspiration." Thomas Edison **Persistence** counts!

Just as it is with free throw shooting in basketball, the development and use of an individualized, disciplined **pre-shot routine** in golf helps a player's mind and body to relax and work in harmony. The process should be kept short, be repeated in the same ordered steps, always consume the same amount of time and be used before *each and every* shot. It is a *positive thought process* that helps to block out negatives and reduce stress. It blocks outside distractions, eliminates uncertainty and frees up the player to sub-consciously perform the correct mechanics. It can be compared to a plane flying on autopilot. The process leads to consistency and confidence and allows attention to be placed on the feel of the shot and reacting to the desired target.

Get lost in the **process** of hitting good shots rather than focusing on the results. Pay attention to the current *task*. This clears the mind of the pressure connected to the situation at hand. This requires **self-discipline**!

"Successful people are willing to do the things unsuccessful people are unwilling to do." Jeff Olson

Focus on **fundamentals**.

Visualization is positive visual and mental imagery leading up to the execution of a particular shot that helps the player to relax and *see* success in their mind. It should be incorporated as part of the **pre-shot routine**. The golfer can clearly *see* the shape and trajectory of the upcoming shot and predict its shape and distance *before* it is played. The imagery might take place in slow motion. The player can *see* the ball go toward the target and into the hole.

Being **in the zone** is experiencing a heightened state of awareness. There is disciplined concentration and flow. Concentration is placed on the process rather than the outcome. Feel is emphasized over swing mechanics. The individual and the task unify. It is allowing one's body to do its thing as *perfectly as possible* through physical and mental training. The mind is kept busy and quiet. *The body is allowed to take over and be able to do the actions it has been trained to do.* Focus on the **task** that needs to be done. The player allows the **sub-conscious** to take over.

Target awareness helps the golfer to produce imagined shots. The target must be *precise*. Focus is narrowed off of extraneous visual stimuli, such as hazards and out-of-bounds.

The shot produced is a reflection of either **positive** or **negative thinking**. If a player is convinced something will happen, they will unconsciously *make* it happen. Think of yourself as being excellent!

"Whether you think you can, or whether you think you cannot, you are right." Henry Ford

Trust is important. Once a player has narrowed their thinking and made a decision on how to hit a shot, they must fully **commit** to it.

Patience is a virtue.

If possible, **walk a strange course backward** before you play it in order to pre-plan strategy and *course management*. There are perhaps five to six dangerous shots that need to be played each round. Be sure to play them smartly and within your capabilities.

Consider it a goal to have **fun** playing the game.

Concentrate in small *chunks*. One cannot concentrate continually over the time span of an entire round. One must learn how to come in and out of concentration. A **signal** or **cue** must be developed by the player to indicate that they are entering the concentration zone. The idea is to focus on the present shot, relax in between and then refocus for the next shot.

Perhaps try using a **cleansing breath** in order to reduce tension.

Attention to ingraining *swing mechanics* is for the **practice range**; *playing the game* is for the **golf course**.

Concern yourself with having a **management game plan** and playing the **golf course** relative to the *strengths* and *weaknesses* of your game.

During the winter, when it is too cold outside to practice or play, or during the season when it is difficult to find time to do so, go to a quiet place, close your eyes and **mentally imagine** yourself performing the correct mechanics concerning the various parts of the game. Try doing this in a darkened room or when you first turn off the lights to go to bed at night. See yourself doing these actions correctly. The idea is to trick your *mind* into thinking that you are actually doing these things.

Be aware of both your **personality** and how you **process information** --- intuitively (creative/impulsive) or analytically (precise).

Focus on what you **can do** rather than on what you *cannot do*. At the same time, identify weaknesses and work to correct them.

Have knowledge of the **things you know you must do** concerning your swing in order to succeed. <u>Do</u> have control over the actions that you know produce quality shots. <u>Do</u> place your full focus on performing these actions each and every time. This is a hugely important concept!

Keep a **notebook** about learning experiences. Also write down key thoughts on a day where your swing worked well. Be willing to learn from both *successes* and *failures*.

Understand that one **does not have to be perfect** in order to play good golf.

The *scores a player shoots* do <u>not</u> determine his/her **self-worth**.

Concentrate on learning the **technique** first and do not worry about results until you have the technique down pat.

Trying harder should be *avoided*.

"Many people have the will to win, but <u>not</u> many people have the will to **prepare** to win." Coach Bobby Knight

How does one get to Augusta National? Practice! Practice! Practice!

Over-learning skills leads to *relaxed* **concentration**. By accomplishing this, on-course distractions are reduced and quality of play is facilitated. The player is less self-consciousness during play. The golfer does not have to think about swing mechanics because they have already been ingrained in the subconscious through repetition during practice. Actions are so well learned they become *automatic*, like driving a car or riding a bike. As a result of repeated success on the course due to the incorporation of correct swing mechanics, the player develops confidence in himself/herself. Under these conditions, one's golf game is confidently portable to any course.

Do not hang your head and quit after a missed shot. After a poor shot, "**throw it away**" with a good practice swing. You will be *rehearsing* the swing you want to make for the next shot.

Place your full **attention** on the *here-and-now*. Stay in the ***present***. Avoid getting ahead of yourself. Play the game *one shot at a time!*

Recall and honor **past successes**.

Make a determined effort to give your **best effort** *all of the time*.

"Make today your masterpiece." John Wooden

Most importantly, do <u>not</u> allow the **negatives** of our world to influence your approach to the *mind game* of golf.

"This is an easy game (sport) until you care!' Roger Maltbie

Always picture the **successful outcome** of a shot.

Before stroking a putt, positively *see* **the ball going into the hole.** *Hear* **it hit the bottom of the cup.**

Maintain an **even keel** --- strive to avoid *highs* and *lows*.

"Failing to **prepare** is planning to fail. **Success** is peace of mind that is the direct result of self-satisfaction in knowing you did your best to become the best you are capable of becoming." John Wooden (1934)

Chapter Twenty-nine
Swing Plane, Ball Flight Laws and Swing Correction

As a teacher and coach, what is your swing diagnosis philosophy?

I do not teach a systems approach. Instead, I meet every student at the point where they currently are with their swing and treat them as an individual. I begin by looking at their **ball flight**. Does the ball fly straight, draw or slice? Working in reverse, I analyze what is happening at impact. Is the club face square, closed or open to the path of the club head? In order to alter ball flight, one must first change what happens between the ball and the club head face at impact. An understanding of **swing plane** is important because such knowledge influences club head **swing path** and the **club head face angle** as it approaches the ball. Is the club head path too outside-in or inside-out? Is the shaft angle too steep or shallow? In order to change swing plane, one must change the motion of one's hands, arms and body. Finally, what is the player's **swing speed**?

What is meant by swing plane? How can understanding it help me become a better player?

Every single golfer has a swing plane which is correct for them, no matter what their height or body type. Assuming the golfer has properly fitting clubs, their swing plane is set by the *angle of their club shaft at address, which is influenced by their posture at address*. This angle is almost the same at both address and impact. Although there is but one plane angle throughout the swing, the club swings through several planes from start to finish.

An understanding of high school geometry is helpful here. We probably all understand *parallel* means everywhere equidistant. One example would be the imaginary latitude lines on the surface of the earth on either side of the equator. An even more familiar example would be the two rails of a railroad track. A passenger on a train forever hopes those rails remain equidistant at all times. The term *congruent* is a little more difficult to understand. Congruent may be defined as having the quality of sameness, agreeing, corresponding, coinciding or being able to be superimposed. All of the angles of a square, a rectangle and an equilateral triangle are congruent.

As a golfer starts their swing, the club travels back along the original plane angle. As the swing continues, the club moves above and parallel to the original plane angle. The club is moving correctly in a circular pattern both in and up, continuously changing planes in the process. The backswing continues to the top, and then the process reverses itself in the downswing. The club again passes through the same planes down to the ball at impact and then on through to the finish. The secondary plane is both above and *parallel* to the original plane. The secondary plane and original plane angles are *congruent*. What we have described, start to finish, is a perfect, circular on-plane swing that produces the proper squaring effect of the club face through impact!

The problem occurs when the golfer swings "off-plane". One possibility is an overly upright, steep straight-line swing path. This outside-to-inside (over the top) pattern (path) produces an opening club face and a usually sliced ball flight. Someone who swings "above" the plane might be good with short irons. The other extreme is an overly flat inside-to-outside swing path. The club face closes too quickly, usually resulting in a hooked ball flight. Someone who swings "below" the plane might be good with the driver or long irons. Characteristics of these extremes are summarized in the diagrams found on the last page of this chapter.

The best method of finding which category you fit into is to hit a driver on the practice range. This is the club having the least loft and producing the most sidespin.

What are the benefits of such knowledge? After enough education and coaching by their instructor, the goal for the golfer is to be able to analyze and remedy their own mistakes. They will be able to develop a plan for overall improvement. They will be able to understand how to maneuver the ball, hitting desired cuts and draws at will. They might even be able to fix their swing in the middle of a round.

What are the different reasons an individual player's swing might be off plane?

There are a variety of reasons why a player's swing might be off plane. Many players simply have an incorrect knowledge of what an upright or flat swing might look like. They might think that having a flat swing is negative and an upright swing is good. This is why 85% of golfers over tilt and slice the ball. Club fitting must be correct. Clubs that are too short will lead to an overly steep, overly tilting swing. When this happens, the player will rotate the right shoulder down in an attempt to get to the ball. The player may stand too far from the ball and thus be reaching for it at address. A fear of trouble, such as a hazard or out of bounds, might cause a brain disconnect, poor mechanics and a less than desirable ball flight. A grip that is either too strong or too weak might create an off-plane swing. Generally, when grip and setup are correct, the plane will usually be correct. Because they cannot come out of their bodies and see themselves, players do not generally get to have a proper perspective of what their swing really looks like. As a starting point toward quality instruction, this is why it might be good for a player to observe what their swing looks like on video. On the other hand, a knowledgeable teacher might simply be able to demonstrate all of these finer points and make the necessary corrections for the student during the course of a lesson.

Why should I be concerned with knowledge of ball flight laws?

As mentioned before, ball flight tells all. Although there are others to consider, the two most important variables are **club head swing path** and **club head face angle** at impact. Additional, secondary variables include the lie of the ball itself, loft of the club being used, shaft flex, swing speed generated, steepness or shallowness of the angle of attack and the hardness of the ball. With a proper knowledge of these cause and effect factors related to these variables, the golfer can go a long way toward fixing their own game. They can become their own coach, especially during a round on the golf course. What is the shape of the ball flight? What is causing the ball to curve as it does? What can I do in order to deliver the club head to the ball correctly *at impact* and to achieve consistency in achieving this goal time after time? Very few golfers are aware of such information!

There are several amazing short videos posted on YouTube for you to look over which contain valuable information about the principles of ball flight laws. The first one is entitled **"Ball Flight Laws from Golf Evolution"** (https://www.youtube.com/watch?v=eEHiY5iv5u4). The second one, a more detailed explanation of the subject by John Dunnigan, is aptly entitled **"The Ball Flight Laws"** (https://www.youtube.com/watch?v=Wnq6TiXw7wU&feature=related). Here is the most basic rule they teach. Club head face angle and the directional path of the club head are *interrelated factors* that cause *sidespin* on the ball at impact. However, assuming sweet spot impact, of the two factors, the club head face angle is responsible for approximately 85% of the starting or takeoff direction of the ball. Club head path is responsible for the remaining 15% of sidespin and path. *The absolute key to controlling ball flight lies in controlling the relationship between club head face angle and club head path at impact.* Shaping a shot in the intended fashion --- creating fades and draws --- requires getting both of these factors to interact in the proper manner.

The ball curves as it does because there is a gap, or difference, between the face angle and the path of the club head. Low lofted clubs, such as the driver, produce the most sidespin, while high-lofted clubs, such as wedges, produce the least sidespin, but the most backspin. *The larger the difference between club head face angle and club head path, the more sidespin is generated.* A **fade** is produced when the club head face angle is *open* to the path of the club head at impact. This produces *clockwise* sidespin on the ball. A fade turns into a **slice** when the differential between the club head face angle and club head path is increased. On the other hand, a **draw** is produced when the club head face angle is *closed* to the path of the club head at impact. This produces a *counterclockwise* sidespin on the ball. A draw turns into a **hook** when the differential between the club head face angle and club head path is increased. A **straight** shot is produced when the club face angle is square to the club head path direction at impact.

It is all about geometry and physics. The ball, an inanimate object, does not have a brain. It has no idea about the intended target line, club head face angle and/or club head path. At the point of impact, it simply reacts to club head face angle, club head path and the speed of the swing. All told, there are three basic club head paths --- inside-out, square-to-square and outside-in --- and three variations of club face angle --- open, square and closed --- for each path. This adds up to nine different ball flight patterns.

The following descriptions provide brief, written explanations of what can be observed in the diagrams at the end of the chapter. The diagrams themselves provide a visual snapshot of the nine common ball flight cause and effect scenarios. By combining the written and the visual information, the reader should now be able to put "two-and-two" together in order to understand what is happening in the relationship between club head face angle and club head path. Note the angle of the leading edge of the face of the club head in relation to the path of the club head, represented by the darker, solid, broken arrows. The lighter, solid, arrow line represents the target line. The line with circles represents the resulting, post impact path of the golf ball.

Ball Flight Descriptions Related to the Ball Flight Laws:

Fade/Slice (diagram 8):
Neutral/square-to-square club head swing path
Club head face angle is *open* to club head swing path and the target line
Clockwise sidespin
Curving, left-to-right ball flight; ball flight starts out right of the club head path and the target line and then curves even farther to the right of it
Greater differential between face and path leads to more sidespin and a bigger ball curvature; a fade becomes a slice

Draw/Hook (diagram 9):
Neutral/square-to-square club head swing path
Club head face angle is *closed* to club head swing path and the target line
Counterclockwise sidespin
Curving, right-to-left ball flight; ball flight starts out left of the club head path and the target line and then curves even farther to the left of it
Greater differential between face and path leads to more sidespin and a bigger ball curvature; a draw becomes a hook

Straight Ball Flight Toward the Target (diagram 3):
Neutral/square-to-square club head swing path
Club head face angle is square to both target line and club head swing path
Straight-line ball flight *toward* the target
Solid feel

Push Fade/Slice (diagram 4):
Club head path is inside-to-outside
Club head face angle *open* to club head swing path
Clockwise sidespin
Curving, left-to-right ball flight to the right of both the club head path and the target line
Greater differential between face and path leads to more sidespin and a bigger ball curvature; a fade becomes a slice

Push Draw/Hook (diagram 6):
Club head path is inside-to-outside
Club head face angle is *closed* to club head swing path
Counterclockwise sidespin

Curving, left-to-right ball flight toward the target or even left of it

Greater differential between face and path leads to more sidespin and a bigger ball curvature; a draw becomes a hook

Straight Push (diagram 2):
Club head path is inside-to-outside
Club head face angle *square* to club head swing path
Straight-line ball flight *right* of target
Solid feel

Pull Fade/Slice (diagram 5):
Club head path is outside-to-inside
Club head face angle is *open* to the club head swing path
Clockwise sidespin
Curving, left-to-right ball flight toward the target or even right of it
Greater differential between face and path leads to more sidespin and a bigger ball curvature; a fade becomes a slice

Pull Draw/Hook (diagram 7):
Club head path is outside-to-inside
Club head face angle is *closed* to the club head swing path
Counterclockwise sidespin
Curving, right-to-left ball flight to the left of both club head path and the target line
Greater differential between face and path leads to more sidespin and a bigger ball curvature; a draw becomes a hook

Straight Pull (diagram 1):
Club head path is outside-to-inside
Club head face angle is *square* to club head swing path
Straight-line ball flight *left* of target
Solid feel

How can I benefit from my newly found knowledge about both swing plane and ball flight laws?

Good coaching must be directed toward evaluating ball flight patterns and tendencies and thus improving club face-ball impact. Swing fundamentals and mechanics must be improved in order to create a correct swing. At this point, I might adjust student grip characteristics (strengthen or weaken), distance from the ball, setup, posture, swing-path and/or club angle of attack. A player who can produce correct and repetitive impact will go a long way toward having control of both the direction, ball flight pattern and trajectory of his/her golf ball.

Here are some thoughts regarding the ideal, most efficient swing. It might be beneficial to evaluate super slow motion videos of top professionals to see what I mean.

Swing shape is important. The most consistent and correct impact has the club approaching the ball at just the right angle and at just the right amount from the *inside*. The club is not *above* or *below* the plane. At impact, the club face is square to the swing arc. The swing has just the right amount of in-and-around and up-and-down. The arms and hands swing out in front of the body just the correct amount. When the club swings on a natural arc, the club face squares up more easily. The arms are swinging while the trunk of the body is turning and/or rotating.

If the golfer desires to play to their maximum potential, their individual grip must naturally return the club face squarely to their swing path. Every golfer has a correct grip for them. Ball flight patterns will help the golfer discover their own optimum grip. Such a grip enables the golfer to face the club in the direction they are swinging at good speed. This may not necessarily be the so-called "standard" grip.

The club face swings along the target line only inches before, during and after impact.

Because the golfer stands inside the swing arc, the club comes into the ball on a circle from inside the target line, to straight at impact, to back to the inside. It is very much a circular or rotary motion. The goal is to contact the inside part of the ball with a closing, released club face. This will produce a slight draw.

With alignment, it is the shoulders, arms, legs and eyes that are the most important.

The club, following a true arc, then moves quickly inside the target line after striking the ball.

It is true the golfer does not hit the ball with their backswing. However, a correct backswing plane gives the golfer the best chance of making a correct and consistent downswing.

In the backswing, there is a feeling of "connection" between the upper part of the left arm to the body, creating a lower top of the backswing. With a one-piece takeaway, the arms and body work in unison. The arms remain out in front of the body.

The upper body coils over the lower body, loading up behind the ball over the right leg.

Be aware of ball position within the stance and distance from the ball. In terms of generating an adequate upper body turn, slicers might consider experimenting by toeing in their left foot and toeing out their right foot. Hookers might try just the reverse.

Golf is a blend of *synchronizing* hands and arms with the turn or pivot of the trunk or body. The body allows the hands and arms to function properly.

From the top, the arms and club "drop".

The plane of the backswing and downswing are mirror images of each other.

The hands are ahead of the ball at impact. In a player's downswing, the roughly ninety-degree club head lag quickly closes down from waist height to almost nothing at impact. When done properly, this helps to generate great club head speed. The golfer's hands get to the ball a fraction of a second before the clubface. You can plainly see this on slow motion replays from P.G.A. and L.P.G.A. Tour telecasts. During the last split second, the club head catapults and releases to the ball. The club head catches up to the hands at impact and the hands release. Another split second after impact, the club head passes the hands and the right forearm crosses over the left toward the finished position. There is a counterclockwise rotation of the forearms and hands. This is better known as releasing the club through impact.

Keep the body turning along with the hands and arms through the ball. There is synchronization. The hands and arms continue to stay in front of the body.

At the finish, the arms fold over, the wrists are re-cocked and the club is positioned across the player's neck and back. This is a folded finish.

Be *creative*! If you are a natural fader, work on drawing the ball. If you are a natural drawer, work on fading the ball. Golf is very much a game of opposites.

What are two different ways to create a ball flight that draws to the left?

A player can create a draw in the following two ways. A **face draw** is caused by slowing the body motion and allowing the hands and arms to rotate past the body, better known as staying behind the ball. This draw is based on timing and breeds inconsistency. A **path draw** is caused by the path of the club through impact, and is thus more consistent and easier to control.

Club Head Path at Impact - Neutral / Square to Square

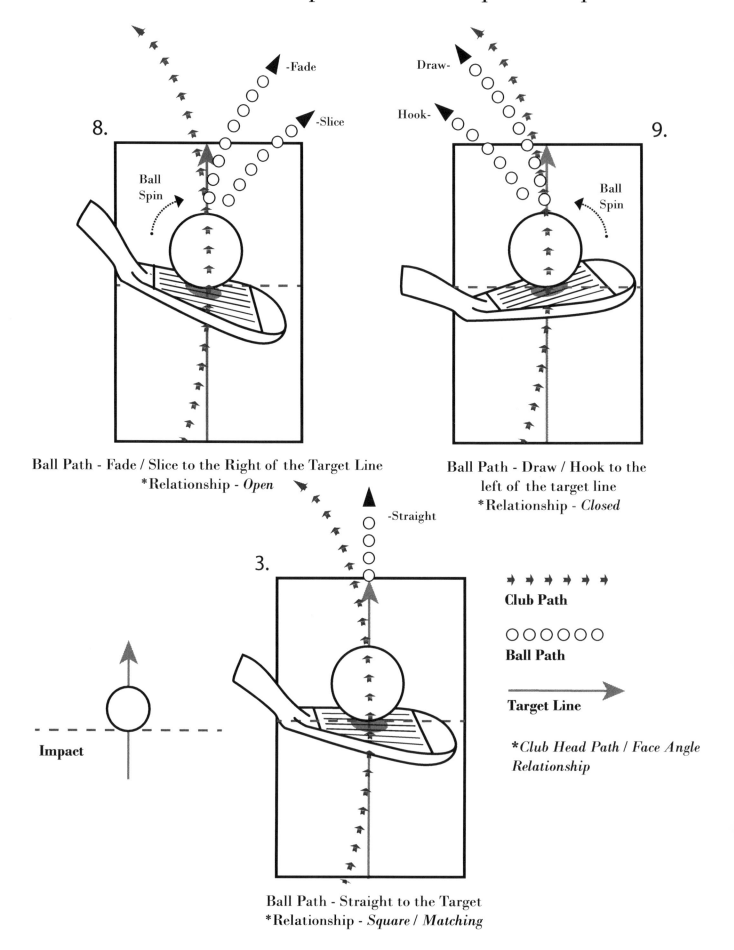

8.

-Fade

-Slice

Ball
Spin

Ball Path - Fade / Slice to the Right of the Target Line
*Relationship - *Open*

9.

Draw-

Hook-

Ball
Spin

Ball Path - Draw / Hook to the
left of the target line
*Relationship - *Closed*

3.

-Straight

Impact

Ball Path - Straight to the Target
*Relationship - *Square / Matching*

Club Path

Ball Path

Target Line

*Club Head Path / Face Angle
Relationship*

Club Head Path at Impact - Inside to Outside

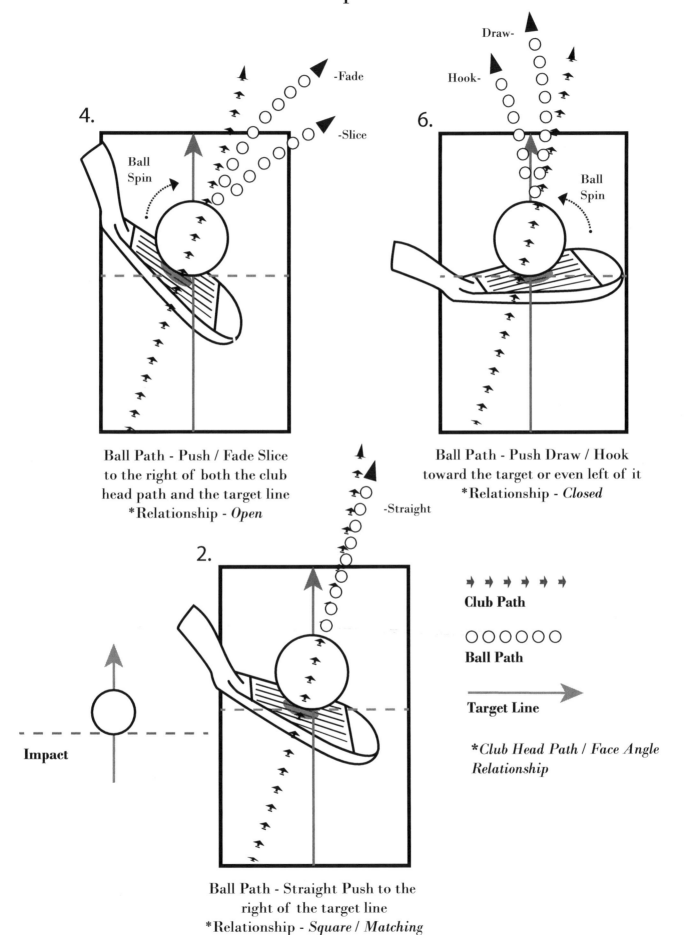

4.

Ball Spin

-Fade

-Slice

Ball Path - Push / Fade Slice
to the right of both the club
head path and the target line
*Relationship - *Open*

6.

Draw-

Hook-

Ball Spin

Ball Path - Push Draw / Hook
toward the target or even left of it
*Relationship - *Closed*

2.

-Straight

Impact

Ball Path - Straight Push to the
right of the target line
*Relationship - *Square / Matching*

Club Path

○○○○○○ **Ball Path**

Target Line

*Club Head Path / Face Angle
Relationship*

Club Head Path at Impact - Outside to Inside

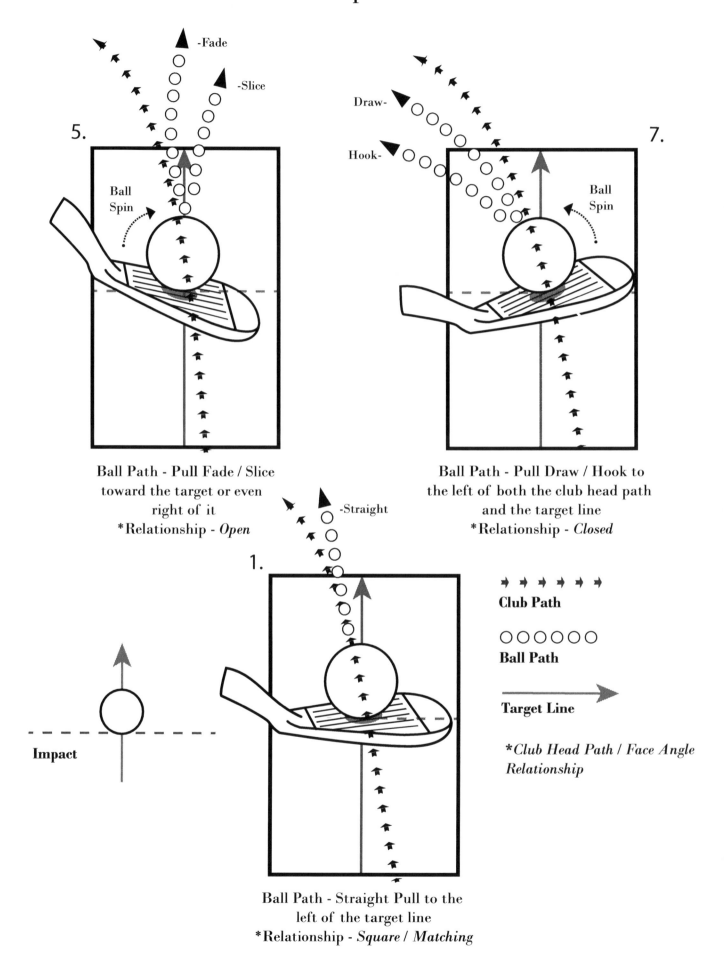

5.

-Fade

-Slice

Ball Spin

Ball Path - Pull Fade / Slice toward the target or even right of it
*Relationship - *Open*

7.

Draw-

Hook-

Ball Spin

Ball Path - Pull Draw / Hook to the left of both the club head path and the target line
*Relationship - *Closed*

-Straight

1.

Ball Path - Straight Pull to the left of the target line
*Relationship - *Square / Matching*

Impact

→ → → → → → **Club Path**

○○○○○○ **Ball Path**

→ **Target Line**

Club Head Path / Face Angle Relationship

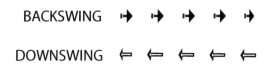
BACKSWING
DOWNSWING

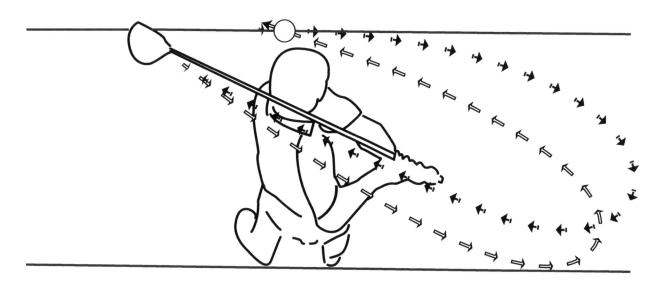

Under Plane Downswing from Inside to Outside

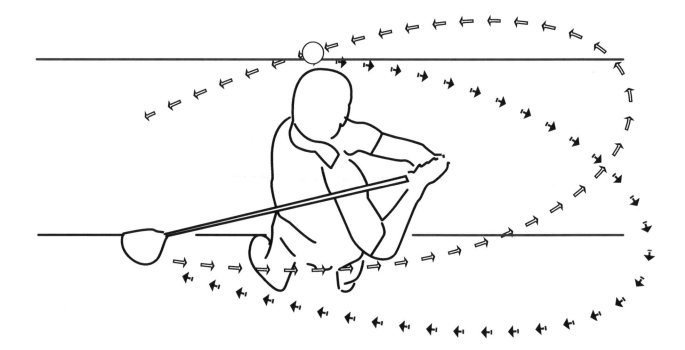

Over the Top Downswing From Outside to Inside

Chapter Thirty
Scoring Better Just by Thinking and Managing One's Game

In 1989, I was working as an assistant professional at Waynesborough Country Club. One weekend, female teaching pro Amelia Rohrer, two of her friends and I teed off for a round at about 2:30 on a Saturday afternoon. I had been out quite late the previous night. On that weekend morning, I had gotten up very early to get to the golf course. Despite having had nothing too much to eat or drink, I proceeded to give twelve scheduled lessons to members. I was flat worn out and dehydrated. As I approached the tenth hole to begin the round, I had a little bit of the shakes and had poor feeling in my hands. On the first few holes, I got off to a decent start. I made a couple of birdies and gradually began to feel better and better. When we finally arrived on the last green, I had an eight-foot birdie putt for a 62. Unfortunately, I missed the putt, made par, but still set a course record. What is the moral of the story? As I began the round, I was not at all physically or mentally prepared. However, I gradually began to develop a *relaxed* atmosphere towards my game. I began to think and feel the right way. My confidence level began to soar and things started to go my way. I was now trusting and believing in myself, thinking I can really do this! The next thing I knew, I found myself near a course record. Did my swing get better all of a sudden? Did I feel great? No! I simply started *thinking* better. There were no negative influences from the outside world in my brain. I had no fear about out of bounds, water hazards, narrow fairways or anything else. My natural ability began to take over. It was like I was on autopilot. I was thinking and managing my way to a course record. I got back into my natural flow because I was making some good mental decisions.

What advice do you have for a golfer who suddenly realizes they are having a career round going?

Some golfers have certain *comfort zones* about the scores they shoot. If they start playing a good round, it might get them out of the zone they are familiar with. Their brain gets involved, they loose focus, do not keep their head in the game and they begin to make mistakes. They become scared and afraid. Players must allow their confidence to continue instead of focusing on score. If you are making net or gross birdies, continue to try to do so. Do not say I need a par-par finish for my career round. Maintain your confidence, play one shot at a time and focus on your visualization and pre-shot routine. Do not play prevent defense as in football. Put the pedal to the metal. The results will begin to be a self-fulfilling prophecy!

Are there two ways of looking at scores?

Absolutely yes! They actually represent two different ways of thinking. A good player will look at a score positively going toward the direction of winning, succeeding, being the best, loving it and wanting it. The negative thinker will be scared, nervous and out of their comfort zone. When the kitchen is hot, they will not be sure they can handle a place they have never been before. They begin to doubt themselves.

How does a player decide what time to arrive at the golf course before the start of a competitive round?

Each person should make this decision based on their personality. What are they comfortable with? The analytical, organized, get up early, look at video, buy a yardage book player who dots their i's and crosses their t's might give themself at least an hour to prepare. On the other hand, the free-wheeling, go-and-get-it, feel player might arrive only 30 minutes before their tee time. This type of player loosens up by hitting 15-20 balls, avoids aiming at targets and finishes up by hitting a few chips and stroking several putts. The bottom line is that each player must match up their personality with their warm-up strategy!

Do you take any stock in the theory that rounds have turning points?

Absolutely! Every round has what might be called a crossroads or turning point. The two roads to choose from are either a success leading to a good score or a negative leading to a less than desirable result. One never knows ahead of time what this crossroads event will be or when it will take place in the round which will influence a player to go in a certain direction. Looking back following the round, one can clearly see how the events played out. Hindsight is always 20-20. Positively speaking, it might be a good lie in the rough which enabled the player to hit a difficult shot. It might be a chip-in at a critical time, an up-and-down from rough or a bunker, a holed putt or a ball hitting a tree and kicking in-bounds. While a round is in progress, I do not want a player to say, "Oh no, here we go, here is the turning point." Analyzing the turning point should never take place during the round itself. Instead, the player should always go back to a round after it is over and then find that critical turning point and learn from it. Was the cause physical, mental or situational?

Can you give a few suggestions about getting off to a good start at the beginning of a round?

This has a lot to do with *attitude* and having the *proper temperament*. In beginning a round, protecting par is important. A player does not want to over-aggressively run a birdie putt way by and wind up with a 3-putt bogey. One cannot win a tournament on the first hole, but they can loose it there. If they do happen to bogey the first hole, they have to be patient. They have to realize it is only one physical stroke out of many. With a smart approach to the game, birdie can be made somewhere else down the road. Perhaps they might have to grind harder. Some great rounds have started off with a bogey, double-bogey or even a triple-bogey. Here is a case in point. In 2014, while playing in the pro-member tournament at Cedarbrook Country Club, I started with a triple-bogey and then made three more bogeys. However, I proceeded to make ten birdies and still shot a four-under 68 and won the event. The lesson to be learned is that one bad hole never puts a player out of a round.

Developing a *game plan* for a particular golf course is important. Players need to know where and when to gamble. In certain situations, gambling does not hurt. One has to know when the percentages are in their favor or against them. They have to know "when to hold em' and when to fold em'."

Before the tournament starts, a ***target score*** should be set to win the event. One should manage their game around this score. The player needs to look in the mirror, discover their golf identity, learn how to play the game and strive toward that goal.

A good player on the brink of becoming a better player should start to change their comfort zone numbers. Instead of aiming at a comfortable three-over 75, they should set their sights on something lower. Players do not do this enough in order to reach a higher level.

How does one improve as a player by not justifying failure of poor results?

Tournament results can be improved by not changing anything physically. After scouting out a golf course and developing a game plan for attacking it, one should, in their *mind* ahead of time, positively *see* themselves hitting each shot on each hole. This would especially be true after not having played in several months. The norm might be to have a lot of negative self-talk. This type of player would not expect much of themselves. They might complain of being stiff, say they are going to score lousy and even pick up several times. Instead, it should be just the reverse. They should only have positive feelings and should quickly get back into the flow of playing. A golfer does not just lose the repetition of what they have been doing all their life. They should relax and rely on the natural ability they do have. There should be no negative demons or insecurities.

How can "looking in the mirror" aid a player's tournament confidence and performance?

It took me a while, but I finally realized and accepted what my peers have always told me. They were amazed how straight I hit the ball for my length. It took me years to accept that I am really a good player and ball-striker. In this regard, I started listening to my positive self-talk. I needed to trust myself fully and know I am skilled. A player needs to see and know who they are and not be afraid. And so it must be for anyone who desires to be a proficient, competitive tournament golfer. Such a golfer must do the necessary "mind work" and realize they belong. This is a huge key to playing solid competitive golf. If people stereotype you as the frontrunner or favorite, accept it and run with it!

Why is it so difficult to be a great player in golf?

From a brain standpoint, there is much time between shots. In a round of golf, only a small portion of the time is needed to actually strike the ball. During the "non-ball-striking time", our *minds* tend to absorb the negatives which in turn create poor shots and higher scores. How many golfers like a ten-minute wait on the next tee? Golfers who block these negatives are the best players in the world. By far, golf is the world's deepest mental athletic event. It is not a reactionary sport such as tennis, football, basketball, hockey or baseball where there is not much time to think. When things get tough, there is no teammate to whom you can pass the ball!

When a good round is developing, what signals an awareness of *getting into* the zone?

There is a feeling of being *relaxed* and having great feel in one's hands. The *mind* is quiet. One's body feels soft, and there is a sense of spring to your walk. The timing and flow of the speed of everything the player does is falling into place. It might even seem that everything is slowing down and is happening in "slow motion." Negative demons are not entering the world you are in. Everything is positive. Confidence begins to build. Good scoring helps to dictate this. One never seems to second-guess themselves. Yardages of shots seem spot on and the player is able to focus on where the ball is going to land. Putting feel is perfect. It is easy to picture successful shots in the *brain*. It feels like being on autopilot. What is happening is the culmination of all of the player's efforts and hard work. They are gaining the acceptance of deserving victory. The player has glimpsed a "snapshot" of his/her potential as a golfer.

Is there a way to *stay* in the the *zone*?

The key is to trust yourself. Let your results be okay. Smile! Have fun! Enjoy the process fully and appreciate the opportunity you have to play a great game. In the process of being in the zone, as I mentioned before, everything seems to slow down. The player is able to positively *visualize* the next shot, seeing it clearly in their mind's eye before it happens. Know that you have gotten into the zone because of good results. Run with this as long as you can. Religiously go through your individual pre-shot routine, but, other than that, try not to think too much. At this point, score is not a concern. Play one shot at a time and add up the numbers later on. Stay in the present moment for each and every shot. In between shots, tell yourself you are a good player. Believe in yourself!

What steps does one go through to come up with an exact yardage?

In the past, the first step would have been to come up with a yardage to the center of the green. Such yardages are commonly found labeled on top of sprinkler heads. Second, add or subtract the number of yards from this point to the location of your ball. Third, add or subtract the number of yards from the flagstick location on the green in relation to the center of the green.

At the present time, my best advice would be to invest in a good rangefinder. Today, most golf courses have installed reflectors within their flagsticks that enable golfers to quickly and efficiently determine yardages. Many golf associations have approved these devices for tournament play. Since a player does not have to walk around searching for sprinkler heads or 150-yard plates and then do the math after consulting pin sheets, time can be saved and rounds can be played faster, an important consideration in the game today. Such devices can be used in order to calculate exact yardages in many situations on the golf course. Here are several common examples. How far is it from my current position in the fairway to the hole location on the green? Additionally, how many yards do I have to carry my next shot in order to clear the bunker or the lake in front of that flagstick location? If the hole location is in the back of the green and there is trouble beyond it, how many yards *might* I have from the flagstick to the back of the green? From the tee on either a par four or five, how many yards it it to clear that bunker or pond? I know that huge tree out there is at the turn of the dogleg? How many yards is it to that point?

Allow me to give some insight about dangerous, back-of-the-green, "sucker" hole locations. Suppose I know the hole location is toward the back of the green, and there is trouble over the green. In another situation, there is a slope short of the flagstick location which, if my ball landed there, would propell the ball over the green. I know all of this because I have scouted the green complexes in an earlier practice round. Keeping these factors in mind and knowing the exact yardage to the hole location, the golfer will be able to make a "wise" club selection choice in order to prevent problems. Knowing exact distances aids the player in making educated decisions related to the many course management situations they might encounter while playing a round.

As aluded to earlier in the book, the following factors should be weighed in with respect to club selection: temperature, humidity, wind direction, firmness of the greens, trouble surrounding the green and the uphill-downhill nature of the shot. Here is an example. You have 167 yards to the pin, the shot is uphill, and it is into a fifteen miles per hour headwind. In reality, now this shot will be in the 185 to 190 yard range. Always pay attention to the ball flights of your playing partners. Their successes or failures may assist you with your own club selection and style of shot.

Are there different ways to handle certain lies in the rough?

I feel there are basically three types of lies. The first is one where *the ball sits way down in thick, three to four inch rough*. That is where one just needs to wedge the ball out into the fairway. The second is where *the ball sits just below the top edge of the grass*. One actually needs to thin this shot or pick it without hitting down deep into the rough. The last lie is where *the ball sits on top of the grass with no resistance to the shot*. This ball should come out normally or even a bit hot. As a result, one might take one less club in this situation. Before hitting any shot in golf, the player always needs to *evaluate the lie* of the golf ball and judge the results before selecting the style of shot and the club to be used in attempting it.

Chapter Thirty-one
Tournament Play: Off the Course Management
{Hotel Rooms, Activities, Meals, Alcohol
and Extracurricular Decision Making}

On a tournament television telecast, Peter Jacobsen offered an interesting insight. "Success on the P.G.A. Tour is largely determined by what the player does between the time he finishes the eighteenth hole today and tees off on the first hole tomorrow."

Quite a few years ago, Joey Sindelar was leading the first round of the Canadian Open with a 64. Following the round, the tournament organizers offered the players the opportunity to attend a special bus trip to a nearby club which featured trout fishing. Twelve players from the field accepted the organizers' invitation to this afternoon event, including Joey Sindelar. You might ask, what does this tell us? Sindelar's plan was to do everything in his power away from the golf course to avoid thinking about the nerve wracking situation of leading a tournament on the P.G.A. Tour. This brings up several important questions. What can a golfer do between rounds to help settle his/her nerves and continue to feel confident about what has been accomplished so far? Is the player out of his/her comfort zone because he/she is in a place he/she has never been before? How does the player handle post-round interviews where the media places him on a pedestal and keeps reminding him this is the first time he/she has held the lead in a tournament of this magnitude? What exactly can the player do to put his/her brain in the right place, calm his/her nerves, feel confident and excited and enjoy the moment? Away from the course, there are ways the player can alter his/her way of thinking in order to downplay the value of being where he/she is in the tournament.

A few years back, Rory McIlroy had a sizable lead going into the final round of the Masters. A couple of people at the driving range where I work asked me if I thought he would win. My response was that if I could witness what he did between the time he left the course on Saturday evening and when he returned Sunday around noon, I could probably answer that question. How did he handle media coverage? Did he watch ESPN on television or read the newspapers? Did he think about what would happen should he win? Was he like a deer in the headlights all night long staring at the ceiling? Did he experience loss of appetite? Taking all of this into account, one might be able to understand why he did not win. At the U.S. Open several months later, under similar conditions, he dominated and won a major. We can surmise he benefited and learned from his real life negative experience at the Masters in handling off-course situations in order to be more successful the next time around. The manner in which between rounds, off-the-course situations are dealt with is a major reason why golf tournaments are won or lost.

After shooting a record-setting thirty-six hole score of 130 in the first two rounds of the 2015 Masters tournament, how did twenty-one-year-old Jordan Spieth spend his time away from the golf course before playing in the third and fourth rounds? He spent the night with his family. He played ping pong. He played cards with his grandfather. No one was allowed to watch golf on television. He got away from the pressures of the game. At the conclusion of play, Phil Mickelson, who finished second, said, "He has that ability to focus and see things clearly and perform at his best when the pressure is on."

A player is competing in an important event (P.G.A. Tour, major tournament, state amateur or open, etc.) away from home and is staying in a hotel. What negatives should be avoided?

This is all about the *mental* part of the game. By far and away, the biggest challenge in golf is how the *brain* gets involved. In this regard, what a player does or thinks can be either destructive or productive to results. It is all up to the player! Concerning a higher level of golf, once the event has started, the player should not watch coverage of the tournament on the Golf Channel or early television coverage of play on a day they have an afternoon tee time. Do not read newspaper coverage about the event or listen to radio or television sports talk shows. Such viewing can trigger the golfer to begin asking destructive questions. How can I hold onto and protect the lead? How might I embarrass myself? In general, society sets us up to think of all sorts of images of insecurity and negativity. More than most people realize, the results of the next day are based largely on what is going on in the player's brain and the insecurities of the individual golfer rather than developing a perfect swing. As we know, golf is an individual sport. I call it a sport rather than a game, as so many bystanders think of it, because it requires both physical and mental components and readiness to play at a high level. While playing and competing, it is just you out there alone. Sure, professionals have their trusted caddies to lean on. But as a competitor, there is no one to help you or pass the ball to if and when things start to go wrong. There is no one else to hit the shots for you. This is why the development of a mental approach to the game is so important. Frequently, after a win, this is part of the reason why you see a player become emotional. They know wins are so hard to accomplish. This is why players rent homes during majors and stay with family and friends during tournament week. They would rather be with others away from the course than to be alone. This is also why you hear the player sincerely thank the members of their surrounding support team for all of the help they have given and continue to give them. This is something important to keep in mind when you watch tournament golf on television.

What about the average club player who is in a similar position?

Every golfer, no matter what their ability, needs to avoid negative thoughts which might appear leading up to actually playing the golf course. In going through the golf course hole-by-hole, examples of such negatives include out of bounds stakes, tough or dangerous hole positions, the bad shot they hit yesterday or who is watching them on the first tee. Instead, they need to concentrate and focus on developing and maintaining an away-from-the-course positive routine of thoughts. They need simply to *enjoy* this great game of golf.

Is it more desirable to have the lead going into the final round of a tournament?

The player might tell you that this would definitely be desirable, but deep down inside their heart, they would probably be more comfortable without it. Instead of having a two-stroke lead and the headlines, they would really rather go to bed at night two shots back, tied for third. This question separates the men from the boys. Great players want the lead and insecure players want to be the underdog.

What about the average club player who is in a similar position?

This sort of thing applies to all ability levels. The difference is comfort zones and the type of personality for each individual player. Jack Nicklaus and Tiger Woods would thrive on having the lead. That might not be the case with an average player, especially if they have never been in this position before.

What advice do you have for someone who is playing well and is on the "hot seat" or in the lead of a multi-round tournament? What exactly would you tell them?

I would tell them to let go of the game of golf as soon as possible. Once they have signed their scorecard, get away from the facility. The media categorizes everything about a player based on their performance on the course. They never talk about what is really most important. The player's time away from golf course sets them up for the next day's round. My advice is to try to keep one's mind off golf as much as possible. Be positive! *In doing so, be creative in what you choose to do!* Do not stare at the clock hoping you could tee off in twenty minutes. Do not try to get the day over with. That type of thinking indicates a player is scared to death of their position. Instead, enjoy life and allow time to simply and normally pass by. *Consider the following list of activities to fill your time.* As I mentioned earlier, if the opportunity presents itself, go fishing. More likely, go to the movies, go bowling, take a trip to the mall and shop or simply take a walk. Play cards with some friends or go shoot pool. Bring along a book to the tournament and read whenever possible. Listen to your favorite music. If family members have tagged along, spend time with them. Play with the kids. Meet a friend for lunch at a nice restaurant. It is important to relax, but if alcohol is being consumed, make sure not to overdo it! In a healthy sense, each player needs to find out what works for them. This may seem crazy and even counterproductive, but Tiger Woods might go to the gym twice a day *even on a day of competition.* This is what he has determined is *correct for him.* It seems to help him keep his brain more confident, stronger and aggressive and perhaps even keeps him from thinking about the out of bounds which may be lurking down the left side of the first hole.

What suggestions can you give about sleep? What do I do if I have trouble sleeping?

Dealing with sleep issues is huge. A player needs to keep a pre-sleep schedule which is right for them. They need to think about the right time to eat dinner which is not too early or too late. When playing in a significant event, do not go on the internet to look at scores and then do forecasting for the next day. Do not go to bed too early. Think about how much sleep is needed and turn in at an appropriate time. If you can not get to sleep or wake up in the middle of the night, do not lie there staring at the ceiling with a "deer in the headlights" mentality thinking about every hole on the course. Such sleeplessness will arouse the insecurities of several important shots in the upcoming round. It will awaken thoughts about the out of bounds or three-putt you had in a practice round. Instead, a player needs a game plan to create drowsiness. If necessary, get up and watch a non-sports movie on television. Do a Sudoku or crossword puzzle. Read an inspirational or humorous book. Listen to your favorite music on an mp3 player. When you feel yourself getting tired, then go to sleep.

What should I eat and drink before competition? Do you have any suggestions for post-competition food consumption?

According to the A.D.A.M. search encyclopedia affiliated with Penn Medicine at the University of Pennsylvania Hospital, proper nutrition can help improve the quality of athletic performance. Before a competitive round, the food you eat should provide the energy you need to perform well and also prevent hunger. The player needs to be well fueled. What you eat should provide the necessary nutrients and calories in addition to the liquids required to avoid dehydration. If a larger meal is consumed, it should be eaten a minimum of three to five hours before the event so that there is adequate time for it to be digested. Smaller meals can be eaten closer to the time of the competition. A small, high carbohydrate snack, such as a cereal bar, could be eaten an hour beforehand or even during the round. Everyone is different, so you have to find out what works best for you! You should not go away from the meal hungry, but, at the same time, you should not overeat. Be aware of what types of food and drink you consume. The player should be wary of soft drinks and/or beverages such as tea or coffee, all of which contain caffeine. Avoid orange juice or any high acid drink. Although water is perhaps the most important nutrient for athletes, it is often overlooked. Water and fluids are absolutely necessary for keeping the body hydrated and are extremely important for maintaining the right body temperature. Keep taking sips of water both during and after the round. Clear urine is a great sign of a player being properly hydrated. Due to the loss of several liters of sweat during exercise, water and sports drinks containing electrolytes are recommended. Make certain you drink plenty of fluids with every meal. This is an important daily consideration no matter whether you will or will not be exercising. The body needs water in order to store glycogen in the muscles and the liver. The basic idea is to eat foods that you like and are familiar with. Due to the time needed to be digested, the meal should be high in carbohydrates and low in fat and protein. The most important thing is the amount of carbohydrates eaten each day. A little more than half of your calories should come from carbohydrates. Carbohydrates, which include whole-grain bread, bagels, multi-grain cereals, pretzels, fresh or dried fruit, waffles, pancakes, a breakfast shake, low-fat yogurt, sauceless pasta, sweet potatoes, rice, apples, somewhat green bananas and some vegetables, such as green beens, keep glycogen stores full for maintaining maximum energy levels. Carbohydrates, which are stored mostly in the muscles and liver, are the most important source of energy during exercise and keep the muscles working hard! Stay away from high fat proteins such as cheese and peanut butter. A small amount of low fat protein foods, such as cottage cheese, eggs and milk, mixed with a carbohydrate, can settle the stomach and prevent hunger. Go easy on high sugar or glycemic index foods before exercise to avoid a "sugar crash" that can happen when blood sugar levels rise and fall. Due to stomach problems, some people find it very difficult to eat before an event. For all athletes, this is why it is vitally important to eat well for several days leading up to the competition. In order to obtain the best possible results, it is usually too late to wait until either the night before or the day of the competition to eat properly.

After the round, it is important to eat carbohydrates. Doing this helps to rebuild stores of energy in one's muscles.

What about protein? Protein is essential for muscle growth. It is also important for repairing body tissues. Protein can be used by the body as a source of energy, but only after carbohydrate supplies have been used up. It is a widely held but false belief that a diet high in protein alone will further the progress of muscle growth. Only a little bit of extra protein is necessary to promote muscle growth. In addition to the proper diet, only strength training and exercise will change muscle. In terms of the amount of protein required for muscle development, most Americans already eat almost twice as much as necessary. Too much protein in the diet has several negative effects. It will be stored as excess body fat. It can increase the possibility of dehydration. It can lead to calcium loss. Finally, an added burden can be placed on the kidneys.

How does a player effectively handle a late-afternoon tournament starting time?

Even most good players would prefer to tee off at 9:30 in the morning rather than 2:30 in the afternoon in a major event. They do not want to have to chase time worrying about what they are going to do before getting to the first tee. In anxiously putting all of their efforts into worrying about passing time, they will not be enjoying the moment as they should be. Once the round gets started, they will generally settle down and be alright. However, getting to the start of the event is difficult. By far, golf is the most analytical and deepest mental athletic event in the world. It is not a reactionary sport. Again, so much depends on one's individual personality and lifestyle. In all that you do, attempt to generate the conditions which promote positive results. Utilize past successes to strengthen the belief in your ability to perform well under difficult circumstances. A player needs to discover what works for them and appropriately fill their mind with as many positive thoughts as possible.

Once the player starts to play the round, what should be the focus?

The player should emphasize the *positive*. Recall the story of Rory McIlroy at the 2014 Open at Hoylake mentioned in chapter twenty-five where he used two words in order to remain calm, stay patient and make good decisions. Next, be sure to rely on the visualization and pre-shot routine discussed in chapter twenty-seven. By doing so, the player is able to stay in the moment and remain in the shot-by-shot process. Have the discipline to go through this process for each encountered situation and remember to play one shot at a time. Finally, make use of some of the focus factors to keep your mind right for golf that are covered in chapter twenty-eight. If you have worked hard at the fundamentals in order to gain control of all aspects of your game, it is now the time to "earn victory." Believe in yourself! Enjoy! Have fun! All of these thoughts will enable the player to remain positive, block out negatives and play at their best. Trust yourself! Do carry something in your bag to eat in order to keep up the energy level necessary to keep playing and competing. Be sure to continue drinking water in order to remain hydrated. An energy bar or an apple or two would be good examples.

During the round, should I encounter a questionable rules situation, what should I do?

All players, especially those playing in competition, should know the rules. You should always call over and consult fellow playing partners as problem-solvers and witnesses when a rules situation arises. However, when competing in a tournament and you are in doubt about a rules situation, be sure to call for a rules' official to help sort it out. Since players on the P.G.A. Tour are vying for big bucks and are trying to keep their reputations in order, you see this happening all of the time. On tour, one rules' official might cover only three assigned holes. In a lower level event, there might be one official assigned to the front nine and another assigned to the back nine. In an amateur event, there might be volunteers with radios on the course who then contact the scoring table at the clubhouse when rules questions arise. Whatever the situation might be, it is always best to get help, especially when there is doubt concerning how to solve the problem. There is also the pressure of the situation to keep in mind. The player needs to be thinking correctly. Remember the mini-tour rules bungle described in chapter eleven. Enough said!

Chapter Thirty-two
Equipment Choices for Modern Course Conditions

In your experiences playing professional golf, have you ever made a mistake which hurt you during competition?

Absolutely! One such instance was during the final stage of the P.G.A. Senior Qualifying School which was held at the T.P.C. Champions Course in Scottsdale, Arizona. Ninety-five percent of the players carried a hybrid to help negotiate the 225 to 245 yard golf shot to small, hard, elevated greens which required a high, soft shot. Meanwhile, I was handcuffing a low 2-iron to a runway which was only ten yards wide instead of a hybrid to a landing area which was thirty-five yards wide. That was a big mistake I made. My style is not a hybrid style. But in that instance, I might have been better off carrying a three or four hybrid in my bag due to the type and length of the course I played.

If you wanted to compete against the best players in the world, should the style of your play or the equipment in your bag possibly be changed in order to be successful?

Yes! Normally, I like to hit a low-to-the-ground 2-iron. Up to this point, I have felt comfortable in Philadelphia sectional events playing with my normal equipment. However, due to the conditions at a national event, there are admittedly times where I need to get away from my history and normal style of golf. I should sometimes probably change to a hybrid versus a long iron.

What style of player functions best with a hybrid club?

In my opinion, a hybrid is best for an armsy, quieter lower body player. Conversely, golfers who have angles and a lot of lower body movement are usually not good with hybrids. They are better off with long irons.

Should equipment changes be made relative to the conditions of the next course to be played?

Yes! Several factors which need to be considered include the tightness of the fairways, sizes, slopes, firmness and speed of the greens, thickness and height of the rough, type of sand in the bunkers, types of trouble surrounding the green complexes, amount of wind and overall length of the course. Is the course playing soft or fast? Of course, much of this depends on the player's skill level and how serious they are about golf. A casual player or a beginner might only own fourteen total clubs.

How might the conditions of the greens influence choice of putter?

Certain players might consider factors into their individual selection process such as green size, speed, slope and grain. Someone who grew up on a course with slower greens reading 7.5 on the stimpmeter might use a heavier-weight mallet putter. If they moved to another course with faster greens averaging a stimp of twelve, they might switch to a lighter-weight blade model. These factors might influence putter choice.

What factors weigh into your choice of the amount of driver loft?

If the course is dry and fast, is longer in length, does not have much rough and it is somewhat windy, I will probably use a lower-lofted 9.5 degree driver. In selecting this loft, the trajectory of the ball will be lower, it will not carry as far in the air but will tumble farther down the length of the hole. In another situation, if the course is more standard in length, is damp and soft, the fairways are more narrow, the rough is thick and the trajectory of the ball is not going to influence the final result, I might go to my higher-lofted 10.5 degree driver. As a professional, these choices would enter into my game plan. The weekend golfer most likely would only own one driver, and thus would not need to make such a decision. Remember, a lot of the new technology allows loft change in drivers up to 1.5 degrees either way.

What helps decide the iron makeup of one's bag?

The choice here might be between a 2-3-4 iron and a hybrid. The player needs to ask themself several questions. Are there any par three holes 230 yards in length with elevated greens? Do the par fives require a second shot in excess of 235 yards requiring a high, soft shot? Keep in mind, hybrids produce ball flights with a higher trajectory. Are the greens hard and fast? In order to carry a maximum of fourteen clubs in one's bag, the player might have to take a mid-iron out of the bag. With the short irons, no change will probably be necessary. Three or four wedges are considered the norm. Golfers who do not play the championship tees might not have to worry about the extra length of the course. In addition, each individual golfer needs to continually evaluate their game and play to their strength. Keep this in mind, everyone hits the ball a different length.

How should the bounce of the club match golf course conditions?

To begin with, the player needs to understand the meaning of the term **bounce**. Bounce is defined as *the measurement in degrees of the angle from the leading edge of a club's sole to the point that actually rests on the ground at address, the trailing edge of the sole*. The center or rear of many soles is lower than the front edge, which helps create the angle between the bottom of the club and the surface of the ground. Bounce is most commonly discussed in connection with wedges. More bounce will keep the leading edge of the club from digging too deeply into grass or sand. It will help the club "splash" through the sand, somewhat like a ski moving through snow.

Golf course conditions should help determine the amount of bounce needed. The amount of bounce should match the firmness of the ground, height of the grass, thickness of the rough and type of sand in the bunkers. More bounce is required when encountering fine, soft, fluffy sand. In this situation, less loft is needed in club selection and a shallow entry is a must. Less bounce will be needed when encountering firmer, harder, coarse sand. The golfer will need to address the ball off the toe, create good angles and strike the sand closer to the ball at impact. Playing from the fairway requires less bounce. Again, all of this depends on the overall proficiency of the individual player and course conditions.

What is your advice regarding matching ability level and the types of available grooves and golf balls?

Shorter hitters should use v-grooves and a harder ball so as to maximize distance. Longer hitters might consider using box-grooves within United States Golf Association guidelines and a softer ball. Manufacturers have stopped making box-groove irons as of 2011. P.G.A. Tour players and golfers competing in U.S.G.A. Open Championships will need golf clubs with conforming grooves. As of 2014, the groove ruling went into effect for the other U.S.G.A. tournaments and top amateur events. If you do not play in these events, the new groove rule does not effect you until at least 2024. Individual equipment choices are based on ability, knowledge and financial situations.

Chapter Thirty-three
Physical Fitness

How important is physical fitness to the golfer today?

It is extremely important! Golfers have begun to realize that physical fitness and staying in shape should be a priority in their lives. As I look at what is going on today on the P.G.A. Tour, these young players are in great shape. The greatest example of fitness related to golf on the Tour is something I found out during the summer of 2010. On the first day of the AT&T tournament at Aronimink Golf Club in Newtown Square, someone suggested to the number one player in the world that he should go to the Ellis Fitness Center in Newtown Square. Since I also go there myself, I found out this player trained *every day* not only before but also after his round. This is a tremendous example of dedication and hard work. As a golf professional myself, I was somewhat shocked by this fact.

How was exercise and working out viewed twenty-five to thirty years ago when you played the P.G.A. Tour in 1986?

Back then, golfers thought it was best to stay away from fitness, weight lifting and too much exercise. It was thought bulking up muscles would create big chests, generate tightness and jam up the player. Instead, they should remain limber and thin. The accepted thinking was that players had gotten themselves to the Tour without working out, so do not do it! It was thought one's feel was based on how their body was at that point in time. Bulking up would cause their body to change for the worse. They would lose feel in their game.

What is the reason the fitness approach has changed for golfers today?

Our society has become tremendously fitness oriented. To begin with, no matter when during the day the television is turned on, someone is involved in promoting fitness, nutritional health and educating the listener how to take care of their body. It seems much is centered around leading a more healthy lifestyle. In doing so, we are asked to consider what we should or should not eat and drink. We are instructed to give serious thought to following an exercise program. All of these factors are important in the world today! Second is the matter of competition. In order to be competitive at a high level of golf, players are going up against other golfers who work out religiously and are fit. As a result, they are less likely to get tired as the competition wears on. In the modern world, a lack of fitness is something which can not happen! It is simply not an option. In many instances, due to weather delays or normal tournament conditions, thirty-six holes of walking is required during play on a single day. This amounts to fourteen miles of walking, often in hot, humid, sometimes soggy weather conditions. In a recent U.S.G.A. Open qualifier, I played the first thirty-one holes in six under par and the last five holes in seven over. Exhaustion set in. The average player competing in such an event is in their mid to late twenties in age. As a fifty-five year old player, in order to remain competitive, I must be in shape. Such invested dedication in terms of remaining in shape also goes a long way towards improving a player's mental approach to the game. If a player feels stronger physically, chances are they will feel stronger mentally too! We all know how important a strong, positive mental approach is to success in golf.

What are the two areas of conditioning and exercise golfers should focus on to improve fitness and reduce risk of injury?

The two areas to focus on include *core strength and stability* and *flexibility* exercises. The muscles of the core are the powerhouse and the foundation of a player's golf swing. Proper conditioning will make a huge difference in the power one generates in producing shots which travel longer distances. Good core strength also allows the player to have more endurance. Their short game is more precise, fresh and controlled. The core exercises work the muscles of the abdominals, back, glutes and hips. Many other muscles attach to this area so the midsection is considered the foundation of all movement.

Golf and flexibility go hand in hand and players need to spend time on range of motion for the perfect golf swing. If your muscles are tight and inflexible, you will have reduced range of motion resulting in a shorter swing. Professional golfers have amazing range and a fluid swing, in large part because of flexibility in the shoulders, torso, and hips. A golf-related yoga program should be strongly considered in building an overall fitness plan.

What exercise is the most effective for strengthening the core of a player's body?

Core strengthening exercises are most effective when the torso works as a solid unit and both front and back muscles expand and contract at the same time. Multi-joint movements are performed and stabilization of the spine is monitored. Abdominal bracing is a basic technique used during core exercise training. To brace correctly, you should attempt to pull your navel back in toward your spine. This action primarily recruits the transversus abdominis muscle. The player should be able to breathe evenly and normally.

What is the newest technique for golfers to improve their overall physical fitness?

TRX training is a unique tool which provides hundreds of different exercises for all fitness levels. A person can use their own body weight and the force of gravity to help build strength as well as core and joint stability. Other benefits gained through TRX training include improved balance, coordination and flexibility. Injuries are also prevented. While working the player's entire body, total training time can be reduced by jumping from one exercise to the next in just seconds.

With each exercise, the core is engaged. Most people believe that the core consists of only the abs. This is simply not true. The core is made up of the pelvis, abs, back and chest muscles. The development of the core muscles is what causes the player's body to have stability, balance and flexibility. The core is the starting point for everything one does in life. No matter what the activity, such as cleaning the house, playing with the kids or even working out, the core is being engaged. Improving the core will only enhance a golfer's performance and way of life.

Another great benefit of the TRX system is that it can be started at any fitness level. By using their own body weight and the force of gravity, a person is able to adjust to their own fitness level by simply moving closer or further away from the anchoring point. This makes it different from traditional styles of training. A person doing exercise does not need to grab a different set of dumbbells or make weight adjustments to machines, thus minimizing wasted time. The body is challenged by completing each exercise. Keep in mind, there are many different methods to golf training. This is just one simple approach.

Chapter Thirty-four
Common Sense Rules Everyone Should Know

At one time or another, everyone has made a mistake within the rules which has cost them strokes. At the 1968 Masters tournament, Roberto De Vicenzo actually shot a final-day 65 and was tied with Bob Goalby at the conclusion of 72 holes. The two should have returned on Monday for an 18-hole playoff. However, De Vicenzo's final-round playing partner, Tommy Aaron, had made a fatal mistake on De Vicenzo's scorecard. Aaron gave De Vicenzo a par on the par four 17th hole rather than the birdie three De Vicenzo had actually made. De Vicenzo failed to catch the error. When he signed the scorecard, De Vicenzo was guilty of turning in an incorrect scorecard. Under the rules at that time, the higher score that De Vicenzo signed for stood, meaning that he was credited with a 66 rather than the 65 he actually had shot. This error meant that he was one stroke off the lead rather than tied and heading into a playoff. De Vicenzo finished second at the 1968 Masters and Bob Goalby was declared the winner. When De Vicenzo realized his mistake, he made the famous quote, "What a stupid I am!" These words live on in golf history. De Vicenzo never won another major, although he did win the PGA Tour's Houston Open three weeks later. Tommy Aaron went on to win the 1973 Masters, where, ironically, he caught a mistake on his scorecard made by his playing partner. In another case, Michelle Wie left the scoring area without signing her scorecard. She was subsequently disqualified. Sometimes it might be not reading a posted rules sheet or perhaps a lapse of concentration as with Dustin Johnson grounding his club in a bunker and earning a two-shot penalty on the seventy-second hole of the 2010 P.G.A.. Whatever the case, the bottom line is that knowledge of the rules will help prevent embarrassing mistakes. Such knowledge will even give you a chance to improve scores by using the rules to your advantage. A game of integrity, golf is the only sport I know where a player acts as a rules official and calls penalties on themself. At the conclusion of each and every round you play, and especially before handing it in at the scoring table during a tournament, be sure to carefully check over the hole-by-hole acccuracy and correctness your scorecard with the fellow-player who has kept it!

The following chapter asks every-day questions which test basic knowledge of the rules of golf each player should know. Virtually all of the rules of golf are tested. This two-part quiz is meant to be both informative and instructional but should not limit a player's efforts or take the place of thoroughly reading over and digesting the rule book. Two kinds of questions are posed, all of which cover situations that come up frequently. The **multiple choice** and **true/false** questions cover general information about the rules, but also test one's knowledge of the practical application of the rules to specific on-the-course situations. Answers are found at the end of the appendix section.

I. Multiple Choice Questions: Carefully read over the following questions and the accompanying choices. In each situation, only one choice is correct. The numbers within the parentheses indicate the rule which applies to that choice.

1. _____Which of the following **regarding clubs & balls** is *false*?
A. A player may carry a maximum of fourteen clubs (4-4),
B. If a player's ball goes out of shape, is cracked or visibly cut, they may replace it only after consulting with their fellow competitor, marking and lifting it and then placing another similar ball on the spot where the original ball lay (5-3),
C. During a stipulated round, a player may continue to use a club without penalty which has been damaged through anger (4-3b),
D. During a stipulated round, a club substantially damaged (e.g. bent shaft, loose club head) in the normal course of play may be replaced without penalty (4-3a).

2. _____With regard to a **player's responsibilities**, each of the following is *true except* . . . . .
A. The player must start at the time established by the committee (6-3a),
B. The player is responsible for the addition of his score on the scorecard (6-6, note 1),
C. Following completion of the round, both the competitor and his marker must sign the card as soon as possible, and then return it to the committee before leaving the scoring area (6-6b),
D. Before the start of his round, the player should identify and mark his ball (6-5).

3. _____Which of the following represents an *incorrect* **order of play**?
A. The player who has the lowest score on the previous hole takes the honor at the next teeing ground (10-1,2),
B. After starting play on a hole, the ball farthest from the hole is played first (10-1,2),
C. If two or more competitors have the same score at a hole, they play from the next teeing ground in the same order as at the previous teeing ground (10-1-2),
D. A player plays his provisional ball before his opponent or fellow competitor has made his first stroke (10-3).

4. _____With regard to **out of bounds**, which of the following is *false* . . . . .
A. A ball is *out of bounds* when any part of it lies beyond the nearest *inside* points at ground level of the white stakes that mark the boundary line of the course (Definition of out of bounds),
B. The penalty for hitting a ball out of bounds is stroke and distance (27-1a),
C. When defined by a line on the ground, the line itself is *out of bounds* (Definition of out of bounds),
D. A player may stand *out of bounds* to hit a ball lying within bounds (Definition of out of bounds).

5. _____Which of the following may *not* be **removed** *without penalty* before hitting a shot if it interferes with your stance and swing?
A. White *out of bounds* stake (Definition out of bounds, 13-2),
B. Yellow *water hazard* stake (Definition water hazard),
C. Red *lateral water hazard* stake (Definition lateral water hazard),
D. All of the above.

6. _____Which of the following is *false* with respect to either a **lost ball** or **out of bounds** situation?
A. You may play a provisional ball, but you must first announce to your opponent or fellow competitor you are doing so (27-2a),
B. In playing the provisional, you must play a ball as nearly as possible at the spot from where the original ball was last played before you or your partner or either of your caddies goes forward to search for the first ball (27-2a),
C. If the original ball is lost or is out of bounds, you must count all of the strokes made with the original ball and the provisional ball, add a penalty stroke and play out the hole with the provisional (stroke & distance) (27-2),
D. If you find the original ball in bounds, you may continue play with the provisional ball and disregard the original (27-2c, 15-3).

7. _____Which of the following choices represents a *mistake* in **searching for and identifying a ball**?
A. In a bunker or water hazard, as many loose impediments or as much sand may be removed to be able to find or identify the ball (12-1),
B. When lifting to identify, you must mark the position of the ball, announce your intention to your fellow competitor or opponent, and allow them the opportunity to observe the marking, lifting and identification of the ball (12-2),
C. You may completely clean the ball when it is lifted for identification (12-2),
D. If the lifted ball is the player's ball, he must replace it (12-2).

8. _____During a *stroke play* competition, *with **no** conditions of competition related to practice in effect*, which of the following **practice** situations would *not* result in the assessment of a penalty?
A. On the day of the competition, practicing on or testing the putting surface on the competition course (7-1),
B. Between the play of two holes, practice putting or chipping is allowed on or near the putting green of the hole last played or on any practice putting green (7-2),
C. Practicing on the competition course between rounds of a competition played over consecutive days (7-1),
D. None of the above,

9._____Which of the following statements **does not** constitute a **breach of the rules** with regard to **giving or asking advice**?

A. Player A looks in player B's bag as player B is selecting a club to hit his next shot (8-1),

B. A competitor suggests to a fellow-competitor that he should play a 6 rather than a 7-iron for the upcoming shot (8-1),

C. While player A's ball is on the green and before his stroke, his partner, player B, points out the line for putting by touching the green (8-2b),

D. Player A positions partner B on the line of play beyond the hole while the stroke is being played from off the green (8-2a).

10._____Which of the following actions incurs **no penalty**?

A. A player tests the condition of the sand by splashing sand with a practice swing (13-2),

B. Within a hazard, a player takes a practice swing without touching the ground, but his club brushes grass or a bush, both of which are growing in the hazard (13-4, note),

C. Within a hazard, during a practice swing, the player touches a loose impediment with his club during the backswing (13-4),

D. During a practice swing, the player breaks a branch of a growing tree and knocks off several leaves in his area of intended swing (13-2).

11._____Which of the following actions incurs a **penalty** in violation of the **loose impediments** rule? (23)

A. On the putting green, a player accidentally moves his ball in the process of removing a twig lying against it, but replaces the ball (23-1),

B. While player A's ball is in motion following his stroke on the putting green, player B removes a twig that would not have influenced A's ball (23-1),

C. Player A removes a twig from the surface of the bunker he is playing from (23-1, 13-4c),

D. Player A removes a nearby twig from the surface of the fairway (23-1).

12._____Which statement is **false** regarding the **putting green**?

A. Player A may test the surface of the *putting green* during play of a hole by rolling a ball or scraping the surface (16-1d, definition putting green),

B. Player A's ball is on the *putting green* when any part of the ball touches the green (Definition putting green),

C. Player A may brush away leaves and repair an old hole plug and a ball mark on the *putting green* without penalty (16-1a{i & vi},, definition putting green),

D. Player A may gently tap down his ball marker on the *putting green* with his putter (16-1a{v}, definition putting green).

13._____In which case does the competitor **not** incur the general **flagstick penalty**?

A. Player A, having his caddy tend the flagstick during his stroke, strikes the flagstick with his ball during his chip shot from the fringe (17-3a),

B. After a stroke from the putting green, player A strikes the flagstick which is unattended and in the hole (17-3c),

C. While his ball is in motion, player A asks his caddie to tend the flagstick; the caddie removed the flagstick, the hole-liner stuck to it, was pulled out of the hole and the ball struck it (17-3a),

D. Providing no one tended the flagstick, in playing from off of the putting green, player A's ball strikes the flagstick (17-1).

14._____When is a player's **ball *not* in play**?

A. As soon as the player has made a *stroke* from the *teeing ground* (Definitions stroke & teeing ground),

B. In the case of having been properly *lifted*, it is again in play when correctly dropped or placed (20-4),

C. A *substituted* ball is in play when it has been correctly dropped or placed (20-4),

D. When lost, *out of bounds*, lifted or substituted (Definition ball in play).

15._____Which of the following actions **does not** incur a **penalty in violation of Rule 18**?

A. While in play, either player A or his partner player B touches or moves player A's ball either on purpose or accidentally (18-2a{i}),

B. Wind or water moves your ball, and you play it as it lies (Definition outside agency),

C. Player A doesn't replace his ball when moved accidentally (Decision 18-2a{i}),

D. After replacing his ball on the green after being marked, player A causes his ball to be moved from its original spot and he doesn't replace it (18-2a, 20-3a).

16._____During stroke play, which of the following actions **does not** result in a **penalty** in violation of the **Rule 19**?

A. Player A's ball is accidentally deflected or stopped by his fellow-competitor's *equipment* or his *caddie*, and he then plays the ball as it lies (19-2, definitions caddy & equipment),

B. Player A's ball is accidentally deflected or stopped by himself, his *equipment*, his partner or his *caddie*, and he then plays the ball as it lies (19-2, definitions caddy & equipment),

C. With a shot hit from on the putting surface, player A's ball hits his fellow-competitor B's ball at rest on the putting green and moves it, player A plays his ball as it lies (19-5a),

D. None of the above.

17._____A player must **always re-drop** his ball in each of the below instances **except** which one? The player drops the ball and it . . . . .

A. Rolls into and comes to rest in a hazard (20-2c{i}),

B. Rolls onto and comes to rest on a putting green (20-2c{iii}),

C. Rolls and comes to rest _less_ _than_ _two_ club-lengths from where it first struck part of the course (20-2c{vi}),

D. Rolls and comes to rest nearer the hole than its original position (20-2c{viia}).

18._____Which of the following is *true* about **lifting and cleaning the ball?**

A. The ball must not be cleaned when lifted to determine if it is unfit for play (5-3, 21a),

B. For identification purposes (12-2), it may be cleaned only to the extent necessary to identify it (21b),

C. The ball may not be cleaned when lifted because it interferes with or assists with another player's play, unless it lies on the putting green (22, 21c),

D. All of the above.

19._____Which is *true* of receiving relief from an **immovable obstruction?**

A. If the ball lies **through the green**, the player must lift the ball and drop it within one club-length of and not nearer the hole than the nearest point of relief (24-2a{i}),

B. If the ball is in a **bunker**, the player may drop his ball outside the bunker without penalty (24-a,b),

C. The player may get free relief from objects defining out of bounds, such as walls, fences, stakes and railings (Definition obstructions),

D. If the ball lies on the **putting green**, the player may lift the ball and drop it, without penalty, at the nearest point of relief that is not in a hazard. The nearest point of relief may be off the putting green (24-2b{iii}).

20._____Which is *true* of receiving relief from a **movable obstruction?**

A. A player could get relief from a folding chair, a golf cart, a spectator blanket spread out on the ground and a portable trash can (Definition obstructions),

B. If the ball **does *not* lie in or on the obstruction**, the obstruction may be removed. If the ball moves, it must be *replaced*, and there is no penalty, provided that the movement of the ball is directly attributable to the removal of the obstruction (24-1a),

C. If the ball lies **in or on the obstruction**, the ball may be lifted and the obstruction removed. The ball must through the green or in a hazard be *dropped*, or on the putting green be *placed*, as near as possible to the spot directly under the place where the ball lay in or on the obstruction, but not nearer the hole (24-1b),

D. All of the above.

21._____Which of the following is *false* in following the procedure in *Rule 28* for putting a ball in play after a player deems his ball is **unplayable?**

A. Drop a ball behind the point where the ball lay, keeping that point directly between the hole and the spot on which the ball is dropped, with no limit to how far behind that point the ball may be dropped,

B. Drop a ball within two club-lengths of the spot where the ball lay, but not nearer the hole

C. If the unplayable ball is in a bunker, the player may proceed under any option under this Rule. The player may only drop outside the bunker if he proceeds under the stroke and distance option of this Rule.

D. When proceeding under this Rule, the player may lift and clean his ball, but may not substitute a ball.

22._____Which is a false statement concerning an **abnormal ground condition**?

A. Such ground conditions include lies in casual water, ground under repair and a burrowing animal hole (Definition abnormal ground condition),

B. The player's ball has come to rest on the putting green in an area where casual water intervenes on his line of putt. He determines his nearest point of relief is in light rough through the green. In taking relief, he must drop the ball at the nearest point of relief in the rough (25-1b),

C. If the ball lies through the green, the player must lift the ball and *drop* it, without penalty, within one club-length of and not nearer the hole than the nearest point of relief (25-1b),

D. If the ball is in a bunker, the player must lift the ball and *drop* it without penalty in the bunker and the ball must be dropped in the bunker or, if complete relief is impossible, as near as possible to the spot where the ball lay, but not nearer the hole, on a part of the course in the bunker that affords maximum available relief from the condition (25-1b).

23._____Which of the following is *false* concerning the situation of a ball lying within a **water hazard** defined by *yellow stakes*?

A. If possible, the ball may be played as it lies (13-1),

B. The player may touch the ground in the hazard or water in the water hazard with his hand or club (13-4),

C. Under penalty of one stroke, the player may play a ball as nearly as possible at the spot from which the original ball was last played (26-1, 20-5),

D. Under penalty of one stroke, drop a ball behind the water hazard, keeping the point at which the original ball last crossed the margin of the water hazard directly between the hole and the spot on which the ball is dropped, with no limit to how far behind the water hazard the ball may be dropped (26-1).

24._____A player's ball last crossed the margins of a lateral water hazard defined by red stakes. In taking relief, which of the following is *true*?

A. When proceeding under Rule 26-1, the player may either clean his original ball, if it is found, or substitute another ball (26-1),

B. Under penalty of one stroke, the player may drop a ball outside the lateral water hazard within two club-lengths of and not nearer the hole than the point where the original ball last crossed the margin of the lateral water hazard (26-1c(i),

C. Under penalty of one stroke, if possible, the player may drop a ball outside the lateral water hazard within two club-lengths of and not closer to the hole than the point on the equidistant and opposite margin of the lateral water hazard (26-1c(ii),

D. All of the above.

II. True/False Questions: If the statement is *true*, write + in the space provided; if *false* write O. The numbers within the parentheses indicate the rule which applies to that choice.

25._____ A ball is lost if it is **not** found by the player, his partner or their caddies within four minutes after the search has begun (27-1a,c).

26._____ Prior to making their stroke, a player is able, without penalty, to repair spike marks and hole plugs on the putting green which are on his/her line of putt (16-1c).

27._____There is **no** penalty if a player makes a stroke at a wrong ball in a water hazard (15-3, exception).

28._____After re-dropping and striking a part of the *course,* player A's ball comes to rest in a position where there is once again interference for his stance by a cart path. He must now play the ball as it lies on the cart path (20-2c{v}) .

29._____*Loose impediments* are natural objects that are not fixed or growing, not solidly embedded or adhering to the ball, such as stones, leaves, branches, dung and worms (Definition loose impediments).

30._____The *putting green* is all ground of the hole being played which is cut to fringe height or less (Definition putting green).

31._____Player A strikes the ball in hitting a wedge shot out of the rough around the green and the ball then makes contact with the club head a second time on the follow-through. Player A takes **no** penalty in recording his final score for the hole (14-5).

32._____*Through the green* is the whole area of the course except the teeing ground and putting green of the hole being played (Definition through the green).

33._____A ball on the putting green may be marked, lifted and cleaned (16-1b).

34._____A ball overhangs the hole after the stroke was made from a bunker. The player reaches the hole without unreasonably delay and then waits 20 seconds before the ball falls into the hole. The player is deemed to have holed out with the last stroke without penalty (16-2).

35._____A player may remove a candy wrapper or cigarette butt, but **not** a pine cone or tree branch, from a bunker without penalty (23-1).

36._____When a player's ball simply rests against the flagstick in the hole, with part of the ball above the lip, the ball has is deemed to have been holed with his last stroke (17-4).

37._____Player A's ball is in play and it moves after he has addressed it. It is known or virtually certain that the wind caused the ball to move. He replaces the ball to its original location, without penalty (18-2b).

38._____Without permission under a Local Rule or another Rule of Golf, there is **no** penalty for a player marking and lifting his ball on the apron surrounding the putting green (18-2a).

39._____When re-dropping under a Rule, player A's ball rolls and comes to rest out of bounds. Player A must now place his ball as near as possible to the spot where it first struck part of the course when re-dropped (20-2c).

40._____During stroke play on hole 16 of a stipulated round, player A makes a stroke at a wrong ball. If he does **not** correct his mistake before making a stroke on the next teeing ground, he is disqualified (15-3b).

41._____Unless otherwise authorized by the Committee, a stipulated round consists of playing the eighteen holes of the course in the correct sequence (Definition of stipulated round).

42._____During stroke play, while both balls are lying on the surface of the putting green, player A putts his ball which strikes player B's ball. **Neither** player receives a penalty (19-5a).

43._____The use of a special putting ball is legal (15-2, 20-6).

44._____Player A's ball at rest is moved by player B's ball in motion after a stroke *from off the green*. Player A's ball must be replaced (18-1,18-5).

45._____During match play, player A's ball is accidentally deflected or stopped by opponent B's *equipment*, his partner or his *caddie*. Player A may, before another stroke is played by either side, choose to *either* cancel the original stroke and play the ball as nearly as possible at the spot from where the original ball was played (20-5) *or* play the ball as it lies, *without penalty* (19-3, definitions caddy & equipment).

46._____Player A drops the ball himself. In doing so, he stands erect, holds the ball at waist height and at arms length. During the drop, the ball accidentally brushes his foot before striking a part of the course and then comes to rest. He has made a correct drop under the rules and the ball is in play (20-2a).

47._____By rule, if the player is going to lift his ball and replace it, the position of the ball to be lifted should be marked by placing a marker or small coin immediately behind the ball (20-1 note).

48._____During stroke play, player A plays a stroke over a *regular* water hazard marked by *yellow* stakes. The ball hits the green and spins backwards and sideways on a different angle into the hazard. Keeping the hole and the spot where the last shot was played in a straight line, under penalty of one stroke, player A now drops a ball at a new spot five yards behind the original position. Player A now successfully plays to the green and correctly completes playing out the hole. He/She has proceeded correctly under the Rules (20-7, 26-1).

49._____If player B's ball interferes with player A's swing or is on his line of play, player A may ask B to mark and lift it (22-2).

50._____A pitch mark on the fringe or fairway made by the player's ball can be repaired before that player plays his next shot (13-2).

51._____If the ball is in a bunker and the player has interference from an *abnormal ground condition* (e.g. casual water) player A may under penalty of one stroke, take the ball outside of the bunker, keeping the point where the ball lay directly between the hole and the spot on which the ball is dropped, with no limit to how far behind the bunker the ball may be dropped (25-1b).

52._____Player A's ball is embedded in its own pitch-mark in the fairway. The ball may be lifted, cleaned and dropped, without penalty, as near as possible to the spot where it lay but *not* nearer the hole (25-2).

53._____When a player discontinues play of a hole under Rule 6-8a, he may lift his ball, without penalty, only if the Committee has suspended play or there is a good reason to lift it. Before lifting the ball the player must mark its position.

54._____In moving loose impediments on the putting green, player A accidentally moves his ball, returns the ball to its original position and penalizes himself one stroke (23-1).

55._____The competitor is responsible for the correctness of the score recorded for each hole on his score card. If he returns a score for any hole *lower* than actually taken, he is *disqualified*. If he returns a score for any hole *higher* than actually taken, the score as returned *stands* (6-6d).

56._____Player A is virtually certain his ball came to rest in an area of casual water and has *not* been found. Through the green, the spot is determined where the *ball last crossed the outermost limits of the abnormal ground condition* (e.g ground under repair). Player A may substitute a new ball, without penalty, and takes relief (25-1c{i}). The nearest point of relief is determined (not in a hazard or on a putting green) and the ball is dropped striking the course within one club length (25-1b{i}).

57._____In stroke play, Player A damages his putter in anger during a stipulated round, altering its playing characteristics and rendering it unfit for play. Player A putts with his hybrid club for the remainder of the round. He goes into a playoff following the round with player B. Player A substitutes a new putter before the first playoff hole and uses it to score a 4 while player B scores a 5. Player A has won the playoff (4-3b, This is a Decision).

58._____The ball may be cleaned when receiving relief from an immovable obstruction (24-1b).

59._____Player B's ball interferes with player A's swing or is on his line of play, so player A requests that player B's ball be lifted . *Neither* of the balls are on the green of the hole they are playing. Player B may clean the ball before putting it back in play by performing a drop (21, 22-2).

60._____Player A's ball went into a water hazard & then was carried downstream out of bounds. The ball is deemed to be out of bounds (Decision...   ).

Chapter Thirty-five
Being in the Zone and Scoring

Do not be afraid to do something good even though it is out of your comfort zone. That is one of the messages from this chapter. For example, before the start of the 1986 P.G.A. Tour Buick Open in Michigan, I remember being very, very nervous. Scores were pretty good that opening day. After the round, fellow Pennsylvania tour pro, Brett Upper, from Lancaster, came up to me and asked me what I had shot. Since I was from nearby Lebanon, we knew each other pretty well. With a look of disappointment, I told him my score had been a 73. Picking up on my mood, Brett said to me, "You do not seem very happy! Are you having any fun?" I said, "No, not really!" He said, "If that is the case, you should get into your car and just head back to Pennsylvania? You are out here in front of all of these people who want to see you play golf. You have got to *enjoy* it. Okay! You are probably uncomfortable --- not just lacking confidence --- to score better and lower than your *comfort zone*. Honestly, would you have felt more confident shooting 71 or 68 today?" I said, "71". He said, "There you go". I realized Brett was exactly right! I was afraid to shoot too low of a score because it was out of my *comfort zone*. My goodness! I might get interviewed. The kitchen might get so hot I would not be able to sleep that night. There is always that boundary of comfort zone that we all want to be in. In driving a car, if the driver is claustrophobic, it might be the experience of going through the Holland Tunnel in New York City. In a like manner, there is always a comfort zone in sports. As a professional in an individual sport, an athlete can not be afraid to win! It is not what most people think, that what separates losers from winners is they are afraid to lose. In my opinion, it is just the opposite. I think people get scared to win because they are out of their *comfort zone*. It is not that they do not want to win. However, trying to get there to win is a very dangerous, slick, curvy road that most players are scared to death to attempt. Instead, they might rather go down another road and be in the middle of the field in scoring, not embarrass themselves and be alright. That is exactly how I felt at the Buick Open that year. I finally realized a player cannot think like that and be successful on the P.G.A. Tour. I learned a lot from that five minute conversation with Brett Upper. I needed to get into the *comfort zone* of setting a lower scoring number. I also came to realize a player will never be able to get into the unified mind-body state of being in the *zone* while being scared. I needed to have more *fun* to accomplish that!

At the awards presentation at the conclusion of Super Bowl forty-nine, the issue of "mental toughness" was brought up by two players. This characteristic is important to the process of being able to get into the zone. Winning New England Patriots quarterback and M.V.P., Tom Brady, stated,
"Our team has a lot of mental toughness. Our team has had it all year. We never doubted each other." Julian Edelman, a New England Patriots' all-purpose player, echoed the point. "We executed when we had to. We have a mentally tough team that works their tails off."

What are some of the thoughts and characteristics of being in the *zone*?

Absorbed in the activity
Automatic - autopilot - no emotions - instinct - easy
Belief
Birdies vs. bogies
Calmness
Clarity
Comfortable
Composed
Confidence that supersedes insecurities - experience – history
Contentedness
Effortless – do not try
Enthusiasm
Enjoyment
Even keel
Feel
Flow state of mind
Focused - target
Fun - enjoyment - pleasure - joy - satisfaction
Gentle
Graceful
Harmony
In command - in charge - govern own destiny
Instinctual
Leisurely
Level of excitation
Making versus missing; success vs. failure
Mellow
Mind-body connection/unison; work together seamlessly
Natural
No fear
Oblivious
"One day chicken, one day egg"
One-putt vs. three-putt
Patient
Peaceful
Perfect state of mind
Positives
Procedure
Quiet mind

Reaction
Relaxation, calmness (breathing)
Remaining silent during the round (Ben Hogan)
Rhythm
Routine
Slowed-down pace
Smile and enjoy
Smooth
Softness
Stay in the present/moment
Step-by-step process
Straight vision
Subconscious
Target-oriented (think about **where** you *want the ball to go*)
Trust
Visualization: see it before it happens

What *does <u>not</u>* enter your brain when you are in the zone?

Negatives
Out of bounds stakes
Trees
Mounds/Slopes
Deep rough
Wrong side of the hole
Short-sided
One's opponent
Hazards
The gallery
Disaster
What if . . . . .
Prior negatives
Comfort of a number scoring
One's hands
Brain attachment to the swing
Scared to succeed
Score

In your professional experience, what descriptive attributes must an individual golfer possess which will enable them to get into the zone?

I feel golf is a sport that is well suited for a player being able to get into the zone. What I am about to say most probably would apply much more to the serious, accomplished golfer than the casual novice. I say this because it seems as if a number of certain *attributes* need to be in place in order for a player to be able to get into this *special state of mind*. Over the course of a lifetime of experience, I believe I have come to be aware of these hallmarks and to appreciate them! Through observing talented players and during my conversations with them, I believe that I have been able to identify these traits in the people I have competed against. I have also come to be mindful of these attributes in my own game. Here is what I have witnessed and discovered!

To begin with, the higher-level player **loves** and **respects** the game. At a competitive level, golf is tremendously **challenging** to them, both mentally and physically. Through their various experiences, they have come to realize it is definitely a very **difficult** sport. They thoroughly enjoy being tested by playing a challenging course and in the tournaments they play. This level of golfer must have a **skill set** that matches the challenges they face. They possess the **ability** to do well. There are components to their game that require both power and finesse. Although there is no denying the game can be very difficult and humbling, it is also very **rewarding** and **worthwhile** for them. It is a game that peaks their **interest**. They realize there is great frustration in playing poorly, but that there is also great elation when they shoot good numbers and win tournaments. The game is **important** to them and they are **proud of their accomplishments**. This player has a deep **connection** with the game and has total **focus** and **concentration** on what they need to do. While playing the course, they get tremendous and immediate **feedback** from observing how the ball comes off of the club face, in seeing the ball either go into the hole or miss and in the total number of strokes they have taken to complete a round. They believe there is **something to be learned** from every round they play. They seek to learn from both their *successes* and *failures*. They **evaluate** their individual rounds and devote great effort into working on their **shortcomings**. A serious player will set specific **goals** for their game improvement. They are not easily discouraged and thus might be described as being very **persistent** in their approach to the game. They continually seek to **improve** and are willing to put **time** into refining *all* parts of their game.

When a player possesses these attributes, it makes it easier for them to get into the perfect flow of the game. This is because everything they are doing concerning their golf really matters to them. They have trained for countless hours to get into this position. The accomplished golfer has labored tirelessly on the fundamentals or mechanics of the game, has corrected mistakes and has come to know what works best for them. They are combining time proven, reliable **physical technique** with a sound **mental approach**. Due to past **successes**, over time, they have developed a deep **belief in themselves** and their fundamental approach to the game. They play with a high level of **confidence**. As I have emphasized before, this flow capacity is true for all nine parts of the game. It applies to all full shots and right on down to the putter. The *marriage* of these *attributes* makes it easier to get into and stay in the zone. Everything seems to **slow down** and become rather **effortless**. When combined with **visualization** and a solid **pre-shot routine**, the *positive* is accentuated and the *mind* and the *body* seem to be in complete *sync* and *harmony*. The player's actions almost seem to be on ***autopilot***. Anxiety and fear are reduced. **Focus** and **concentration** are heightened. The game appears to become easier and the player is able to reach the maximum level of their performance! Complete attention can be placed on the **golf course** and playing it with the proper **management strategy**.

What steps can I take to get into the zone?

As indicated above concerning personal attributes, the player must be fully invested in their game. Distractions must be eliminated. I know I have said it before, but that is why the visualization and pre-shot routine process is so important. Relaxation through breathing is another component. There should be *joy* and *fun* in playing the sport. Can a player learn how to get into the zone? With attention to the proper concerns, I believe the mind can be trained to accomplish this.

Stu, can you recall a recent time when you were in the *zone*?

It was while driving the golf ball at the 2011 Senior P.G.A. at Valhalla in Louisville, Kentucky. I felt a total connectedness of mind and body. My brain was tremendously in tune with my vision down the middle of the fairway. My focus was totally on a target relationship. The feel in my hands was so relaxed. My grip on the club felt very soft. The swing felt natural. My brain was <u>not</u> at all attached to the speed of the swing. My timing and flow was perfect! I did not allow any outside demons to get in the way. It was one of the greatest feelings I have ever experienced on a golf course. If I could make a wish, it would be that I could have bottled up that feeling and never lose it. In addition, I wish I could market and sell it.

July to September, 2011: I won 8 out of 10 tournaments.

I was totally focused on winning. I was confident I could win each and every time I teed it up. I had the feeling I was in a zone of success. I could take advantage of a situation where things were going well. My goal was to allow my good feelings to put myself in a confident place I could get back to and repeat time after time. I would not get nervous about a target score I had in mind. I did not put pressure on myself to shoot a certain score. I simply played shot-for-shot golf.

At age fifty-five, why do you feel you have been able to get into the *zone* more than ever before?

Is the attainment of confidence a chicken or egg type of situation? Which comes first? Is it belief or confidence? Depending on the situation at hand, I believe it goes both ways. Over the years, people have told me I am a good player. For a variety of reasons, I have finally chosen to accept this fact. I now have a relaxed feeling of enjoyment about me. Why is this so? These days, I keep several very important thoughts in mind. To begin with, I know I have forty-six years of experience in both playing and teaching the game. Over this time, I have taught over nineteen thousand lessons. As a result of playing tournament golf, I feel I have accumulated knowledge concerning how to play the game. I now believe in my natural ability and shot making capabilities. Within my level of competition, I know I am a good player. I have had success winning tournaments and have been Philadelphia Section P.G.A. Player of the Year numerous times. I have experienced success, have learned to trust myself, and I know my scoring comfort zone. Now, when I find myself leading a tournament with three holes to play, I do not allow the kitchen to get too hot.

What helps to keep a player "in the *zone*"?

Blocking the negative demons
Thinking positively (affirmations)
Staying focused
Being comfortable
Expect to win (stated positively)
Do *not* be afraid to win (not be afraid to loose)
Visualization - imagining motions - training the mind
Process of a pre-shot routine
Meditation
Breathing
Exhileration

Can any level of golfer get into the *zone*?

It largely depends on your identity as a player. Remember to consider the player attributes I covered earlier in this chapter. To accomplish reaching the zone, I still think it requires a higher level of proficiency within the game. I am not so sure about the average player and the high handicapper. The book is still out on that one. It is all based on one's choice of thinking. A player must also keep their scoring range in perspective. Growth, improvement and success comes to golfers who accept the comfort zone of a scoring number. They accept being able to beat a median score. Their comfort zone is expanded enough to accept playing a good round and scoring low.

Does comfort level of score influence a player out of the *zone*?

Absolutely! This again speaks to the mental aspect of golf. When the "kitchen gets too hot" and a player finds himself/herself scoring lower than normal, nerves take over. The player is not ready for this new feeling or scoring level. What then is the basis of a golfer picking a target score? Should it be the comfort zone of their ability or winning? One or two things, or both, need to take place here. Either the player needs to play shot for shot and not think about score, *or* they need to pick a lower scoring range prior to starting the round. In order to succeed, they must attempt to forget about the comfort level of a score being too good. However, and most importantly, whatever target score is chosen, they must make sure there is a *realistic* chance of successfully reaching the score being predicted. They must have the discipline to keep focus on their visualized pre-shot routine.

Based on the level of competition, should a player have a *target score* in mind prior to the start of play?

Yes! This is huge. Most players do not do this! In order to become a better player, one has to learn to know what results are needed for success. The answer to success is whatever they want it to be. The question now becomes how high do you want to set the bar? What is it going to take to succeed in this round of golf? This is one very important area for golfers to improve on during their careers. I find that many aspiring players --- juniors, collegians and assistant professionals --- never seem to get much better in the results of their game. Keeping within the scope of *reality*, one needs to put into perspective a lower target score. For example, if the player shot a 36-hole score of 150 last year during an event, a reasonable goal might be to try to shoot 145 this year. The player must keep things in perspective based on history and ability. Furthermore, one must keep the level of competition as the influence to this number, making sure that whatever tournament they are playing in, they must try to pick a target score that can make them succeed. This would be the case in a club championship, member guest, state amateur qualifier, U.S. Amateur qualifier, U.S. Open qualifier, U.S. Senior Open qualifier, making the cut at a Senior P.G.A. and in a P.G.A. Senior Tour School qualifier. For example, as a professional, I know I need to shoot a minimum of twelve strokes under par for four rounds to have a chance of succeeding at Senior Tour School. A target score of 70 or 71 is simply unacceptable. I have to change my feeling of success and comfort based on my competition. On the other hand, if I were playing in a four-round section event, I might win at seven under par. One has to put into perspective what success is going to be.

Chapter Thirty-six
P.G.A. Tour Success with Different Choices

This chapter is not about my acceptance of success. It is about hindsight vision being twenty-twenty. What could I have done better to still be successful out there in the arena of the P.G.A. Tour? I learned that satisfying my own arena was not good enough. My main problem was that I accepted my own personal arena as success. I did not set my sights nearly high enough. My aim certainly was not what was required out there on the Tour. If I was not all out for success on that highest level, then I had a bad formula. A bad formula is exactly what we are talking about here. If a player's goal is to be successful on the P.G.A. Tour, then they have to put their acceptance of success and goal setting up there at the level where they belong.

The information I am giving here is not only applicable to a club professional stepping up from the Philadelphia Section of the P.G.A. to the national stage of the P.G.A. Tour, but also for the club amateur jumping up from competing in their club championship to the regional events of the Golf Association of Philadelphia and the Pennsylvania Golf Association and then to the national events of the United States Golf Association.

Stu, you were fortunate enough to accomplish the rare feat of qualifying for and playing on the P.G.A. Tour. If you could look back again, knowing that hindsight is twenty-twenty, what would you possibly change in your thoughts and approach to success? What would you have done differently?

I could have done better both *physically* and *mentally*.

Physical:

1. I would have switched to the *long putter* in 1986 instead of 1990.

2. I should have focused much more on and worked harder at improving both my *wedges* and *chipping*.

3. I should have worked on *fitness* and being in better shape. It was not thought to be a priority at that time. Today, it is of the utmost importance if one wants to compete, especially on the highest stage of the game.

4. My style of play was never *aggressive* enough to win. I hit a lot of conservative irons off of the tee. Today, players gamble a lot more than I did then.

<u>Mental:</u>

1. I needed to accept the fact that I had earned my P.G.A. Tour card. My attitude should have been that I definitely was *welcomed* out there and *belonged* playing on the Tour.

2. My flawed approach was that I was simply going through and enjoying the experience. This seemed to justify any results I accomplished. Just getting out there, walking the walk and going through the experience was good enough for me at the time. It helped me to justify the fact that even if the results were not good, then I was successful. That is not the way it should have been. A player cannot do this, but somehow I allowed it to happen. I accepted my performance as pretty successful. Some people would say what was happening was good enough, but in reality, it was not. This is like getting to the World Series, N.B.A. finals, the Stanley Cup finals or the Super Bowl and just being content to get there. It is just not good enough to show up. *One must have the attitude they want to win, not just get there.*

3. My attitude many times was just to get a score that did not embarrass me instead of actually trying to win. No matter what the level of competition might be, we have all done this. As an example, we might say to ourselves, "If I shoot 77, I will not be embarrassed, but if I gamble on the fourteenth hole and mess up, I might shoot an 85." On the Tour, a player cannot do that. I allowed it to happen to me. I was comfortable shooting 72 even though I knew I probably was not going to make the cut, but I did not embarrass myself shooting 81. A player must possess the *confidence* and *trust* to push himself/herself to shoot the best score possible.

4. Looking in the mirror, my sense of success and attitude seemed to be just fine where it was. On the other hand, my peers, friends and fellow competitors thought I was much better than that. I did not appreciate this fact at the time. What I am saying is that when I looked in the mirror, I really did not know my *identity*. All of my friends and peers knew how good I was. I never swallowed this concept. If you do not swallow your identity as an athlete, you are never going to maximize your ability, and that is exactly what I did <u>not</u> do. Believe me when I say I never did that. It took me *years* to realize that many people looked at me as an incredible athlete and golfer with God-given skills. I was a legend in some people's terms and the best ball-striker they had ever seen. However, I never used this as a tool of confidence to allow me to succeed. I never did it back then in the 1980's on the P.G.A. Tour. It is a huge crime when a player *underestimates their ability*, does not trust and accept their identity and simply goes through the motions in playing the game. It took me many years to realize and accept how good I was.

Chapter Thirty-seven
Conclusion

I have been afforded the God-given opportunity to live a sporting dream through the game of golf. Golf has provided me with a job, an income and happiness that not many people get a chance to experience. The past chapters of this book have uncovered the events which I have lived. I only hope to make you smile at these remembrances and help you to become a better golfer. After thirty-three years of teaching and forty-six years of playing on all levels, I have come to realize that golf is not so much about swinging like Ernie Els or Fred Couples. It is also not about keeping your head down or your left arm straight or swinging easy. It is about uncovering the secrets and insights of the game which have been presented herein. It is about managing one's self both off and around the golf course. During a typical round, how does one handle hard versus soft sand, rules situations, reading the greens, bad lies or even getting into the zone? In the final analysis, it is about knowing your own golf *identity*. This is really what this sport is all about.

As a player, you have all chosen golf as either a business investment, a sport, entertainment, competition, a family activity, a professional career or maybe even just as a source of fun. I think we all agree we do not play golf just to play. We challenge ourselves with the result of a score because each and every one of us feels pride in great accomplishments. In my opinion, golf is the single most mentally challenging sport in the world. At the same time, I believe it is the most rewarding sport. More professional athletes in all sports would rather play golf than any sporting activity other than their own. I also think it is the easiest sport to learn but the most difficult at which to be great. I hope all of you treat this book like a journal where important thoughts can either be highlighted or notes can be written down in the margins. Another approach would be to think of it like a cookbook where the reader can go back to certain topic "recipes and ingredients" and remind themselves about newly learned secrets and insights. To all readers, I want to sincerely thank and congratulate you for being involved in a game of a lifetime, this great game of golf!

Finally, and most importantly, I want to thank my parents, who were very good golfers in their own right, for giving me the opportunity to experience this wonderful journey. I also want to thank my co-author and friend, Bob Ockenfuss, for his patience, insights and total golf investment in helping me write this book. The process of this creative adventure has allowed me to share and express my total golf heart and knowledge with anyone who wants to absorb what I have to say in order to work toward becoming a better golfer. I want to thank each and every one of my students over the past thirty-three years. Thank you to all those golfers who attended camps, clinics, and those who received individual and playing lessons. You have sincerely placed your trust in me and believed in my ability to educate and communicate to the betterment of your game. I have learned much from you as well. All of these interactions have helped me to become a better teacher. Thank you for sharing this experience together.

Epilogue

As I look back over the four-and-a-half year journey it has taken to write this book, it gives me pause to think about the true meaning of its title, <u>Mind Game</u>. This title was actually agreed upon almost two years ago. Having said that, the title appears to have a lot of relevance to what is currently going on in the game. Now, in late February 2015, it seems to be a very unique topic for a very special player in the game, Tiger Woods. Tiger is considered by many to be the most-recognized athlete in the world. In my opinion, he is the greatest and most dominant athlete I have ever seen. There can be no doubt Tiger has been the most influential athlete and game-changing individual in the entire golf industry. During his years of dominance, I truly believe he has possessed the most powerful mind in sports. However, as I have witnessed and then thought about Tiger's recent tournament appearances in Phoenix and San Diego, I have come to realize we are seeing a very different person than the golfer who has dominated the game during the past fifteen to twenty years. Considering everything that has happened to him, I truly feel that Tiger's poor play and tailspin is much more *mind-related* than mechanical or swing-related. Consider the following concerns he has had to endure since 2008. How about the social-media jabs and the negative questions that are constantly thrown at him through sports media? This occurs every single place he goes. "What's wrong with Tiger?" they say. What about the know-it-all comments constantly made by sports announcers? Is it possible that the "yips" have entered his brain? Many of these critics have never had to deal with the pressures of competing at a high level in a high-profile sport! Yet, they seem to think they have all of the answers. As a P.G.A. Tour player, what is the real meaning and effect of the long-time number one player in the world shooting 82 in a tournament? Adding a little icing on the cake, why not throw in the injuries and personal issues that have beset him over the past few years. Then there is the final straw. With all of the apparent signs of insecurity and lack of confidence, is he now actually scared to compete? By withdrawing from some tournaments and not entering others, is this really a sign of *avoidance*? As one might be able to see, my analogy is directly related to *his state of mind*. For the past few months, it seems as if all Tiger has constantly been talking about has been his current or past teachers and the mechanics of his swing. It just seems so situational, ironic and symbolic that the problems he is having with his golf game are somehow closely coinciding with the release of this book and how it relates to the title concerning the mental aspect of golf. From the bottom of my heart, and for his sake, I really hope he can block the negative demons and get back to just playing and enjoying the game. I hope he can come to allow his own mind and natural ability to take over and smother society's comments and judgments. No matter where his future lies in golf, we, who love this great game, all owe Tiger Woods a sincere gratitude of thanks for making golf what it is today. I personally want to thank Tiger for his accomplishments in winning and his influence in making golf something special. Above all else, one thing appears to be certain. Tiger's current problems seem to justify a close examination of the contents of this book, <u>Mind Game</u>. It might help you too!

Sincerely,

Stu Ingraham

Appendix

Power Outages

As a P.G.A. teaching professional, approximately 85% of the students who come to me for help have a power outage problem. Their shots might be described as weakly slicing to the right. Here is a list of factors that can lead to a ***reduction*** of power in the golf swing.

Weak left hand

Weak right hand

Too much tension

Standing too far from the golf ball

Poor club fitting

Bad ball position

Poor setup and posture

No wrist hinging

Grip in the palm of one's hand rather than the fingers

An outside to inside path of one's golf swing

Too *shallow* of an entry of one's downswing

Hitting the golf shot too thin

Hitting the golf shot too fat

Hitting the golf shot on the heel

Hitting the golf shot on the extreme toe

Deceleration through impact

High, fake finish on one's follow through

A very short backswing

Staring at the golf ball too long

Trying to make a perfect, mechanical golf swing

Poor flexibility

A very stiff back

Fanning the club on the backswing

Over *tilting* of the shoulders

Holding onto the club at impact

Using jumbo, over-sized grips

A grip that is worn out and slippery

A grip that is too thin for a big hand

Worn-out golf glove

Moisture on hands and grip

Head-down syndrome

Power Producers

Some students inquire about how to increase their power output. Here is a list of factors which can lead to an **increase** of power in the golf swing.

Stronger grip (proper grip in the fingers, not the palm)

Strength and flexibility (being in better physical condition)

Creating proper *angles* during the golf swing

Hips spin (turn) through impact

Maximizing the *hinging* of the club during the *backswing*

Unhinging of the club on the downswing: (1.) reduction of lag angle leading up to impact, and (2.) the right hand releasing over the left past impact (forearms rotate counterclockwise)

Toe of clubface is *more valuable than* heel

Lighter grip tension

Downswing comes from the inside (not straight-on or from the outside)

Maximize shoulder turn (backswing and downswing)

Stand closer to the golf ball at address

Proper *setup* to the golf ball

Correct *posture*

Match equipment correctly to body build and needs (proper fitting)

Load up weight in the backswing on the rear foot

Allow the head to move naturally on the backswing turn

Eye alignment is inside out (to right field)

Head coming up through impact as fast as possible

Folded finish of the arms over the left shoulder

Tee height proper for the driver

Match the golf ball to one's needs

Trap the golf ball when playing iron shots

Accelerate the golf swing through impact

Swing as hard as possible based on individual ability and personality

Keep a "green light" thought during the swing

Match grip size to hand size

Swing Opposites
*Right-Handed Golfer

Too Upright		Too Flat
	Arc (angle of attack)	
Steep, Tilting		Shallow, Circular, Around
	Plane	
Over --- Above		Under
	Swing Path	
Out to in		In to out
	*Arm & Hand Rotation (Backswing)	
Counterclockwise		Clockwise
	*Arm & Hand Rotation (Downswing)	
Clockwise		Counterclockwise
	Impact	
Face open		Face closed
	Shot Pattern	
Slice (left to right)		Hook (right to left)
	Divots	
Too much ground ground		Won't hit enough Thin
Deep --- Dig --- Hit fat		Hit thin
	Club Head Face Impact	
Toe		Heel
	Grip Pressure	
Too tight		Very relaxed

Backspin Factors

More Backspin

Higher club face loft (wedges)
Soft, balata-type ball
Square grooves
New and clean grooves
Hard, aggressive swing
Steep angle of attack
Soft green surfaces
Short, tight grass
Dry grass
Strong left hand

Less Backspin

Lower club face loft (3-iron)
Hard, surlyn ball
V-grooves
Worn out and dirty grooves
Gentle swing
Shallow, "scoopy" angle of attack
Hard green surfaces
Long, wide-blade grass
Wet grass
Weak left hand

Rules Quiz Answers

I. Multiple Choice:

1. C - club damaged in anger and as a result rendered non-conforming cannot be used or replaced during the round; penalty for breach of rule: disqualification

2. B - the Committee is responsible for adding the score. The player is only responsible for the correctness of the hole-by-hole scores and his and his marker's signatures

3. D - the player has played out of turn, however there is *no penalty*; ball played as it lies

4. A - inside points at ground level of the white stakes

5. A - Stakes defining out of bounds are deemed to be fixed and may not be removed

6. D - must continue with the original ball if it is neither lost nor out of bounds

7. C - ball may not be cleaned beyond the extent necessary for identification; breach of Rule penalty: penalty is the same in both forms of play . . . one stroke – see Rule 12-2 and Rule 21

8. B

9. A

10. B - Note to Rule 13-4

11. C – must not touch or move a loose impediment lying in or touching the hazard; breach of Rule penalty: Match Play – Loss of hole; Stroke Play: 2-stroke penalty

12. A – must not test the surface of any putting green by rolling a ball or roughing or scraping the surface; breach of Rule penalty: Match Play – Loss of hole; Stroke Play: 2-stroke penalty; however see Exception to Rule 16-1d

13. D

14. D

15. B

16. A

17. C

18. D

19. A

20. D

21. D

22. B. Must place the ball in the rough

23. B

24. D

II. True/False:

25. False - 5 minutes

26. False – This question is meant to test the player's knowledge related to what may or may not be repaired on the putting green (ball plug ands spike marks) prior to taking a stroke. Spike marks may not be repaired

27. True

28. False - re-drop again without penalty

29. True

30. False - specially prepared

31. False - one-stroke penalty and play the ball as it lies

32. False - exception also includes hazards

33. True

34. False - reasonable time without delay to reach the hole plus an additional 10 seconds

35. True

36. False - move or remove flagstick and fall in

37. False - No penalty, but must play the ball from its new position - New Exception to Rule 18-2b

38. False - part of ball must be on the surface of putting green

39. True

40. True

41. True

42. False - Player A incurs a 2-stroke penalty

43. False - 2-stroke penalty

44. True

45. True

46. False - drops from shoulder height; ball hitting the person or his equipment must be re-dropped without penalty

47. True

48. False - the player has played from the wrong place; <u>match play</u>: breach of Rule penalty is loss of hole (20-7b); <u>stroke play</u>: penalty of two strokes under the applicable Rule; he must play out the hole with the ball played from the wrong place without correcting his error unless serious breach, which must be corrected; failure to report the to the Committee so they may determine the facts before turning in his scorecard results in disqualification.

This question is meant to simulate the Tiger Woods situation a few years back on the 15th hole of the Masters. In the end, we want the reader to understand that a player in this situation has three options:

a. Proceed under the stroke and distance provision of Rule **_27-1_** by playing a ball *as nearly as possible* at the spot from which the original ball was last played (see Rule **_20-5_**); or
b. Drop a ball behind the **_water hazard_**, keeping the point at which the original ball *last crossed the margin of the* **_water hazard_** directly between the **_hole_** and the spot on which the ball is dropped, with no limit to how far behind the **_water hazard_** the ball may be dropped.
c. If there is one marked, drop a ball in the drop zone and play from there.

49. True

50. False - pitch mark must be on the green; 2-stroke penalty. can repair after the stroke

51. True

52. True

53. True

54. False - correct procedure used; no penalty in this situation

55. True

56. True

57. True - Decision, Def. Stipulated Round

58. True

59. False - Player B may not clean his ball in this scenario and it must be placed at the spot it was marked

60. True

Student Questionnaire

Name: Mr./Mrs./Ms._____

Street & Number/Box Number_____

Town_____ **State**_____ **Zip Code**_____

Home Phone_____ **Work Phone**_____

Cell Phone_____

e-mail address_____

Course/Club *affiliation (if any)*_____

How did you **find out** about *my teaching?*_____

_____

Describe how you would like to **benefit** from lessons_____

_____

Describe your *realistic* **goals** and **expectations**_____

_____

A*ctual* **average score**_____ Approximate number of **rounds/year**_____

Briefly **describe your game**_____

_____

Identify personal **strengths**_____

_____

Identify personal **weaknesses**_____

_____

Identify any **major issues:** top, fat, thin, shank, duck hook, etc._____

_____

Favorite **golf club**_____ **Short game** *rating*_____

Physical problems/limitations_____

Identify any personal **swing keys** or **thoughts**_____

Area of my game I'd like to *focus* on_____

Golf shot about which I'm *insecure*_____

Describe your **golf history** and **level of experience**_____

_____

_____

What is your *level of* **commitment** to the game (0=low to 10=high)_____

Amount of *time* I'm able to devote to **practice/week**_____

Describe a *typical* **practice session**_____

_____

Place a "check mark" next to the choices that apply to you:

I am _____**left-handed**, _____**right-handed**.

My most frequent **miss is to the** _____**left,** _____**right.**

My **learning style** may best be described as . . . . .

_____Visual (seeing), _____ Auditory (hearing), _____Kinesthetic-Tactual (doing).

My ball flight pattern is best described as (a) _____hook, _____straight, _____slice.

Distance (in yards) I *honestly* hit the ball: _____driver, _____5-iron, _____Wedge

_____I spend time during *practice* on my **short game (chipping, loft shot and bunker play).**

_____I spend time during *practice* on my **putting.**

_____I am able to **maneuver the ball** right-to-left and left-to-right.

_____I am able to **vary the trajectory** of my shots (high, medium and low).

_____I have developed a **game plan** to become a better player.

_____I have had **lessons** _before._

_____I have thought about purchasing **new equipment**.

_____I have been **fitted for clubs**.

_____I have had a **short game** _lesson._

_____I have had an _on-course_ **playing lesson**.

_____I would like to receive a **golf lesson critique** today.

_____I wear a **golf glove**.

_____I _wear out_ the heel part of my **glove** as it gets older.

_____I play **competitive golf**.

Place a "check mark" next to the golfing statements that you have ever tried or thought about:

_____Keep your **head down.**

_____Keep your **head still.**

_____Keep your **eye on the ball.**

_____Make sure you **see the club hit the ball.**

_____Do not **sway.**

_____**Transfer your weight and use your legs.**

_____Keep your **front arm straight and firm.**

_____Take the club **straight back and straight through.**

_____**Extend your arms.**

_____Make sure you **swing slow and easy.**

_____**Finish real high on the follow-through.**

Made in the USA
Middletown, DE
02 June 2015